The Khamsis: A Cradle of True Gold

BORIS HANDAL

Copyright © Boris Handal 2020
Published: July 2020
Boris Handal

The Khamsis: A Cradle of True Gold (print)
ISBN: 978-0-6489014-0-2

The Khamsis: A Cradle of True Gold (e-book)
ISBN: 978-0-6489014-1-9

All rights reserved.

The right of Boris Handal to be identified as author of this Work has been asserted by him in accordance with sections 77 and 78 of the Copyright, Designs and Patents Act 1988.

No part of this publication may be reproduced, stored in a retrieval system, copied in any form or by any means, electronic, mechanical, photocopying, recording or otherwise transmitted without written permission from the publisher. You must not circulate this book in any format.

To my mother

All [the Khamsi brothers] are remembered before this Most Resplendent Beauty. We beseech God to graciously aid each and every one to achieve that which is conducive to everlasting remembrance. *Bahá'u'lláh*[1]

---

[1]Provisional translation authorised by The Universal House of Justice.

Foreword

Biographies are written not to sanctify or to deify nor to enlist men and women in the immortal pantheon. They are written so that we may cultivate our religious instinct – to transform belief into compelling wonder and the attitude of prayer into the imaginative life of labor, work, and action ('vita activa'). Meaning must be moving and truth to prevail as aroma to the Light otherwise religion means as little to us as the atomic structure of water – a barren and profitless look onto that other most valuable giver of life. The human tale here told embodies in sumptuous detail this very special aspect of religion owing its presence and transformative power to how it really should be understood. The greatness of our enraptured lovers of God lies precisely in the description itself – the greatness of what they loved – and it is this frenzy that gives birth to remarkable human powers and achievements which makes the life of these selfless consorts, these most beautiful of mortals, exemplary suppliants, 'recipients of heavenly grace', ever more haunting. In this most recent biography of the faithful, exceptionally researched by its author, we learn the fascinating narrative of a family most 'fortunate, blessed and successful' – three meanings captured in one name Mas'ud, the multilayered prominent figure which occupies a good half of the book.

The inspiration of the Khamsi-Báqirof family lies not in any array of mundane possibilities but in the untrodden region of unalloyed divine love. Together with their spiritual brethren, these early believers, small in number and dimly islanded, interpenetrated two worlds, one enabling, the other harshly inhibiting – the new, aborning community of the Greatest Name opposed to the fierce rule of an oppressive, fanatical underworld. On the one hand, we read how the patriarchs of the Sádát-i-Khams (The Five Siyyids, in Arabic) designated as such by Bahá'u'lláh, (and from where comes the surname Khamsi) were trampled, betrayed and faced tyranny from all sides. On the other, they had to outgrow these vicissitudes digging ever deeper roots of faith to resist fiercer tempests as the unrelenting ire and hatred of the local population reacted with even greater intensity. A brutal and lashing anomaly understood only by God but accepted by unfailing resignation and unshaken trust by these faithful admirers in the parched dust of battle. All this suggests that there is an alternative way of thinking about history that has a different structure from the idea of history as a stream of causes and effects, structures and events. Here is an account of what people thought and believed in a particular epoch; what they wanted; and what social and environmental conditions framed (or suppressed) their choices – illustrated vividly by the conversion of five brothers in 1881 in Persia and which led to particular states of knowledge, belief, and agency. Is history composed of objective causal relations that exist among historical events and structures or is history an agglomeration of the actions and mental frameworks of individuals, high and low? This book seems to suggest the latter view.

The publication of *'The Khamsis: A Cradle of True Gold'* is auspicious as it coincides with the hundredth anniversary of the extended travels of the 'star servant' Martha Root to South America in 1919 to announce the advent of the Promise of all Ages. Unconcerned about the harvest, this small, frail and often ill, middle aged American covered the territories of Brazil, Argentina, Peru and Chile and, undaunted, even crossed the Andes on top of a mule in wintertime ('huddled on the edge of jagged peaks, frozen chasms, and stiffened mountain torrents') to reach the western coast of South America from Buenos Aires so that she may travel up the western coast of South America in order to reach Panama and beyond.

Such implacable audacity displayed from our indomitable 'herald of the Kingdom' and 'harbinger of the Covenant' as 'Abdu'l-Bahá was moved to describe her, bids fair to be renewed in several shades in the life of Mas'ud Khamsi who, on one his private visits with the beloved Guardian, was told portentously that soon he will start his 'international services'. This goes to show that we really do not know anything of ourselves as the true heading of who we are is inscribed elsewhere, by angels, perhaps, who make possible the extraordinary idea of communion, independent of proximity, to be felt only by extra-sensory perception, extraordinary sensitivity and the gift of hindsight. Indeed, a life of true service in the path of God is never sketched in visible ink and our destiny remains vaulted in the 'abysm of time'.

FOREWORD

Four years after meeting the beloved Guardian, Mas'ud, his wife Jane and two children, Ahmad and Dorothy, had settled in South America.

In today's eclipsed world, a polluting multitude scorns the divine, too insensitive to venerate anything that has no rational premise and yet hails pagan virtues and senseless pageantry. In these pages lies an advertence to such ambiguity. Fruits of sacrifice endure more ages than the tinsel of lineage but when lineage itself becomes indistinguishable from the highest form of the adorning bondage of selflessness it deserves an accolade which cannot be disparaged, an intriguing thesis rightly chosen for scrutiny and literary effort.

I am sure that the story of the Khamsis shall weave its spell over successive generations of readers because it translates religious imagination on an exalted plane but with no extravagant display. 'Abdu'l-Bahá was once asked what to say when people enquired who He was. 'Tell them, He said, that He was a person calling men to the Kingdom of God, a promoter of the Faith of Bahá'u'lláh, a herald of peace and reconciliation, and an advocate of the oneness of humanity.' A family's extensive eulogy recounted here is testimony to this unassuming call to greatness, made especially poignant when we consider that a noble scion should be most remembered for bringing the Bahá'í Faith to the humble indigenous masses of South America.

The message of this indispensable and very moving book is clear: it is saying that if we are to illumine mankind we must surrender ourselves, an unassailable prescription of the beloved Master that '[w]e must release the kernel from the husk'. The unique individuals portrayed here adhered nobly to this advice and delivered themselves from the husks of earthly trappings, traditions and dogmas to boldly construct the divine in the unedifying realms of kites, crows and owls.

Shahbaz Fatheazam
Paraná, Brazil
February 12th, 2019

Preface

I first learned about the Bahá'í Faith through the Khamsi children when they settled in my neighborhood in 1969. They had just arrived by sea from Iran to pioneer in Lima, Peru's capital, having decided to live temporarily on the upper floor of the National Bahá'í Headquarters.

This was a two-storey building standing next to a huge 91-acre park known as the Mars Field. The latter was located less than 3 km away south-west from the presidential palace and used to be the capital's hippodrome, the stage for military parades and the place for the "Six Peruvian Hours", the largest endurance and most important annual car race in the country. This huge green area was by surrounded by many *casonas* (grand luxury houses) creating a pintoresque landscape for the other middle-class homes spread on the adjacent *barrios*. Either escaping from the hot summers or from the tedious winters, the Mars Field offered a space for the adults and children to relax and have a breath of fresh air during daytime and in the evenings. Particularly populated during the weekends for family picnics, the site was ideal for having a Bahá'í Centre, let alone the place for ocassional teaching campaigns.

For the neighbours, the Bahá'í Centre was a sort of lonely property sitting at the extreme of the street without much human activity. A regular residence converted to offices with the big living room transformed into a small hall that could accommodate about sixty people, this pink building stood five doors –fifty meters- away from my home where I grew up from birth. It had been bought in 1954 through a donation of the Hand of the Cause of God Amelia Collins during the Ten Year Crusade launched by the beloved Guardian, ten years prior to the formation of the first Spiritual Assembly of Lima thanks to the efforts of Eve Nicklin, an American pioneer who arrived to Peru in 1941.[1]

Certainly, the Bahá'í Centre was a historical and hallowed

---

[1] Handal, Boris. *Eve Nicklin, She of the Brave Heart.* SC, CreateSpace, 2011.

building. Various sacred relics were deposited there such as the locks of Bahá'u'lláh's hair presented by Shoghi Effendi. The Blessed Beauty had referred to His Hair as "My Phoenix", "My Cord", "My Veil" and "My Messenger" that "is calling aloud at all times upon the branch of fire within the hallowed and luminous Garden of Paradise". [2]

To add sanctity to the spot, twelve different Hands of the Cause had blessed its premises including Amatu'l-Bahá Rúhíyih Khánum, Rahmatu'lláh Muhajir, Abul-Qásim Faizí, Jalal Khazeh, Adelbert Muhlshlegel, Leroy Ioas, Hasan Balyuzi, Ugo Giachery, Alí-Muhammad Varqá, Enoch Olinga, Colin Featherstone and Hermann Grossmann. Due to Lima's strategic geographical location in the subcontinent, the Spiritual Regional Assembly for ten South American countries (Argentina, Bolivia, Brazil, Chile, Colombia, Ecuador, Paraguay, Peru, Uruguay, and Venezuela) had this Hazíratu'l-Quds as it seat during Shoghi Effendi's life having also been the center of his communications to and from the region. It was also a welcome sojourn for many international visitors and travel teachers.

Another world, however, existed outside its walls. The building had an exterior simple garden ideal for the noisy street kids to gather there since the place seemed uninhabited during the day. A bunch of about twenty rascals from middle-class Catholic families populated the same street who were known to be notorious for their poor behaviour and loudness, depriving residents from any tranquillity from morning to night. The Bahá'í Centre garden had become our self-designated territory to play with marbles, yo-yos and wooden spinning tops, not to mention the scene of occasional fights, and games that went wrong sometimes such as when Ahmad (whose name we hispanicized as "Asmat") almost lost a finger for playing with fire crackers. Their garden was an oasis where the harassment from the unhappy neighbours could not reach us and away from our parents' sight. Certainly our soccer ball was the terror of people's windows.

Strangely, the solitary building appeared to irradiate a sense of serenity and holiness from the other extreme of the street, the "barrio", attracting natural reverence, while being also immersed by a halo of mystery. Nobody knew who the Bahá'ís were, from which place

---

[2]Bahá'u'lláh. *Bahá'í News*, 121, p. 11, 1938. Available online at: https://bahai-library.com/bahaullah_alwah_shaarat

on earth they came and what was their mission. I remember one or two people coming in and out of the building every day, despite that, the house appeared totally empty. The centre had a distinct pattern, nearly every month it hosted a gathering with its lights illuminating the street, the rustling from dozens of people happily talking, reaching the ears of the residents, and the sight of delicious food being served capturing a passersby's imagination only to disappear and appear again the next month. For us kids in our teens, the Bahá'ís did not fit our concept of conventional religion but rather looked like a happy philosophical society with an oriental name embracing all.

Later I realized that those peculiar evenings were Nineteen Day Feasts and the lady was the secretary of the National Spiritual Assembly while the American man was the caretaker, a pioneer. As a way to illustrate to the public who the Bahá'ís were, they had placed a bronze plaque on the façade with a rather enigmatic inscription in Spanish: "Bahá'í National Centre: The Unity of Humanity through the Unity of Religions".

No doubt, such a strange pattern of things had led the neighbourhood to develop the weirdest theories about the Bahá'í Centre ranging from being an esoteric group to a secretive lodge, although, in general, they were happy with its quietness, a precious element of any communal life. Most of all, the centre kept "the plague" or the "piranhas", as they called us, away from them let alone that we had our own territory where to engage our prolific imagination and mischief. The "Bahá'ís" were the only ones who never complained, greeted us warmly with smiles, waving always their hands to us and never interfering despite how disruptive we were. This must have produced a good impression on the older residents and parents – what is in the Bahá'ís that can tolerate these wild children who only made a nuisance of themselves.

When the Khamsis came to the street a sense of reality came to the building. For us outsiders, it was difficult to relate the mysterious Bahá'í Centre to an authentic and bubbling family. The four children quickly became integrated with our crowd - the two boys went with the boys and the two girls with the girls. We never before had associated with foreign kids particularly when they were coming from places unbeknown to us or only recognisable in our geography school books. It was beyond our mental scheme to imagine a family whose children were all born in four different countries, Iran, United States, Argentina and Bolivia, and having a Persian father and an American mother. They also appeared rich because their pocket money was substantially higher than ours. And here they were, playing with us like brothers and sisters from day one demonstrating through word and deed that we were all part of one human family. Ultimately the Khamsi children were found playing with us inside our homes to our parents' pleasure and warmly welcomed because they were much better behaved than their own children.

One afternoon while playing in the dirt with Gary, an eight-year old freckled boy and the youngest of the Khamsi kids, I could not resist asking the question that had been puzzling me for so long, "What is the Bahá'í Faith?" His sole, candid and yet profound response was "We believe in all prophets", five words alone which immediately put me to be in a reflective mood. The enigma had been solved and all clicked together coherently: the Bahá'ís were a religion accepting all religions. This brief conversation, I have to admit, was one of the most substantive that I have ever had, opening a new window in my life and naturally leading me into a path that changed me for the better.

Mr and Mrs Khamsi were the type of kind neighbours that all would be so fortunate to have. For them, we were like their own children and as such they could understand our hormonal helplessness, accept us for who we were and never reprimanded us. They used to come to where we were sitting and talked to us, with a spirit of love, asking how we were which was contrary to the approach of other residents who governed us with shouts and threats. One hot day Mr Khamsi came out of the Bahá'í Centre to buy an ice cream from a street vendor's cart when he was pushed away from one of the "piranhas" who were running around. Mr Khamsi began a friendly conversation with the remorsed boy and also bought him an ice cream and for all the group. Through their example we came to realize that, like the National Assembly secretary and the resident American pioneer, all the Bahá'ís were friendly people and can even love naughty children, the best assurance that they would never throw us out of their garden, our refuge!

The Khamsis stayed for one year or so and I was sad to see them go to their new home far away in the other extreme of the city close to a big racecourse. Due to this juvenile friendship, in the years to follow the "piranhas" began developing a binding relation with the new caretakers who from time to time invited us for supper and to play board games. Their ping-pong table was certainly their main attraction. Rumours were that my older brother had been converted after spending much time with the Bahá'ís. Five spinster aunts living also fifty meters from the Baha'i Centre had been warning us about the Bahá'ís since we told them that this is a new religion. "Be careful of the devil", the old and sanctimonious aunts told us, but by then we could not resist visiting and mingling with them. Their warning was disregarded because our mom had given us her spiritual endorsement. Although a very Catholic person, she had a lot of respect for the Bahá'í Faith. Her respect came from her admiration to Dr Sánchez, a physician working with her at a local public hospital where she was a chemist. My mother respected him not only for his professional knowledge but also because she herself witnessed how he helped his patients and went beyond his duties. Dr Sanchez and my mother had been helping patients, Bahá'ís and non-Bahá'ís, obtaining free medicines and hospital services either because they could not afford them or because they were overseas pioneers without public health access. Although not entirely interested in the teachings, my mother matched the Bahá'í Faith with Dr Sánchez and for that reason my brothers, unlike my other neighborhood friends, had to enter the Bahá'í headquarters with a lot of respect and politely convey her regards if we saw him. With those admonitions, we had no choice but behave better than the other *piranhas*! Dr Sánchez always asked us about our mother and that made us connect more to the Bahá'í Center.

Despite their change of residence, we used to see the Khamsis, parents and children, from time to time. One of *piranhas* told me that while he walked to the Bahá'í Centre apparently with a despondent face which met Mr Khamsi's smiling remark "behind each suffering there is a blessing", a compassive advice that still rings true for him fifty years later despite he never became a Bahá'í! We were also invited by the center residents to Bahá'í celebrations where we devoured their cakes and sweets. I remember, however, one occasion when we crossed the red line and the whole gang of piranhas was literally asked to leave the festivity.

When I became a Bahá'í at the age of seventeen, on that wonderful auspicious night, a copy of the *Hidden Words*, my first Bahá'í book, was presented to me by a Khamsi child and not long after I was found teaching the Faith with them on the streets. During that magical evening the Bahá'í Centre was again resplendent, full of lights with people chatting heartily on the street, and me at the centre of the celebration. It was Ayyám-i-Há, the Days of God.

Growing as a new Bahá'í in the years to follow, I partook of the Khamsis' hospitality at their well-attended Bahá'í picnics organised in their beautiful gardens. Because of his immense wisdom, love and mentoring, Counselor Khamsi had become a father figure to all the youth. Mr Khamsi turned up again in my life in 1980 when he was called by the National Assembly to appease my very disgruntled non-Bahá'í mother seeing her son leaving both university studies and a career for a remote isolated pioneering post. One year later he appointed me as his Auxiliary Board member for propagation in the Andes region, a relationship from which I learned so much about oriental wisdom and reverence. I remember myself delivering a well-prepared talk at a summer school about the Covenant. I first wrote on the board a quotation from 'Abdu'l-Bahá and underneath a passage from Baha'u'llah's writings. He quickly corrected me – although the relevance of the statements were in the correct order, Bahá'u'lláh's name had to be come first. For us, that was a small and beautiful concept that we Latin Americans never heard before. Firmness in the Covenant and service to Bahá'u'lláh, were always present in his talks, always holding high expectations on the teaching front. His wise guidance to all of us working in Radio Bahá'í of Peru was always there, on the other end of the phone and asking for constant reports. "Radio is noise", he used to say, "and you have to make a lot of noise with your radio", of course, for spreading the Faith.

Later, when Mr Khamsi was appointed member of the International Teaching Centre in Haifa in 1983, he facilitated my first pilgrimage to the Holy Land the next year, me being a penniless homefront pioneer. In Haifa, also my grandmother's birthplace, he entertained me as his guest with considerable hospitality and generosity. I was overwhelmed and humbled when he arranged for me to meet with the International Teaching Centre to consult about the progress of the

Faith among Indigenous believers, his favourite topic. He visited us in the Andes again in 1988 for a teaching campaign where over 1,700 new believers were enrolled as new believers in one week. There he was, the veteran general one more time marshalling his ground troops to victory emboldened by an ironlike reliance on the Concourse on High.

Years later when Parvin and I were pioneers to Macau we kept in touch through correspondence and telephone. Actually, he was instrumental in encouraging us to go to that part of the world in 1993. When the Khamsis returned to Peru I had the opportunity in 2004 to enjoy again their warm friendliness at their home in Lima. In 2018 I journeyed to the beautiful Baku, the Khamsi family town, and while mingling with the friends there I recalled in their faces the history of its early believers and the old spaces where their consecration took place. The Bahá'í friend who drove us back from the Bahá'í centre to our hotel that evening told us that his grandfather had been 'Abdu'l-Bahá's secretary demonstrating the infancy of this universal Faith and how tantalisingly fresh the story was. Members of the Khamsi family in Baku were active members of the local community.

I always will remember how after completing my first book "The Concourse on High" in Spanish[3], written at his initiative despite being afflicted with self-doubt when I was still twenty-five years old, Mr Khamsi said to me, "Once you have started writing, you should not stop writing". Since then I have focused on immersing myself in the field of Bahá'í research and writing making it one of my preferred fields of service. How interesting, one could say how providential, that this chain of events has now connected forty years later to this new book celebrating the distinguished achievements of the Khamsi family throughout almost 150 years of continuous history.

At the memorial service for his father in the Sydney House of Worship in April 2013, the oldest of the Khamsi children and also my old street mate, suggested the idea of writing a biography. Ahmad Khamsi, who was then visiting the country, said that I was the most suitable person for the task, a thought that I found difficult to reconcile at the beginning. The timid initial exploration of the topic grew in

---

[3] Handal, Boris. *El Concurso en Lo Alto*. Lima, PROPACEB, 1985.

intensity as I found myself discovering a fascinating storyline running continuously from Bahá'u'lláh's time till the present day with three brilliant characters taking the stage: Mas'ud Khamsi, his father Siyyid Ahmad and his great-uncle Siyyid Naṣru'lláh.

To my delight, my research took me to visit unimaginable places such as the Caucasus where East meets West. For this historical narrative, over 100 collaborators assisted and supported me during the process of data collection, analysis and reporting. I was also able to communicate with Bahá'í scholars from all over the world and old believers who like Mr Khamsi had the privilege of meeting the beloved Guardian and were part of the story.

I know that Mr Khamsi would not like anybody to write about him. At a conference where long Bahá'í records of services were read before a talk was delivered, Mr Khamsi gave an imperturbable response to the presenter who was asking for one: "Just call me Khamsi". In a short sketch of his over 50-year pioneering services, both homefront and international, he wrote at the beginning:

> On several occasions, the Universal House of Justice asked the pioneers to write their stories, achievements and experiences in the field of service. On many occasions I tried to write my experiences, but as I am a Persian when the word "I" was to begin it discouraged me and I gave up. Now, the wisdom of the Universal House of Justice's instructions is clear and my duty is to obey, this is why I am writing these lines and I hope they become a guide for other Bahá'ís, particularly for the youth.[4]

Noblesse oblige, and the purpose of this chronicle was not to intended to exalt people but to illustrate important attributes of services and the struggles they went through to serve the Cause with the most dedicated and unassuming disposition in a different time and before us.

I am humbled at the thought of all those blessings, all which started from an informal chat between two children in front of a Bahá'í Centre. It is with these feelings that I make *A Cradle of True Gold* available to my readers and to posterity, in brief, paying with ink

---

[4] *Pioneering and Services of Mas'ud Khamsi,* unpublished manuscript.

labour a personal debt of love to Counselor Mas'ud Khamsi, a person who touched many other lives in his services to the Faith of God.

Boris Handal
Sydney, Australia

Acknowledgements

My deep appreciation goes to Hoda Seioshansian, Mary Victoria, Habib Hosseiny and Dr Stephen Lambden for their assistance in translating a number of tablets revealed by Bahá'u'lláh and 'Abdu'l-Bahá to the Sádát-i-Khams family and to Dr Moojan Momen for generously sharing his own translation of the Law-i-Ihtihad (Table of Unity). I also would like to thank the Research Department of the Bahá'í World Centre for reviewing and approving the translations of original Tablets into English.

I am much indebted to Mansour Adami for orally translating the text of Khándán-i-Sádát-i-Khams with so much patience while I was taking notes and to Shahram Khozoei for double-checking the accuracy of my notes with the original text. Also, my thanks to Qodrat Motallebi for reading me the Tablets to the Khamsi-Baqirof family and explaining their content. Likewise, I would express my appreciation to Farzad Naziri for assisting in rendering an accurate translations from historical documents in Farsi.

For the English/Spanish translations I was generously assisted by John and Pati Kepner, Jimmy Jensen, Dorothy Khamsi-Samandari and Kurt Grove. I also would like to express my gratitude to Ulviyya Afaridan, Robin Mihrshahi and Helene Safajou for their assistance with the Russian, German and French translations, respectively.

Dr Adren Alinejad, John and Pati Kepner, Nur Mihshahi, Dr Felicity Rawlings-Sanaei and Masud Samandari (in alphabetical order but all equally helpful) assisted me with the proofreading, editing and suggestions to improve the narrative and the text.

There was an army of Mr Khamsi's admirers who out of their own hearts provided me with their own memories to enrich the content of the book through interviews, personal communications and other means. The names of these believers are: Payam Ala'i, Jamshid Ardjomandi, Jesus Ascencio, Dr Iraj Ayman, Houshang Balazadeh, Dr Omar Brdarevic, Shahnaz Brdarevic, Cesar Cortes, Pedro and Mirna Donaires, Dunia Donaires, Shanny and Gerson Elias, Augusto

Erquinio, Shahbaz Fatheazam, Leski Franco, Iran Furutan, Dr Miguel Gil, Dr Grover Gonzales, Zia and Molok Ghofrany, Maria Eugenia Gonzales, Alberto and Rosario Guerrero, Violette Haake, Nasser Haddadan, Roxana Hadden, Camelia Handal, Juan Handal, Jimmy Jensen, Dorothy Khamsi-Samandari, Ahmad Khamsi, Bahiah Khamsi, Gary Khamsi, John and Pati Kepner, Lina Leon, Maria Loayza, Dr Augusto Lopez-Claros, Yessica Lopez, Vicente Lopez and Marta Tirado de Lopez, Mehran Manie, Martin Mansilla, Azam Matin, Moojan Matin, Sally McAllaster, Tahereh Mohammadi, Shapoor Monadjem, Ali Nakhjavani, Carlos Núñez, Hector Núñez, Sabino Ortega, Eshraghollah Ouladi, Clemencia Pavon, Amparo Polanco, Steve Pulley, Dr Shapour Rassekh, Patrick Ravines, Abraham Reyes, Jose Luis Reyes, Conrado Rodriguez, Donald Rogers, Oscar Rojas, Manuel and Fariba Rosas, Sandro Ruju, Ana Maria Saavedra, Dr Mahmud Samandari, Masud Samandari, Enrique (Kiko) and Veronica (Ore) Sanchez, Monica Sanchez, Fernando Schiantarelli, Marko Sebastiani, Mohiman Shafa, Manoucher Shoaie, Dr K. Dean Stephens, Shahnaz Talebzadeh, Farid and Roya Tebyani, Yolanda Torres Urteaga, Rolf von Czekus, David Walker and Luis Wong. The Khamsi-Samandari family provided the author with important primary sources and comments that certainly enriched the book.

My gratitude also goes to Alex Kaefer for permitting me use quotes from his book about the history of the Bahá'í Faith in Austria and to Ruhu'lláh Mihrabkhání for his permission to quote from his book Khándán-i-Sádát-i-Khams.[1] This book was based on the historical material about the early Khamsi family, compiled and gathered by Mr Ruhollah Khamsi.[2][3]

My sincere thanks to the National Spiritual Assembly of Peru for giving me access to their national archives, for continuously supplying with photographic material and for responding to my requests for information. I am similarly grateful to the National Spiritual Assembly

---

[1] Rúhu'lláh Mihrabkhání. *Khándán-i Sádát-i-Khams.* Darmstadt, Mu'assassih-'i `Asr-i Jadid, 1994.
[2] Ruhollah Khamsi (1915-1997).
[3] Bahá'í World Centre. *The Bahá'í World - In Memoriam* (1992-1997). Haifa, 2010, pp. 185-186.

of Azerbaijan for providing documents from the early years of the Faith in Baku. I also would like to show my appreciation to the National Spiritual Assembly of the Bahá'ís of Australian for reviewing and approving the manuscript for publication.

The audio-visual resources supporting the production of the book were kindly facilitated by the World Centre Audio-Visual Department, the United States Bahá'í Archives, the Khamsi-Samandari family, Pedro Donaires, Cesar and Rolando Cortes, Roxana Hadden, Sally McAllaster, Conrado Rodriguez, Stephen Pulley, Leski Franco, Mehran Manie and many other friends. The credits for cover concept design go to Fariba (Heydari) Rosas. Pedro Donaires drew the Caspian Sea map with skill and talent.

I cannot close this acknowledgment page without expressing my gratefulness to my wife Parvin for being so helpful, patient and loving while immersed for years researching and writing the book.

A Short Note on Bahá'í Orthography

Readers are advised that to a feasible extent the author has used the transliteration standard adopted by Shoghi Effendi in 1923 for Bahá'í literature in the Persian and Arabic language. The system was adapted from the standards set by the Tenth International Congress of Orientalists held in Geneva in 1894.

Due to the lack of a uniform system before Shoghi Effendi's ministry, the writing of Bahá'í terms was inconsistent. For early texts, this book has kept as much as possible the integrity of the original source although sometimes the correct transliteration has been used to ensure the smoothness and flow of the narrative.

In order to facilitate the understanding of some oriental words the table below outlines the variations of some Bahá'í terms that the reader may come across. In some cases, for practicality reasons, the most popular form of the name has been kept such as Mas'ud Khamsi instead of Mas'úd Khamsí [4], or Tehran instead of Ṭihrán.

---

[4] The sound Kh is enounced as in the English pronunciation of *house*.

Bahá'í transliteration	Variations
Báqirof	Baqirof, Baguerof, Baqiroff, Baqirov, Bakeroff
Naṣru'lláh	Nasrollah, Nasru'lláh, Nasroullah
Jináb	Jinab, Jenab, Jenabe
Siyyid	Sayyed, Sayyid
Asadu'lláh	Asadollah
Bahá'u'lláh	Baha'o'llah
Riḍá	Reza, Rida
Mahmúd	Mahmoud
'Ádhirbayján	Azerbayjan
Áqá	Aqa, Agha

Before first names and surnames were enforced in Iran in the 1920, people used to be called according by their single first name, title and/or their original town. Some of those titles were:

Ḥájí: A person who has successfully completed the pilgrimage to Mecca.
Mírzá: If the term precedes the name it refers to an educated person. After the name it stands for Prince.
Abu'l: Father of ...
Shaykh: A religious leader
Áqá: Master, Sire
Siyyid: A descendant from Prophet Muhammad.
Jináb: His/Her Excellency
Mullá: An Islamic clergyman

Titles can be combined in a single name such as in *Ḥájí Mírzá Siyyid 'Alí Shírází*, meaning a person whose name is 'Alí, from an educated background, a descendant from Prophet Muhammad, having born in the city of Shíráz.

Table of Illustrations

Figure 1: Tablet of 'Abdu'l-Bahá to Siyyid Naṣru'lláh. Source: Khándán-i Sádát-i-Khams. 21

Figure 2: A street scene in 'Akká, c. 1914. Courtesy: Bahá'í Media Bank 22

Figure 3: The Caspian Sea and Neighbouring Countries. Courtesy: Pedro Donaires. 23

Figure 4: Three of the Báqirof brothers are standing on the front. Left to right: Siyyid Naṣru'lláh, Mír 'Alí Naqí and Siyyid Asadu'lláh. Source: Khándán-i Sádát-i-Khams.. 23

Figure 5: Receipts by 'Abdu'l-Bahá for Khamsi-Báqirof family's contribution to the Bahá'í Fund. Courtesy: Khamsi-Samandari family. 24

Figure 6: Siyyid Naṣru'lláh. Source: Khándán-i Sádát-i-Khams. 25

Figure 7: Siyyid Naṣru'lláh with some of his children. Source: Khándán-i-Sádát-i-Khams. 26

Figure 8: Siyyid Naṣru'lláh with Bahá'ís of Tehran. Sitting on right side of second row. Source: Khándán-i Sádát-i-Khams ... 27

Figure 9: Siyyid Ahmad with 'Abdu'l-Bahá in Paris. Third standing from the left. Source: Khándán-i-Sádát-i-Khams. 28

Figure 10: Siyyid Ahmad with 'Abdu'l-Bahá in Paris. Third standing from the left. Courtesy: Khamsi-Samandari family. 29

Figure 11: 'Abdu'l-Bahá in Budapest. Siyyid Ahmad is second from the left. 68

Figure 12: 'Abdu'l-Bahá in Stuttgart. Courtesy: Bahá'í Media. 68

Figure 13: The Grand Hotel of Tehran in the 1900s. 69

Figure 14: Shahpoor Avenue, Rasht, 1934. Source: Shahre Farang. 69

Figure 15: Reza Shah in 1941. Source: Wikimedia Commons 70

Figure 16: Siyyid Ahmad's family. Mas'ud Khamsi is standing behind his father Siyyid Ahmad on the left side. Source: Khándán-i Sádát-i-Khams.............................. 71

Figure 17: Shoghi Effendi's map at the beginnning of the Ten Year Crusade. 71

Figure 18: Khonsar nowadays. Courtesy: Nasser Sadeghi, CC BY-SA 3.0 72

Figure 19: Jane and Mas'ud Khamsi wedding. Source: Bahá'í Peruvian National Archives. 72

Figure 20: Jane and Mas'ud at the 1953 Kampala Conference. Source: Bahá'í Peruvian National Archives................ 73

Figure 21: Shoghi Effendi's letter to Mas'ud Khamsi 104

Figure 22: Last photograph of Shoghi Effendi. Source: Bahá'í Media 105

Figure 23: Pioneering in Argentina 1959. With Ahmad and Dorothy Khamsi. Source: Bahá'í Peruvian National Archives. ... 106

Figure 24: Travel teaching in the Andes. Courtesy: Bahá'í News, December 1961 107

Figure 25: Addressing the Bahá'í World Congress in London in 1963. Source: Bahá'í Peruvian National Archives.. 107

Figure 26: With indigenous believers in Bolivia. Source: Bahá'í Peruvian National Archives. 108

Figure 27: Discussing teaching plans with Hand of the Cause Dr Muhajir in Bolivia. Courtesy: Stephen Pulley........... 108

Figure 28: With Hand of the Cause Mr Faizi in Lima. Source: Bahá'í Peruvian National Archives. 109

Figure 29: In Tehran before departing for Peru. Source: Bahá'í Peruvian National Archives. 109

Figure 30: At the Green Light Expedition. Source: The American Bahá'í Archives..........110

Figure 31: At the Green Light Expedition. Source: The American Bahá'í Archives..........242

Figure 32: Leonora Armstrong, Spiritual Mother of South America, Amatu'l-Bahá Rúhíyih Khánum and Counselors at the Lopez residence. Courtesy: Vicente Lopez..........242

Figure 33: In a Bolivian village with Amatu'l-Bahá Rúhíyih Khánum. Source: The American Bahá'í Archives..........243

Figure 34: El Viento Canta. Source: Bahá'í World Centre..........243

Figure 35: Hand of the Cause Amatu'l-Bahá Rúhíyih Khánum, members of the Universal House of Justice Mr Ali Nakhjavani, Mr Borrah Kavelin and Dr David Ruhe with El Viento Canta team at Mr and Mrs Khamsi's home in Haifa in 1988. Source: Rolando Cortes..........244

Figure 36: Consulting with the National Spiritual Assembly of Peru. Source: Bahá'í Peruvian National Archives..........245

Figure 37: In a summer school in Lima next to Eve Nicklin (centre), Spiritual Mother of Peru. Source: Bahá'í Peruvian National Archives..........245

Figure 38: At the inauguration of Radio Bahá'í of Lake Titicaca in Peru in 1981. Mas'ud Khamsi is standing on the left hand side. Andres Jachakollo is sitting on the front row second from the left. Courtesy: Mehran Manie..........246

Figure 39: Members of the International Teaching Centre featuring the Hands of the Cause of God Amatu'l-Bahá Rúhíyih Khánum and Ali Akbar Furutan (front row, third and fourth from right). Mr Khamsi is standing second on the back row..........247

Figure 40: Mr Khamsi with Hand of the Cause of God 'Alí-Akbar Furútan. Courtesy: Iran Furutan..........248

Table of Contents

Foreword i
Preface v
Acknowledgements xv
A Short Note on Bahá'í Orthography xvii
Table of Illustrations xix
Introduction..1
Part I: The Five Brothers..................................9
1. Introduction 9
2. The Báqir's Descendants 10
3. Siyyid Mahmúd.. 12
4. Siyyid Asadu'lláh.. 14
5. Mír 'Alí Naqí 17
6. Siyyid Riḍá 18
Part II: Siyyid Naṣru'lláh Báqirof (1859-1924) 31
1. Introduction 31
   1.1 Settling in Baku...................................... 32
   1.2 Sakineh Khánum 33
   1.3 Wealth and Socio-Economic Development................. 34
   1.4 Mode of Living 37
   1.5 A Russian Citizen 38
2. **Relationship with Bahá'u'lláh** 39
   2.1 Passing of Bahá'u'lláh................................ 42
   2.2 Guidance from 'Abdu'l-Bahá. 43
   2.2.1 Firmness in the Covenant 45
   2.2.2 Advice on Politics................................... 46
   2.2.3 Tributes to Siyyid Naṣru'lláh 47
3. **Service**... 48
   3.1 Teaching the Faith 48
   3.2 Teaching the Faith to Prominent People................ 48
   3.3 Defending the Bahá'ís................................. 51
   3.4 The Central Assembly of Tehran 55

    3.5 Diplomatic Missions 56
    3.6 Communications between Iran and the Holy Land 61
    3.7 Contributions to the Funds 63
4. Relationship with 'Abdu'l-Bahá 64
5. Passing and Significance 65
Part III: Siyyid Ahmad Khamsi-Báqirof (c1880-1950) 75
1. Family Life 75
2. Homayoun Khánum 76
4. Spiritual Dimensions of his Business 79
    4.1 Trustworthiness: The Inheritance 79
    4.2 Competency: The Government Finances 79
    4.3 Socio-Economic Development: Tea Plantation Innovation . 80
5. Trip to Europe 81
    5.1 Paris 81
    5.2 Stuttgart 86
    5.3 Budapest 90
    5.4 Vienna 91
    5.5 Second Visit to Stuttgart 94
6. Services to the Cause of God 96
    6.1 Helping Non-Bahá'ís 97
    6.2 Protecting the Bahá'ís 97
7. Teaching the Faith 101
Part IV: Mas'ud Khamsi (1922-2013) 111
1. Childhood and Youth in Iran 111
    1.1 Childhood 111
    1.2 The Tuman 112
    1.3 Youth Activities in Iran 113
    1.4 Schooling 116
    1.5 Homefront Pioneering 116
    1.6 University Studies 119
    1.7 Work in Tehran 120
    1.8 Mary Jane Snyder Khamsi 120
2. Meeting the Guardian 124
    2.1 The Kampala Conference 125
    2.2 Thinking of Going on Pilgrimage 126
    2.3 Travelling to Haifa from Kampala 126
    2.4 Meeting the Guardian 127

TABLE OF CONTENTS

3. First Pioneering to South America **133**
   3.1 Planning to Pioneer to South America 134
   3.2 Settling in Argentina 139
   3.3 Settling in Bolivia 141
   3.4 The Beginning of Mass Teaching in South America 143
   3.5 Teaching the Faith in Bolivia 146
   3.6 His Love for Bolivia 154
   3.7 Returning to Iran 156

4. Return to Iran (1963-1969) **159**
   4.1 Activities in Iran after returning from Bolivia 159
   4.3 Appointed Counselor in Iran 162
   4.4 Returning to South America 165

5. Second Pioneering to South America **165**
   5.1 Learning to Travel Teach 167
   5.2 Learning to Grow 168
   5.3 Learning to Teach 178
   5.4 Learning to Fast 180
   5.5 Learning to Give 183
   5.6 Learning to Nurture Scholarly Ability 185

6. Amatu'l-Bahá Rúhíyyih Khánum **187**
   6.1 Introduction 187
   6.2 The Green Light Expedition 188
   6.3 A Sense of Reverence 190
   6.4 The Green Light Expedition in Lima 193
   6.5. At the World Centre 197

7. Pioneering **198**
   7.1 Encouraging New Pioneers 199
   7.2 Nurturing Current Pioneers 205

8. Bahá'í World Centre Services **208**
   8.1 A Member of the International Teaching Centre 208
   8.2 Youth Programs in Haifa 209
   8.2 Latin Nights 210
   8.3 El Viento Canta 210
   8.4 External Affairs 212
   8.5 International Trips 214

9. Socio-Economic Development **215**
   9.1 An Entrepreneurial Mindset 216
   9.2 Bahá'í Radio Stations 217

9.3 Nur University..220
9.4 Institutes..221
9.5 Rural Schools..221
10. Protecting the Bahá'í Community 225
   10.1 Looking after the Youth...............................226
   10.2 Covenant-breaking...................................227
   10.3 Proclaiming the Faith................................228
   10.4 The Street Quarrel: A Teaching Story 231
11. Returning to Peru......................................234
   11.1 Serving at the National Spiritual Assembly.............234
   11.2 Generosity 236
   11.3 External Affairs 237
   11.4 Last Years..239
Appendix 1: The Robbery, a Green Light Expedition Story ..249
Appendix 2: The Green Light Expedition Film Narrative (extracts)..255
   Venezuela - the Amazonas...................................255
   Suriname – The Bush Negroes...............................260
   Brazil – Manaus...263
   Colombia – Leticia 264
   Peru – Iquitos and Pucallpa................................265
   Peru – Lima...266
   Bolivia – Oruro...267
   Peru - Cusco 268
Bibliography 271

Introduction

Looking at the immensity of the Caspian Sea from the terraces of my hotel in Baku, the capital of the Republic of Azerbaijan, I keep wondering about the monumental scope of the research I am undertaking taking me aback from my native Peru. Two countries so culturally different from each other but nevertheless united by a singular thread that only God mysteriously could have woven.

With sources from English, Spanish, Persian, German, French, Arabic and Russian that I struggled to translate, I immersed myself in a fascinating saga traversing across three centuries, two falling Iranian royal dynasties, three generations, two world wars and four continents.

This is a story taking us to Iran, Russia, the Holy Land, the main European capitals, Africa and even to exotic places such as the Amazon rain forest and the magnificent Andes mountains, showing that love for humanity also travels and it never gets tired in giving if inspired by higher principles. It touches on the lives of Bahá'u'lláh, 'Abdu'l-Bahá, Bahíyyih Khánum, Shoghi Effendi and a number of Hands of the Cause, particularly Amatu'l-Bahá Rúhíyyih Khánum, intertwined with momemtous events of the Faith's Heroic and Formative epochs.

To borrow Foucault's words, this narrative is more about "a historical awareness of our present circumstance".[1] More than a chronology, this book is a collection of teaching stories with a current morale told mostly by primary sources who were themselves protagonists in the narrative. Each story intends to highlight a spiritual attribute focusing more on the actions that on the persons themselves. These teaching accounts will always be valid inasmuch as they were all laden with devotion and sacrifice and they have something to tell us as we strive to spread the Message of Bahá'u'lláh to our fellow human beings in any part of the world.

These tales are about a wealthy family adopting a nascent religion

---

[1] Foucault, M. The Subject and Power. *Critical Inquiry*, 8(4), p. 778, 1982.

struggling to survive in the midst of a fanatical establishment. It reminds us of the story of the seed striving to come to the surface and to evolve into a magnificent tree. It is the narrative of a clan that preferred to put their spiritual obligations above others of a financial nature, benefits that will never perish. Bigotry, persecution and harassment could not abate the inner spiritual forces impelling the family members to get their religion accepted, protected and flourishing.

From becoming a persecuted underground movement in the 19th century, despite all odds, the Iranian Bahá'í community found itself in the last century, gaining continuous strength and consolidating through the establishment of hospitals, schools, endowments and government-accredited governing bodies, both in rural as well as in urban areas. Reluctant to give in to religious-based intimidations and adamant to uphold the truth of their beliefs, the Bahá'ís of Iran opened their own windows to modernity in a country still submerged in antiquated Dark Ages.

In all these developments, some prominent families like the Khamsi-Báqirof were able due to their social position, to defend, overtly and covertly, the worth that their newly espoused religion had brought to a country already on an accelerated material and spiritual decline.

As I kept unravelling the Khamsi-Báqirof family story, I marvelled at the tradition of devoted and creative services to the Bahá'í Faith as honoured in the numerous Tablets from Bahá'u'lláh and 'Abdu'l-Bahá, and writings from Shoghi Effendi as well as in the testimonies from the Universal House of Justice. It all began with the declaration in 1881 of five brothers, known in Bahá'í history as Báqirof-Khamsi, whom Bahá'u'lláh designated as Sádát-i-Khams (The Five Siyyids[2], in Arabic) from where the surname Khamsi (Five, in Arabic) comes from. Going through various tumultuous Iranian social scenarios three main waves in the Báqirof-Khamsi family are easily recognisable and characterised in the persons of Siyyid Naṣru'lláh Báqirof (1859-1924), Siyyid Ahmad Khamsi-Báqirof (c1880-1950) and Mas'ud Khamsi (1922-2013).

---

[2] A Siyyid is a descendant from Prophet Muhammad.

INTRODUCTION

Siyyid Naṣru'lláh Báqirof's life could be characterised by his disposition to valiantly protect the vulnerable Bahá'í community using his social influence at a time where there was no administrative or legal mechanisms to defend them. Enabled to serve and visit Bahá'u'lláh and 'Abdu'l-Bahá during his lifetime, Siyyid Naṣru'lláh was also able due to his wealth to generously contribute to the needs of the Cause. His nephew and virtual son, Siyyid Ahmad, also lived up to those standards as a result being privileged to accompany 'Abdu'l-Bahá to His historical travels across Europe as well as contributing to the organic development of the Iranian Bahá'í community as it turned to the 20th century. Highly respected because of his widely known business integrity, Siyyid Ahmad did reach the highest governmental and social circles of the country to protect the believers and contribute to the protection and respect of the Cause. The privilege was left to Mas'ud Khamsi, Siyyid Ahmad' son, to visit the beloved Guardian and, while pursuing his predecessors' lines of action, more distinctively with intrepidity and great detachment, left the native Iran and took the Cause to tens of thousands of people in South America, mostly indigenous, a path that was eventually crowned by distinguished international services throughout the globe. Generations to come will certainly draw inspiration from the valiant services of this selfless and honoured family in the pathway of the Beloved.

Blessed by those sacred encounters the Khamsi-Báqirof also received tablets from Bahá'u'lláh and 'Abdu'l-Bahá with continuous guidance, encouragement and reassurance. Specifically, Baha'u'llah prayed for and assured the Khamsi-Báqirof family members that they will be remembered eternally. Likewise, 'Abdu'l-Bahá wrote that the distinction of the Sadat-i-Khams will remain for centuries and ages to come. He called them the Stars of Khams ("Five Stars", in Arabic) which are shining from the "horizon of guidance".[3]

Like passing magic from one generation to the other, they brilliantly infused their own zeal into their offspring confirming them to even greater heights of service. This was a family where the Faith was constantly at the centre of the table, with memories of visits to Bahá'u'lláh and 'Abdu'l-Bahá, and always accompanied by a

---

[3] Rúhu'lláh Mihrabkhání. *Khándán-i Sádát-i-Khams.* Darmstadt, Mu'assassih-'i `Asr-i Jadid, 1994.

permament influx of prominent believers. How important therefore is the role of the Bahá'í family as a divine fortress, one would reflect upon, in ensuring that the next generation is spiritually well nurtured akin to a chain of memories that provides daily accompaniment. Acknowledging such a principle, Mas'ud Khamsi once wrote: "In order for you to understand my origin, it is important to mention my family's history".[4]

Hence, the learning and prayerful attitude from the first Khamsi-Báqirof generation were passed to the second one as the latter, in turn, handed on and augmented to the third family wave, ultimately leaving their mark on the faithful and the wider community in which they operated. Mathematicians call this phenomenon the multiplicative effect but the author (also a mathematician), recalls 'Abdu'l-Bahá's words: "... an especial blessing is conferred on some families and some generations".[5]

The weighty decision made by the five Báqirof brothers to declare their belief in Bahá'u'lláh, as the proceeding narrative will attest to, had a pivotal and unprecedented impact on many generations of that family and the societies in which they lived. In a Tablet revealed for the auspicious occasion of the Birth of the Báb, Bahá'u'lláh emphatically summoned all to heed the following counsel:

> Make thou every effort to render service unto God, that from thee may appear that which will immortalize thy memory in His glorious and exalted heaven.[6]

It is from the heroic and courageous decision made by the Báqirof brothers, and the distinguished services they rendered, that countless generations have benefited and their memory has been immortalized both in this world and the next.

The three generations of Khamsi-Báqirof who are the subject of this book can be characterised, among many factors, by their devotion to the Bahá'í Faith but also by their innovative acumen. The latter was manifested in their own successful business enterprises where

---

[4] *Pioneering and Services of Mas'ud Khamsi*, unpublished manuscript.

[5] 'Abdu'l-Bahá, *Some Answered Questions*. US Bahá'í Publishing Trust, 1990, p. 305

[6] Bahá'u'lláh. *Tablets of Bahá'u'lláh Revealed After the Kitáb-i-Aqdas*. US Bahá'í Publishing Trust, 1988, p. 233.

they were ahead of their times. Innovative and creative projects were initiated by them such as establishing and disseminating tea planting practices in northern Iran to avoid imports as well as the first cinema and the first modern hotel in Iran adhering to European standards. They were second in the country to acquire an automobile sharing this innovation only with the royal family. Conscious of the benefits of Western civilization, the Khamsi-Báqirofs were also among the first Iranian families to send their children to European universities. They owned entire villages around Tehran where the inhabitants were taught literacy and children had formal education. The family also ventured into radio, television, oil, hospitality, publishing, road infrastructure, trading, real estate and mining interests, among other businesses revealing a strong commercial and industrial expertise, let alone a strong sense of practicality.

Such a progressive mindset was also manifested in their Bahá'í endeavours through socio-economic development projects such as radio stations and schools, medical centres, teacher training institutes, summer schools, encouragement to Bahá'ís to establish universities, creation of new Bahá'í literature and engagement with the arts. They were also pioneers in learning complex undertakings such as connecting with diplomats, networking with prominent people and developing the indigenous population. Through mass conversion, certainly the original five Khamsi-Báqirof burgeoned scores of tens of thousands of new believers mostly in Latin America.

My research also pays tribute to three amazing women who, besides their husbands' public figures, were at all times working hand-in-hand in service to the Faith of God, namely, Sakineh Khánum, Homayoun Khánum and Mary Jane Snyder. Although not broadly visible to the public eye except for some glimpses included in historical records, and within the scope of what women could do in the public arena in their times, these three heroines had their own joy of service as well as the responsibility of bringing the family together to be able to navigate in the arena of service, despite the constant presence of physical danger or constant moves. As 'Abdu'l-Bahá had said: "Among the miracles which distinguish this sacred dispensation is this, that women have evinced a greater boldness than men when enlisted in the ranks of the Faith".[7]

"I was born in a cradle of gold", Mas'ud Khamsi sometimes observed. And yet, the family was the embodiment of the wealthy Bahá'í individual consecrating their wealth to the promotion of the Cause of God just as Bahá'u'lláh said in the Hidden Words:

> Well is it then with him, who, being rich, is not hindered by his riches from the eternal kingdom, nor deprived by them of imperishable dominion. By the Most Great Name! The splendour of such a wealthy man shall illuminate the dwellers of heaven even as the sun enlightens the people of the earth![8]

Nowadays, we find Khamsi family members settled in many countries mixed with a variety of races and excelling in diverse teaching or administrative serving capacities, carrying Bahá'u'lláh's blessings conferred on them for eternity.

This book is about a celebration of well-spent lives, a feast of the spirit and a rendezvous of consecrated souls. These stories testify that if you live by higher principles the result is always spiritual triumph, that although the destination is unknown you are always safe, because you have to learn to trust in higher powers, relinquish yourself in larger hands to the Will of the Almighty, surrendering your lives and possessions to God, irrespective of how much you have, because, in the end, nothing matters but pleasing the Beloved, just as 'Abdu'l-Bahá had wished:

> It is clear that life in this fast-fading world is as fleeting and inconstant as the morning wind, and this being so, how fortunate are the great who leave a good name behind them, and the memory of a lifetime spent in the pathway of the good pleasure of God.[9]

But above all there was another and more powerful force

---

[7] *The Compilation of Compilations: Prepared by The Universal House of Justice* (vol. 2). Maryborough, Victoria, Bahá'í Publications Australia, 2000, p. 403.

[8] Bahá'u'lláh, *The Hidden Words of Bahá'u'lláh*. US Bahá'í Publishing Trust, 1985, p. 41.

[9] 'Abdu'l-Bahá. *The Secret of Divine Civilization*. Wilmette, US Bahá'í Publishing Trust, p. 70, 1983.

motivating the characters of this narrative. It was their immense love for Bahá'u'lláh expressed in the service to His Cause. A love that was unconditional, contagious and courageous bringing at the same time spiritual joy and inner happiness to the soul. Such a love, nurtured in the family nest, permeated their everyday conversations, inspired their steps and gave them an authentic Bahá'í identity among their peers. Most importantly, that love for Bahá'u'lláh became a bliss to serve, a disposition that can be better summarized in these words of Mas'ud Khamsi around the last years of his life:

> ... That nothing is sweeter, that nothing gives more happiness than working for the Faith. All the things that you can do in any day are going to be forgotten. However, the work of the Faith is never going to be forgotten. So everyone has their chance to serve the Faith wherever they may be because that will remain forever in this world and the one to come. Please continue to work, continue to help the Faith because it is the only thing that will remain for you in this world and the world to come. It is the only thing that remains. All the other things that you gladly want to do are fine but will not remain as much as your efforts for the Faith. What you do for Bahá'u'lláh will remain now and for eternity. [10]

---

[10] Talk by Mas'ud Khamsi in July 2010 at the National Bahá'í Centre. Peruvian Bahá'í Archives.

PART 1:
The Five Brothers

1. Introduction

This narrative begins on the shores of the Caspian Sea.

The Caspian Sea is strategically and historically important because it separates Europe from Asia. Five countries surround this immense mass of water, comparable in size to Japan. These countries are the republics of Iran, Russia, Turkmenistan, Kazakhstan and Azerbaijan – the last four representing the remnants from the collapsed Soviet Union and the Russian empire.

The Caspian Sea is actually not a sea but the largest lake in the world. It was always called a sea probably due to its vastness, the relative salinity of the water, and sometimes rough waves — actually, surfing is practiced on its waters. In ancient times people thought it was even connected to a big ocean.

Its European name came from the Greek historian Strabo (64 BC – AD 24) who named it after a tribe, now extinct, called the Caspi. The Caspian Sea is a great blessing from the Lord sustaining the life of dozens of ethnic groups. Although each one has their own culture and language they were for millennia profoundly influenced by the ancient Persian empires and its civilization and past glory.

Rich in natural resources, particularly oil and fish, the Caspian Sea displays an amazing and unique array of fauna and flora. For instance, the world famous caviar is the flagship of those waters. Diverse and rich as the neighbouring ethnic cultures were, this life-giving lake was also surrounded by an even more beautiful coastal geography, creating a landscape of awe and promise, one which was destined to include Núr, Bahá'u'lláh's ancestral home.

On the southwest side of the lake lie the most strategic cities of Rasht and Baku located in the former Persian and Russian empires, respectively. Both were like twin cities because the main bulk of commerce between the two nations was traded between their ports for centuries. The strategic location of the region made it the scene of the famous Iran-Russia wars between the 17th and 19th centuries. Russia succeeded in defeating Iran and consequently seized a considerable amount of Iranian territory, including Baku. Russian imperialism was growing within the region and was at its peak by the first half of 19th century.

It was in Rasht where the Russian influence was most felt. As early as in the eighteenth century the Imperial Russia had plans to take India from the British[1] with Iran being the landmass interposing between Russia and India. Russian military expansionism was supported by the advances of the industrial revolution with increasing travel infrastructure such the new railway joining the Caspian and the Black seas and linking Asia and Europe. Because of this, Rasht and Baku became the safest and most comfortable gateways to travel to Europe and to the Middle East, using a combination of steamship and trains.

Rasht, on the Iranian shores of the Caspian Sea, is where our story begins. As the capital of the Iranian province of Gilan, Rasht was by then the most densely populated province of Iran perhaps because of its intense and favourable agricultural environment and certainly because of the commerce with neighbouring Russia.

A humid subtropical climate allows a lush forest to grow in the region throughout the year and occasionally outbreaks of malaria. It is called the City of Rain. With tile roofs, Rasht resembles an English town and is also being known as the most westernized population in the country and the main gateway to Europe.

2. The Báqir's Descendants

Our narrative commences with Siyyid Báqir Musavi Tulami, a wealthy Iranian landlord in the district of Lahijan in the northern province of Gilan. Báqir, in short form, was a *siyyid*, one whose lineage could be traced to Prophet Muhammad. Being a siyyid was a sign of respectability among the native population mostly from an Islamic religious background.

---

[1]Jennifer Siegel. *Endgame: Britain, Russia and the Final Struggle for Central Asia*. IB Tauris, 2002.

Siyyid Báqir died in 1897 having begotten seven sons by the time of his death. Twenty years before, around 1879, the youngest five of these seven brothers became followers of Bahá'u'lláh. In a country where the Bahá'í Faith was, and still is, considered a heresy, the Shariah law automatically disqualified them from obtaining a share of their father's large inheritance when the patriarch died. The five brothers were disinherited by the two elder siblings who at their father's death obtained an order from the clergy to keep all the family's state and wealth for themselves. [2]

Notwithstanding that, God blessed the five brothers with fortune and they became very prosperous business people on their own. According to Mas'ud Khamsi:

> .... as they were among the first ones to discover oil in Baku (Russia) they were given Russian nationality because at that time there were no passports or identification cards in Persia. The wealth, on one hand, and due to the Russian government's influence in Persia, besides their natural honesty when dealing with Muslim priests, made them exemplary citizens. As a result, in their native city of Rasht (Persia) there were not any martyrs in the history of the Faith and the mullahs (priests) and ordinary people did not dare to insult or persecute the Bahá'ís. [3]

Their business activities involved Russia and Iran, and in their Russian civil documentation they were known by the surname Báqirof, a patronymic meaning "son from Báqir". Their newly adopted nationality gave them a degree of independence and legal protection in Iran at a time when Russian political power was feared.

The five Báqirofs became known among the Bahá'í community by the Arabic designation that Bahá'u'lláh gave them, Sádát-i-Khams[4], in short, the *Five Siyyids*. Their descendants are currently named Khamsi. According to Mas'ud Khamsi (1923-2003), a third generation

---

[2]Soli Shahvar. *Forgotten Schools: The Bahá'ís and Modern Education in Iran, 1899-1934.* I.B.Tauris, 2009.

[3]*Pioneering and Services of Mas'ud Khamsi,* unpublished manuscript.

[4]*Sádát* is the plural form of *siyyid*. The word for *five* in Arabic is *Khams*. Hence, Sádát-i-Khams means the *Five Siyyids*.

from the Sádát-i-Khams clan, his grandfather:

> ... was a very rich man at that time, so much so that it was said that the pearls and diamonds from his deposits were moved with shovels. We all witnessed this fortune with his granddaughters who were not Bahá'ís and received their grandfather's heritage. Every time my mother took me to their house, upon leaving they filled my small pockets with golden coins, pound sterling, Russian manat and Persian ashrafi ... [5]

The names of the five brothers were Mahmúd, Riḍá (Reza), Asadu'lláh, 'Alí Naqí and Naṣru'lláh. The province of Gilan where they resided had already been opened for the Faith by various early believers particularly 'Ali Ashraf Lahijani, known as Andalib, a renown Bahá'í teacher as well as a gifted poet. The story of each of these five brothers follows.

3. Siyyid Mahmúd

The famous Bahá'í poet Andalib was also a native of the Gilan province where the five brothers used to live and commenced the process of teaching them the Bahá'í Faith. The brothers appeared to be attracted to the new teachings from the beginning but referred them to Mahmúd, the eldest brother, for commenting due to his special knowledge of religious matters.

Mahmúd was not only a successful jeweller but also a man of profound spirituality and theological knowledge. He was the one who took a particular interest in the new religion that was sweeping across Iran. According to Rúhu'lláh Mihrabkhání:

> ... This brother [Siyyid Mahmúd] studied religious studies when he was young in Karbilá and Najaf, not to become a cleric but because he had an intense interest in religion and in considering its teachings, attaining virtues and understanding its truths. That is why when Andalib started teaching those brothers, the other four brothers came to him to accept the Bahá'í Faith, surrendering to Andalib's arguments to accept the new Faith with more certainty.

---

[5] *Pioneering and Services of Mas'ud Khamsi,* unpublished manuscript.

... Siyyid Mahmúd was in Karbilá [Iraq]. He always had this doubt whether the brothers were really the descendants of Prophet Muhammad. This is because being attributed to the Prophet brought with it material and spiritual advantages, meaning Sádát were always respected by people and received "khoms"[6]. As recorded in many histories, many people used to call themselves Sádát and were known in public as descendants of the Prophet, and this title was passed on to their children and grandchildren. When the Blessed Beauty confirmed in writing that they came from Muhammad's lineage, Siyyid Mahmúd was relieved of his suspicions. [7]

We also know that Siyyid Mahmúd attained the presence of Bahá'u'lláh and received at least one Tablet in his honour. In that Tablet Bahá'u'lláh also proclaims Himself as the Concealed Treasure and the Hidden Mystery, and among other guidance, reveals a prayer for him.

> O Mahmúd! Upon thee be the Glory of God, the Almighty, the Loving. I bear witness that thou hast renounced worldly cares, turning towards the celestial sanctuary of the Lord of all that hath been and shall be. Thou didst proceed from the House in order to seek out the Lord of the House, until thou didst arrive and behold His Countenance, hearkening unto the call of God, the Lord of all beings. We bear witness that thou didst attain unto that which was inscribed by the Exalted Pen in this Prison, a Prison where the Cause of God was proclaimed, and His Sovereignty, His Majesty and His Might were revealed, and every hidden secret was brought to light. Convey My greetings to thy brothers and rejoice them with the glad-tidings of that which was ordained for them by the Pen of God, the Almighty, the All-Powerful. We have remembered them in the past and do so again, with that which doth enrapture their hearts and souls.
>
> Say: Be not grieved by the actions of those who have been held

---

[6] One fifth of revenue paid as a religious practice.
[7] Rúhu'lláh Mihrabkhání. Khándán-i Sádát-i-Khams. Darmstadt: Mu'assassih- 'i `Asr-i Jadid, 1994.

back by their vain imaginings from pondering the outcome of their deeds. By the righteousness of God! That which they have committed shall not avail them. Erelong will they find themselves chastised as decreed by God, the Lord of Hosts.

Say: O God, my God! Cast me not out from the gate of Thy generosity, nor suffer me to be kept back from the ocean of Thy bounty or severed from the cord of my hope, by Thy power and might. O Lord! Thou seest this thirsty one seeking the soft-flowing waters of Thy mercy, this quintessence of nothingness Thy confirmations, this meagre rivulet the ocean of Thy wealth. I beseech Thee, O Thou Preserver of those who are nigh unto Thee, Thou Saviour of the sincere ones and Refuge of the sore oppressed, to illumine his Majesty the King with the light of Thy justice, and adorn him with that which will draw him nigh unto the court of Thy bounty and the throne of Thy Providence. Aid him, O my God, with the hosts of earth and heaven, and the battalions of the seen and the unseen. Potent art Thou to do what pleaseth Thee. No God is there save Thee, the Strong, the Most Powerful, and in Thy grasp are the reins of all that are in heaven and on earth. [8]

4. Siyyid Asadu'lláh

Siyyid Asadu'lláh was also a prosperous businessman whom the people called the *financier*. Siyyid Asadu'llah eventually moved to the city of Qazvín, 170 km southeast from Rasht, and later to the capital Tehran. Moojan Momen wrote in this regard:

> In 1899 a paved road had been completed by the Russians from Anzali [Rasht's port] to Tehran and soon became the main trade corridor of Iran. Together with Mír 'Alí Naqí [his brother], Sayyid Asadu'llah was part of the consortium who negotiated with the Russians for the concession to run a carriage and postal service on this road and to provide all travellers' services (rest houses, changes of horses, food and accommodation) along the route until 1910. As a result these two brothers became very wealthy. By 1903, following the

---

[8]Provisional translation authorised by The Universal House of Justice.

death of Mír 'Alí, Sayyid Asadu'lláh had moved back to Rasht to administer the contract.[9],[10]

He visited Bahá'u'lláh in 'Akká and is more known for having received the famous Tablet of Unity (Lawh-i-Ittihad) where Bahá'u'lláh explains, at Siyyid Asadu'lláh's request, the meaning of unity. In this Tablet, the Blessed Beauty explains six types of unity, namely, unity of religion, unity of words, unity of ritual acts, unity of rank or station, unity of wealth and unity of souls. He also received many Tablets from 'Abdu'l-Bahá honouring his services to the Faith. A passage of the Tablet translated by the Bahá'í World Centre reads as follows:

> And among the realms of unity is the unity of rank and station. It redoundeth to the exaltation of the Cause, glorifying it among all peoples. Ever since the seeking of preference and distinction came into play, the world hath been laid waste. It hath become desolate. Those who have quaffed from the ocean of divine utterance and fixed their gaze upon the Realm of Glory should regard themselves as being on the same level as the others and in the same station. Were this matter to be definitely established and conclusively demonstrated through the power and might of God, the world would become as the Abhá Paradise.
>
> Indeed, man is noble, inasmuch as each one is a repository of the sign of God. Nevertheless, to regard oneself as superior in knowledge, learning or virtue, or to exalt oneself or seek preference, is a grievous transgression. Great is the blessedness of those who are adorned with the ornament of this unity and have been graciously confirmed by God.[11]

While living in Qazvín his faith was severely tested due to the influence of the Azalis, the followers of Mírzá Yahyá, Bahá'u'lláh's half-

---

[9]Moojan Momen. *The Bahá'í Communities of Iran.* George Ronald, 2015, p. 331.

[10]Mírzá Yahyá 'Amídu'l-Atibbá Hamadání. *Memoirs of a Bahá'í in Rasht: 1889-1903* (Translated by Ahang Rabbani). Explorations in Bahá'í History, vol. 9, 2007.

[11]Bahá'í World Centre. *Messages from the Universal House of Justice 1963–1986.* Compiled by Geoffrey W. Marks. Wilmette, Illinois: Bahá'í Publishing Trust, 1996, p. 376.

brother, also called Subh-i-Azal which means Morning of Eternity. At that time Mírzá Yahyá had risen in direct opposition to Him claiming to be the spiritual successor of the Báb. Samandar, the famous Bahá'í travel teacher, has written in his chronicles how Siyyid Asadu'lláh's was successful in passing that spiritual test:

> One of the Azalis sent his brother to Siyyid Asadu'lláh to be his servant, using this as a way of coming into contact with him. This man caused suspicions and doubt to slowly enter Asadu'lláh's heart, making him hesitate and have doubt in his belief. As soon as they found out that he was not well aware of what was going on, they did not leave him alone, at home or in his store, and began to destroy his faith. From the words that this Jináb-i-Siyyid [12] [Asadu'lláh] was uttering, I found out that this person had fallen in doubt. One night I told him that because you are not fully informed of the topic in question, it is better that in your own presence we have a discussion with them. You sit aside and listen and ask God to guide you to show the truth. Asadu'lláh said the Azalis will not come to argue with you. Eventually they decided that Siyyid Asadu'lláh informs Samandar whenever the Azalis came to his house. Therefore one night, Áqá Mírzá Hasan [13] and Mírzá Abu-al-Fazl who were known to each other, went to the house of Siyyid Asadu'lláh without knowing that someone from this side was going to join them; I also attended the meeting. After greetings the way of discussion opened. I sent someone home to bring the Báb's Holy Book, the Bayan-i-Farsi, and had a deep discussion regarding all the things that caused doubt. First they expressed their doubts. So, one by one I gave the answers, referring to the Bayan. And as Siyyid Asadu'lláh was all ears, paying attention to the arguments and reasons of both sides and weighed them against each other, the topic became obvious for him and the confusion was removed, his mind became clear of doubts and his faith became stronger and he found peace of mind. Then he asked for that book, the Persian Bayán. So I gave him one book in the handwriting of Jináb-i-Mírzá Ahmad-i-Kateb as a gift.

---

[12] Jináb or Jenab is a courtesy title that can be translated as His/Her Excellency.
[13] Áqá is a male courtesy title that can be translated as Sir.

He read that book, and to the last days of his life he rendered many great services and in 'Akká he attained presence of the Blessed Beauty. In that meeting he asked, when he was in the presence of Bahá'u'lláh, a question about the unity of God. A detailed Tablet was revealed and then he passed away in Gilan, ascending to the Abhá kingdom. After his passing, a Tablet of Visitation to his tomb was revealed by the pen of the Centre of the Covenant in honour of him and the rest of the members of that family. [14]

5. Mír 'Alí Naqí

Mír 'Alí Naqí was another of the five Sádát-i-Khams brothers. He settled in Tehran where he became a wealthy merchant. One whole section of the Great Bazaar of Tehran was owned by Mr 'Alí Naqí and named after him. According to Rúhu'lláh Mihrabkhání:

> His involvement in gathering wealth in commerce did not prevent him from developing spiritual values and rendering services to the Cause. Because he was so famous and credible in his lifetime, the enemies of the Faith could not cause him much harm. But after his passing, the enemies provoked thugs to destroy his grave. [15]

Mír 'Alí Naqí died in on 29 December 1902 and was buried in the Sar Qabr Áqá cemetery where Bahá'ís used to be buried. However, they were not allowed to undertake public burial ceremonies. The neighbourhood was very hostile, for instance, when the believers were building a tomb for one of the Bahá'í martyrs the neighbours destroyed it.

Next to the cemetery there was an alley where a number of Bahá'ís had settled and where they used to teach the Faith. This passage was known as the Bábí Alley where some Bahá'ís lived along a small property known as Baghe Ferdowsi (the Garden of Paradise) that functioned as a Bahá'í centre. Usually, the Bahá'ís of Tehran came first

---

[14] Rúhu'lláh Mihrabkhání. *Khándán-i Sádát-i-Khams*. Darmstadt, Mu'assassih-'i `Asr-i Jadid, 1994.

[15] Rúhu'lláh Mihrabkhání. *Khándán-i Sádát-i-Khams*. Darmstadt, Mu'assassih-'i `Asr-i Jadid, 1994.

to the centre, visited the Bahá'ís and then went to visit the graves.

A number of notable early believers such as Rúhu'lláh Varqá and his father are buried there. Mír 'Alí Naqí was interred next to Mulla 'Alí Jan, a Bahá'í martyr. Mír 'Alí Naqí's mother was grief-stricken after the passing of her son and wanted to build a burial chamber for him. For this reason, the neighbours became very upset and began attacking the Bahá'í places in the Bábís' Alley. According to Fazel Mazandarani, "the enemies in large numbers, in particular some from the Royal mule regiment, whose commander's house was in that neighbourhood, swarmed the cemetery, and began destroying the graves and taking the dead bodies from their resting places".[16]

The mob started shooting and a bullet hit a person. It happened that at that time a number of the Bahá'ís who belonged to a regiment called the Cossacks, led by a Russian Colonel, were present having prayers, studying the Writings and listening to talks. These friends reacted immediately and counter attacked the mob, pushing them out of the house and the alley and even injuring some of them. Interestingly, the regiment commander praised these soldiers and rewarded them somehow preventing further attacks.

6. Siyyid Riḍá

Siyyid Riḍá (also written as Reza) passed away around 1881, that is, a few years after becoming a Bahá'í. There is little information about him except that he was steadfast in the Faith of Bahá'u'lláh and that along with his older brothers "rose to the service of the Cause and helped with the victory of the Faith as far as they had time and capacity". [17]

Siyyid Riḍá was the father of Siyyid Ahmad and Siyyid Mihdí, both well-known and active believers. Siyyid Ahmad's brilliant life is outlined in Part III.

As with Siyyid Mihdí, we know that his son Mírzá Riḍá with his family pioneered to Austria as early as 1911 and was instrumental for

---

[16] Fazel Mazandarani. *Zuhúru'l-Haqq (The Manifestation of Truth)*. Tehran, vol 7, p. 232-233, 1944.

[17] Rúhu'lláh Mihrabkhání. *Khándán-i Sádát-i-Khams.* Darmstadt, Mu'assassih-'i `Asr-i Jadid, 1994.

'Abdu'l-Bahá's visit to that country in the company of Siyyid Ahmad in April 1913. A personal testimony of an early German believer in the book *Die Geschichte der Österreichischen Bahá'í Gemeinde* [The History of the Austrian Bahá'í Community] indicates:

> The Bahá'í Faith took root in Vienna in 1911: That year, the Persian Mírzá Riḍá Khamsi Baqiroff settled with his family in what was then the main city of the Danubian monarchy [Vienna]. He had been a Bahá'í from childhood and became a pillar of strength for the gradually emerging Bahá'í community in Vienna over the two decades until his passing in January 1931. A eulogy prepared by the Bahá'í community of Vienna at the occasion of the passing of Riḍá Khamsi Baqiroff states that "the community of spiritual labourers of Vienna owes much to him, because the departed was a zealous co-worker and propagator of the sacred teachings who was mindful of the commandments of Bahá'u'lláh throughout his entire life".
>
> His daughter, Miss Roghi Khamsi, tragically died only months after her father's death. She died on 2 July at the age of 28 years of severe lung disease. As a devoted Bahá'í, she had also contributed much to the growth and progress of the new Faith in Vienna. The Viennese Bahá'í community honored her achievements in spreading the Bahá'í teachings in the capital in the following words: "She brought the glad tidings to countless people from the most distinguished circles. Even during her illness, she was always ready to serve the holy Cause and to spread it ... The widow of Riḍá Khamsi, Khánumgol Khamsi, returned to Persia at the beginning of the Second World War".[18]

The youngest of the five Sádát-i-Khams brothers and the most prominent was Siyyid Naṣru'lláh for whom the next section is dedicated. After Andalib led them to accept the Faith he wrote to Bahá'u'lláh mentioning their names and requesting blessings upon them. By that time the Blessed Beauty had already moved to the Mansion of Bahji. Siyyid Naṣru'lláh, Siyyid Mahmúd and Siyyid

---

[18] Alex Käfer. *Die Geschichte der Österreichischen Bahá'í Gemeinde.* Horizonte Verlag, pp 18-19, 2005.

Asadu'lláh attained His presence in the Holy Land and it is probably in that residence in the countryside of 'Akká where the visits took place.

Figure 1: Tablet of 'Abdu'l-Bahá to Siyyid Naṣru'lláh.
Source: Khándán-i Sádát-i-Khams.

Figure 2: A street scene in 'Akká, c. 1914.
Courtesy: Bahá'í Media Bank

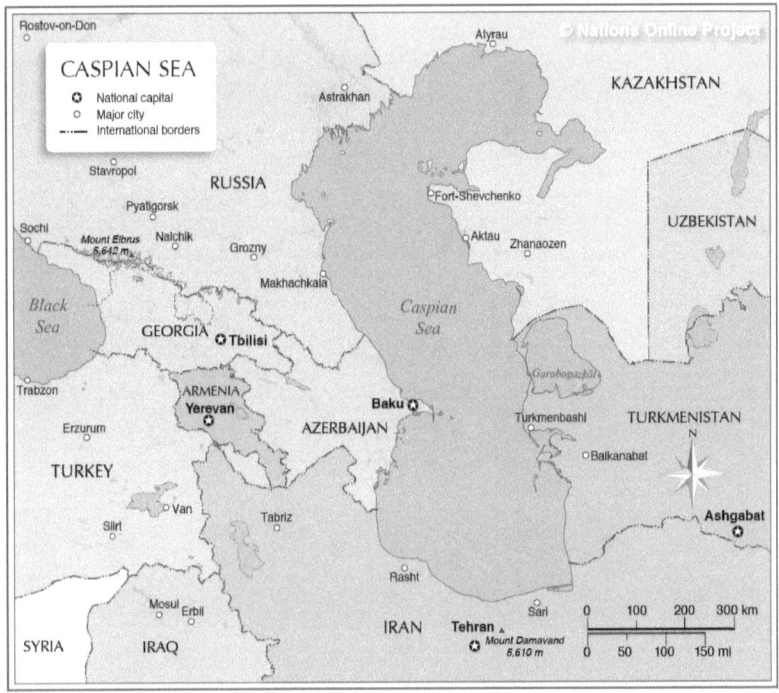

Figure 3: The Caspian Sea and Neighbouring Countries.
Courtesy: Pedro Donaires

Figure 4: Three of the Báqirof brothers are standing on the front. Left to right: Siyyid Naṣru'lláh, Mír 'Alí Naqí and Siyyid Asadu'lláh.
Source: Khándán-i Sádát-i-Khams.

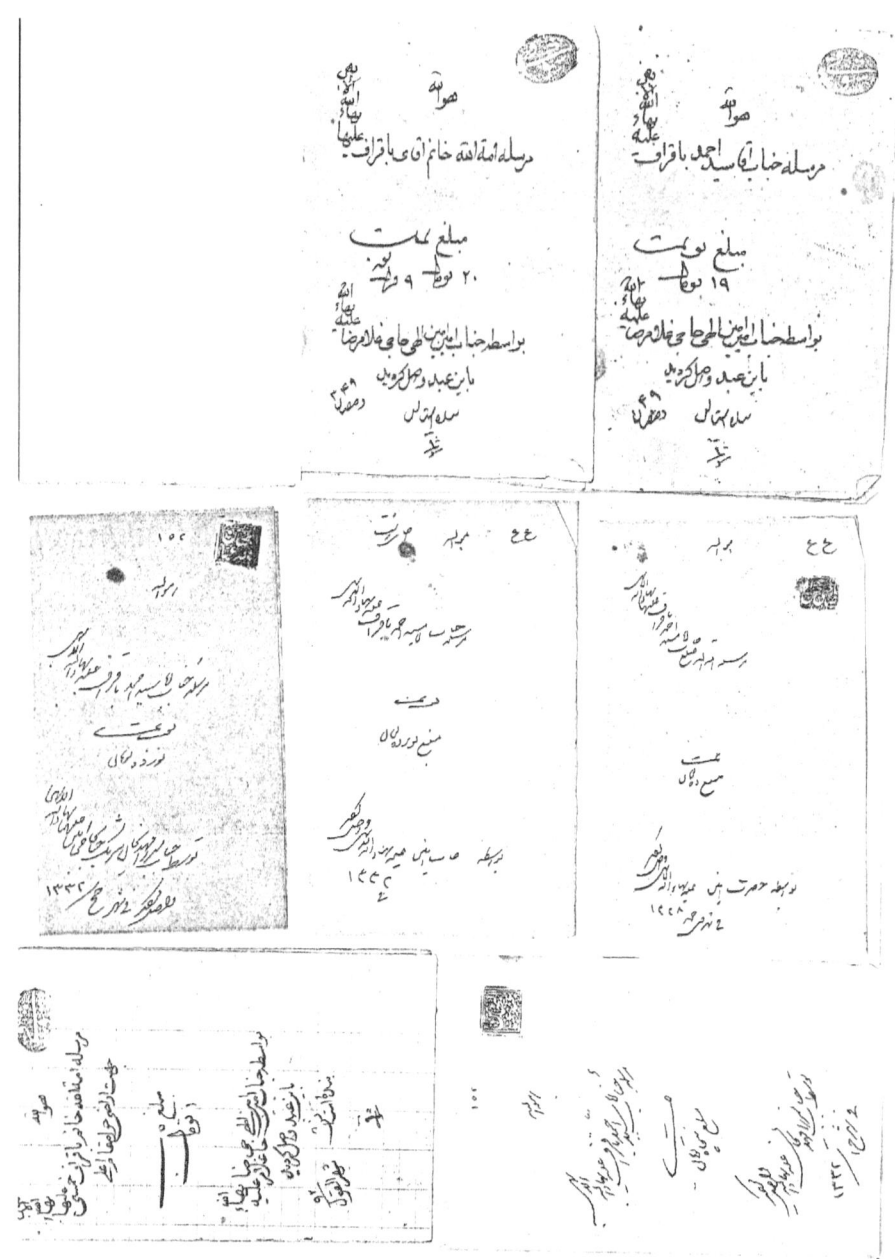

Figure 5: Receipts by 'Abdu'l-Bahá for Khamsi-Báqirof family's contribution to the Bahá'í Fund.
Courtesy: Khamsi-Samandari family.

Figure 6: Siyyid Naṣru'lláh.
Source: Khándán-i Sádát-i-Khams.

Figure 7: Siyyid Naṣru'lláh with some of his children.
Source: Khándán-i-Sádát-i-Khams.

Figure 8: Siyyid Naṣru'lláh with Bahá'ís of Tehran.
Sitting on right side of second row.
Source: Khándán-i Sádát-i-Khams

Figure 9: Siyyid Ahmad with 'Abdu'l-Bahá in Paris.
Third standing from the left.
Source: Khándán-i-Sádát-i-Khams.

Figure 10: Siyyid Ahmad with 'Abdu'l-Bahá in Paris.
Third standing from the left.
Courtesy: Khamsi-Samandari family.

PART 2:
Siyyid Naṣru'lláh Báqirof
(1859-1924)

1. Introduction

Naṣru'lláh was a great man, one that attained the presence of Bahá'u'lláh and 'Abdu'l-Bahá in 'Akká and for over forty years served the Cause of God in Russia and Iran with unquestioning devotion. He distinguished himself for the way he used his social influence, being a rich and respectable businessman, to protect the Bahá'í community from the constant onslaught of the ecclesiastical Muslim hierarchy which in turn instigated the establishment and the populace to harass the believers. Naṣru'lláh was also very successful in teaching the Faith to prominent people in Iran. The meaning of his name Naṣru'llah in Arabic, the Victory of God, was certainly befitting of his achievements in the Cause of Bahá'u'lláh.

Abundant words from the Blessed Beauty[19] and the Center of His Covenant confirm his elevated station. For example, Bahá'u'lláh revealed to him:

> O Naṣru'lláh! Thou hast attained unto the precious and incomparable Word of God. Know this and be of the thankful. The Pen of the Most High enjoineth steadfastness upon the people of God, for loud clamour hath been raised in every land. Those souls who, when affliction befell them, concealed themselves shamelessly as behind a veil, have now emerged into the open like serpents, ready to strike at the Lord of Names. They opposed the One Who hath revealed from the heaven of His Will the equivalent of every Book of former or more recent times, while they strive to misguide the people with their vain imaginings and idle fancies.

---
[19] A title of Bahá'u'lláh.

Woe betide them for that which their hands have wrought in opposition to God. They have repudiated and denied Him, closing their eyes unto that which was sent down from the Kingdom of His wondrous Utterance.

Convey the greetings of this Wronged One to the friends, and rejoice their hearts with the bounties of the One True God, exalted be His Majesty. The glory which hath dawned above the horizon of My loving-kindness rest upon thee, and upon every steadfast and righteous one.[20]

In turn, 'Abdu'l-Bahá wrote to him that he had been the cause of guidance of the prominent men of Iran, a service very difficult to succeed. He advised Naṣru'lláh to thank God because of this blessing that can be compared to a crown conferred by the Hand of the Merciful Himself.[21]

1.1 Settling in Baku

Siyyid Naṣru'lláh was not highly educated. Actually, he regularly apologised for not being able to write well. However, he was gifted with brilliant business acumen, and although deprived of his inheritance he achieved great commercial success. Naṣru'lláh left his native Rasht and travelled to Baku on the adjacent shore of the Caspian Sea to begin a new life when he was 18 years old. Baku was thriving commercially and, being under Russian sovereignty, meant that the hostile Muslim ecclesiastics and popular hostility was under governmental control.

Baku is a short form of Badkube which stands for *city of winds* due to its strong gusts. This city port, situated on the northern section of the old Silk Road connecting China and Rome, had plenty of caravanserais (inns) where caravans packed with travellers stopped. It was, and still is, the centre of the remarkable Azari culture with a variety of languages spoken such as Persian (Farsi), the native Azari and Russian. As discussed earlier, Baku was formerly part of Iran and therefore it was not a strange place for Iranian. Iran was defeated by Russia during the Russo-Persian War of 1804-1813 and Baku was

---

[20]Provisional translation authorised by The Universal House of Justice.

[21]Rúhu'lláh Mihrabkhání. *Khándán-i Sádát-i-Khams.* Darmstadt, Mu'assassih-'i `Asr-i Jadid, 1994.

ceded to Russia in the Treaty of Gulistan in October 1813.

In Baku, Naṣru'lláh began to work for a firm in the nascent petroleum industry. Baku was booming in oil extraction because at that time extraction was done manually and no complex technology was needed. Oil naturally emerged from the surface or was found manually at very close depth. By the end of the 19th century Baku was supplying more than half of the world's oil production.

Rúhu'lláh Mihrabkhání stated:

After arriving in Baku, Siyyid Naṣru'lláh began working for a merchant exporting oil to Iran. Because he was very clever in commerce, it did not take long for him to achieve great success. He succeeded so much that when that merchant became bankrupt, Naṣru'lláh took over the business and slowly paid back the merchant's debts to his debtors. An accident also helped him in this. From the two oil tankers that were travelling and bringing oil to Iran, one belonged to Siyyid Naṣru'lláh and the other to another merchant. The one that belonged to the other merchant sunk while the one that belonged to Siyyid Naṣru'lláh safely reached Iran. So, the oil was sold at a better price and his business flourished.[22]

1.2 Sakineh Khánum

In Baku Siyyid Naṣru'lláh married Sakineh, a Russian citizen, who was a devoted Bahá'í and the sister of the celebrated poet Mírzá 'Abd al-Khaliq Ya'qubzadih. Sakineh bore ten children to Naṣru'lláh: seven boys and three girls although the first one died at a young age.

According to Rúhu'lláh Mihrabkhání, "'Abdu'l-Bahá always had a great feeling of kindness towards Sakineh Khánum and revealed some Tablets in her name".[23] In one of His Tablets, 'Abdu'l-Bahá reminded her of Siyyid Naṣru'lláh's special reverence shown at Bahá'u'lláh's shrine and how he carried water on his shoulders to water the surrounding gardens. The Centre of the Covenant advises her that his pilgrimage

---

[22] Rúhu'lláh Mihrabkhání. *Khándán-i Sádát-i-Khams*. Darmstadt, Mu'assassih-'i 'Asr-i Jadid, 1994.

[23] Rúhu'lláh Mihrabkhání. *Khándán-i Sádát-i-Khams*. Darmstadt, Mu'assassih-'i 'Asr-i Jadid, 1994.

on her behalf has been accepted and prays for the well-being of her family. In another Tablet, 'Abdu'l-Bahá compares two of her sons with jewels that God has given to her and praises Siyyid Naṣru'lláh's parental virtues. In a Tablet written in His own handwriting 'Abdu'l-Bahá addressed them as descendants from a pure soul and promised that the light of their children will radiate for centuries to come.

Further, the Master asked Siyyid Naṣru'lláh to choose one of his talented sons and send him to the Holy Land for His personal training. Rúhu'lláh Mihrabkhání wrote:

> This was 'Abdu'l-Bahá's blessing and loving attention to Jináb-i-Báqirof, but Jináb-i-Báqirof answered subtly that both of his sons were talented! So he sent both of them and for years they were studying at the University of Beirut under the guidance of 'Abdu'l-Bahá. In the University of Beirut they were together with Shoghi Effendi and on holidays they would go attend the presence of 'Abdu'l-Bahá. Then from there, 'Abdu'l-Bahá sent them to England to carry on with their studies and because it was not possible to send money to England from Iran, due to the First World War, 'Abdu'l-Bahá supported them. [24]

1.3 Wealth and Socio-Economic Development

As stated previously, Siyyid Naṣru'lláh became a wealthy and successful businessman. For example, he managed to get the concession to administer the road between Anzali, Rasht's port, and the capital Tehran. The concession included the franchise to establish motels and restaurants along the 370 km route. Previously transportation was based on animal caravans and traveling on foot but they were innovatively replaced by wagons and carriages. The concession also included the maintenance of the road.[25] About ten stations were established along the road where tired horses were replaced by rested ones ensuring a quicker and more comfortable trip as well as the faster delivery of merchandise and the postal service. Many Bahá'ís were employed in that business.

His business combined private entrepreneurship, innovation and

---

[24]Rúhu'lláh Mihrabkhání. *Khándán-i Sádát-i-Khams*. Darmstadt, Mu'assassih-'i 'Asr-i Jadid, 1994.

[25]Marzieh Gail. *Summon up Remembrance*. George Ronald Oxford, p. 98, 1987.

socio-economic development. Eventually Siyyid Báqirof transferred his wealth to Iran and settled in Tehran.[26] Along with his four brothers, he owned an important publishing house in Tehran. He also invested in agriculture, hospitality and entertainment. For example, he bought extensive properties in the rural areas of Gilan, Mazindaran and the Rayy area of Tehran where he employed mostly Bahá'ís. According to Moojan Momen:

> Sayyid Nasru'llah Khan Báqirof owned a group of six or seven villages south of Tehran in the area known as Ghar. These included Hasanabad (pop. 380 in 1951), Ja'farabad (5 km southwest of Rayy on the main Tehran to Qumm road, pop. 20 in 1951) and 'Alíyabad (9 km south of Rayy, 1 km west of the Tehran to Qumm road, pop. 150 in 1951). A former resident of Báqirabad states that in 1950s Báqirabad consisted of a population of 110, of whom 65 were Bahá'ís. From about 1910 Báqirof encouraged Bahá'í villagers to move to these villages, especially from the villages of the Kashan area, which was being ravaged by Na'ib Husayn Kashani and the Sultanabad area. They farmed the area, growing grains and sugar beet and herding livestock. In 1918 'Abbas Mahmúdi moved to these villages and began to teach the Bahá'í children there. The Bahá'í villagers often talked about the Bahá'í Faith with the Muslims in these villages and in the surrounding villages such as Sayyid-abad, Khalazir (6 km northwest of Rayy, pop. 395 in 1951) and Pala'in (8 km west of Rayy, pop. 176 in 1951). Among those who tried to spread the Bahá'í Faith in this way were Mírzá Husayn Jawshqani Masiha'I and his son Mírzá Amanu'llah Mudir Masiha'i; Mírzá Hatim Khan (of Ahl-Haqq origin), the clerk at the mill in Hasanabad; Ustad Habibu'llah Vadqani, the master miller; and Haji Ulya. These individuals would invite those Muslims who showed interest to meetings at which 'Abbas Mahmúdi spoke.

> Primary schools were established in three of these villages.

---

[26]Hossein Abadian. *Armenians Socio-Political Activists & Iranian Constitutional Revolution (1905-1911).* In Proceedings of International Academic Conferences (No. 2503649). International Institute of Social and Economic Sciences, June 2015.

The largest was at Hasanabad. At Ja'farabad there was an established primary school teacher, who for some years was Ustad Ibrahim 'Ubudiyyat. At Báqirabad, Sakinih Sultan would teach during the week and a Bahá'í would come from Tehran on Fridays to teach arithmetic. The children from this school would go to Ja'farabad for a short time at the end of their studies in order to get a signature from the teacher there and then go to Rayy to have the certificate issued.[27]

Siyyid Naṣru'lláh also introduced the first cinema and the first modern hotel with European style. These were known as the Grand Hotel and the Grand Cinema built on the exclusive Lalehzar Street, which Násir'd-Dín Sháh had built to emulate the explendor of Parisian Avenue des Champs-Élysées, a landscape that impressed him in his last European tour. The hotel and the cinema complex included a ballroom and a theater. Representing progressive thought the Grand Hotel hosted in 1924 the first female singer, Qamar-ol-Moluk Vaziri, without wearing a hijab.[28]

The Grand Cinema became a recreational space for the people of Tehran. In turn, the Grand Hotel was built in the hope that 'Abdu'l-Bahá would visit Tehran and count on a comfortable place to stay. 'Abdu'l-Bahá Himself blessed this enterprise and approved Siyyid Naṣru'lláh's wishes that the hotel be registered as a property of the Bahá'í Assembly. Several Western travelled teachers lodged there such as the Hand of the Cause of God Martha Root in February 1913. For the Bahá'í Magazine she wrote:

> Coming into the Grand Hotel, I saw that covers had been laid for nearly one hundred and fifty guests; the owners were giving this dinner in my honour. Many of the famous national dishes of Persia were served - chicken pilaw with pistachio nuts, raisins, dates and orange peel for flavour. Also they had the many delicious fruits for which Persia is so celebrated.
>
> This hotel has been my headquarters. It is one of the most beautiful and comfortable hotels in all Persia. It is an

---

[27] Moojan Momen. *The Bahá'í Community of Iran*. George Ronald Oxford, 2015, pp. 105-106.

[28] A headscarf worn in public by Muslim women.

interesting fact that the builder of this hostelry, Mr Seyid Nasroullah Bakeroff [Siyyid Naṣru'lláh], a most ardent Bahá'í, constructed this luxurious "palace" built round a central court and with a great theatre, in the hope that the Centre of the Covenant 'Abdu'l-Bahá, would come again to His native land and this hotel would be His home! Some religionist opposed him and tried to have the construction stopped. They said, "he is building such a hotel for his God". Well, indeed he did build it to the glory of God. One feels the love and the spirit in this house.

Ordinary travellers are impressed with the courtesy, the completeness of everything; but coming as I did as a Bahá'í (and it will be the same when you come), it is infinitely sweet to hear "Alláh-u-Abhá'" every time a boy comes to serve you; and he does not walk, he runs to fulfil your wish! The three brothers Mir Aminoullah Bakeroff, Mir Kamal Bakeroff and Mir Jalal Bakeroff own this hotel, and with them I feel their love, their thoughtfulness, their efficient care are showered upon this humble Bahá'í from the west as it would have been poured upon 'Abdu'l-Bahá who never came during His lifetime, and the builder, too, has passed on to the Other World. [29]

1.4 Mode of Living

Siyyid Naṣru'lláh, as well as his brothers, used their wealth to develop a good relationship with a number of high-ranking people of Iran in order to protect the Faith. They were well known for their wealth but also for the integrity with which they conducted their business. Notwithstanding their prosperity, Siyyid Naṣru'lláh and his family lived a modest life because he was in essence a simple man. According to Rúhu'lláh Mihrabkhání:

> Despite the fact that he was not as well educated as his brothers and would feel embarrassed when he wrote something to the presence of 'Abdu'l-Bahá for not having proper dictation and writing style, he had a very important status in the country, which allowed him to declare the Cause to the greatest and

---

[29] Martha Root. Pilgrimage through Persia. Part 3: Qazvin and Tihran. *Star of the West,* 21, 6 (September 1930), p. 177.

most knowledgeable men in Iran at that time.[30]

He built a magnificent house on the prestigious Amiriyih street opposite the residence of Prince Kamran Mírzá, the Shah's son and also vice-regent. According to Rúhu'lláh Mihrabkhání:

> Jináb [Siyyid Naṣru'lláh] Báqirof, despite the glory and majesty he had in the eyes of the people, led a very simple life himself. His home had two parts: Biruni (outside) and Andaruni (inside). The outside area, which was to meet and welcome the Prime Ministers, the ministers, ambassadors, the rich and the famous people of Iran, the people of capacity, was extremely luxurious and rich. But the Andaruni, where he lived, was absolutely simple and unadorned. At the dinner area, in the Andaruni division where he was, at the time of lunch, men and women, servants or maids, labourers and gardeners, all of them sat next to him and ate together. He led a very simple life and if one of his servitors was wasteful, he rebuked him. However, if he was to spend for the Faith he was extremely generous.[31]

1.5 A Russian Citizen

Since his wife Sakineh was Russian, Siyyid Naṣru'lláh obtained Russian citizenship. Those were very interesting times in Iran and Baku. In Iran, the Qajar dynasty was absolutely corrupt extracting money from the rich who for this reason were trying to get hold of either the Russian or the British citizenship. Such citizenships would provide them some degree of protection for any abuse through their embassies.

At the global level the First World War (1911-1914) was raging all over the world. The Russian front was being attacked by Germany which was allied with the Turkish Empire. After massive failures during that conflagration, perennial social inequalities and the economic crisis that surrounded the country, Czar Nicholas abdicated

---

[30]Rúhu'lláh Mihrabkhání. *Khándán-i Sádát-i-Khams*. Darmstadt, Mu'assassih-'i `Asr-i Jadid, 1994.

[31]Rúhu'lláh Mihrabkhání. *Khándán-i Sádát-i-Khams*. Darmstadt, Mu'assassih-'i `Asr-i Jadid, 1994.

in 1917. His empire had finally collapsed and was left in the hands of a politically intolerant Communist regime taking charge of the country. Some ethnic groups found in this chaotic land an opportunity to be emancipated from the Russian colonial yoke.

Having its centre in Baku, Azerbaijan was proclaimed as an autonomous republic comprising the old provinces of Azerbaijan, Armenia and Georgia but it did not last long because two years later Azerbaijan was forcefully invaded by Russian forces and declared a satellite Soviet republic. In the meantime, Iran was in tumult as everything had become very expensive and there was an acute shortage of bread that led people to massive protests. There was political chaos everywhere with people demanding a modern constitution which was finally adopted in 1910 by the Shah after five years of intense debate and convulsion. Siyyid Naṣru'lláh must have sensed such instability as he eventually settled in Tehran during those turbulent years. The decrepit Qajar monarchy finally collapsed in 1925 and was replaced by the Pahlavi dynasty led by Reza Shah who was proclaimed king by a majority of the parliament.

2. Relationship with Bahá'u'lláh

Having accepted Bahá'u'lláh at the beginning of his new spiritual identity, Siyyid Naṣru'lláh then received two additional bounties. First, from Baku he visited Bahá'u'lláh in the Prison of 'Akká and secondly, he received various Tablets from Him.

Siyyid Naṣru'lláh had the enormous privilege of attaining the presence of the Manifestation of God during his lifetime. We do not know exactly the year, but must have been before he was 33 years of age, while still a young man. What we know is that Siyyid Naṣru'lláh must have been twenty years old when he became a Bahá'í along with his four older brothers. In any case, in various Tablets, the Blessed Beauty reminded him of these two blessings: the blessing of belief and the blessing of pilgrimage. Such blessings accompanied him for the rest of his life's journey, assisting him to become a star in the firmament of the Faith.

On the inestimable grace of reaching the presence of 'Him Whom God shall make manifest', that is, Bahá'u'lláh, the Báb had revealed in the Bayán:

There is no paradise more wondrous for any soul than to be exposed to God's Manifestation in His Day, to hear His verses and believe in them, to attain His presence, which is naught but the presence of God, to sail upon the sea of the heavenly kingdom of His good-pleasure, and to partake of the choice fruits of the paradise of His divine Oneness.[32]

We do not know how Siyyid Naṣru'lláh travelled to the Holy Land but being in Baku he could have travelled the new Western route opened between the strategic Caspian and the Black Seas. The Russian Empire had built the Trans Caucasus railway around 1883 connecting Europe and Asia. The 1,200 km line joined the ports of Baku and Poti, on the Caspian and Black Seas respectively. From Poti, comfortable steamships took passengers to Istanbul, the capital of Turkey, and from there the voyage proceeded smoothly towards the Holy Land via the Mediterranean Sea.

On this pilgrimage to His sacred presence, the Blessed Beauty revealed to him:

To Jináb-i-Áqá Siyyid Naṣru'lláh, who attained Our presence

> He it is Who beholdeth all from the Abhá Horizon

The victory hath indeed arrived, and by it the banners of dominion have been raised above all other standards by God, the Incomparable, the Almighty, the All-Knowing. He it is Who standeth victorious before all creation, summoning all towards the All-Glorious, the All-Bounteous One. Through Him the pillars of godlessness have trembled, and the daystar of Divine Unity shone forth from the Horizon of the Heaven of Understanding. Through Him the Divine Secret was divulged, and all created beings proclaimed: "The Kingdom is God's, the Lord of the beginning and the end".

O Naṣru'lláh, thou didst turn towards the Supreme Horizon while this Wronged One was in the Prison of 'Akká. Thou didst enter therein and beheld Us, hearkening unto the Call as it was raised betwixt earth and heaven; thou didst believe in Him

---

[32] The Báb. *Selections from the Writings of the Báb*. Haifa: Bahá'í World Centre, 1976, p. 77.

Who was seated upon the throne of testimony, endowed with wisdom and utterance. Remember My loved ones on My behalf and rejoice them with the glad tidings of My loving providence that hath encompassed the whole world. Say: Your names have been sent down from the most exalted Pen as a token of the bounty of God, the Lord of Lords. We counsel you to preserve whatsoever hath been given you by God, the loving, the Lord of grace. By My Life! My remembrance cannot be compared to that of any in the world. Unto this beareth witness He with Whom is the knowledge of the Book.

Say: O God, my God! Thou seest my sad condition and hearest my lamentation. I beseech Thee by the splendours of the Thine omnipotence and Thy dominion, and by that which was concealed in Thy knowledge, to ordain for me that which shall draw me nigh unto Thee. Praised be Thou, O my Lord, for Thou hast made known unto me Thy hidden mysteries and treasured symbol, and hast given me to drink from the living waters of reunion with Thee by the hands of Thy grace and bounty. Thou hast enabled me to hearken unto Thy most beauteous call, and hast shown me the splendours of Thy Countenance shining forth from Thy exalted horizon. I beseech Thee, O Thou the Lord of the kingdom of eternity, by the sovereignty of Thy Name, to graciously aid me to serve Thy Cause among thy servants, and to remember and praise Thee in Thy lands.

O Lord! This stammering one hath turned towards the kingdom of Thine Utterance; this longing heart seeketh the realm of Thy providence, and this remote soul the court of Thy nearness. I beseech Thee not to deny him that which he craveth from the clouds of Thy mercy and the heaven of Thy grace. Write down, then, for him the good of this world and the world to come. Potent art Thou to do what pleaseth Thee. No God is there but Thee, the Ever-Forgiving, the All-Glorious. No God is there but Thee, the Almighty, the All-knowing. [33]

In another Tablet the Blessed Beauty gives him the following exhortations:

---

[33] Provisional translation authorised by The Universal House of Justice.

O Naṣr! Upon thee be the glory of God, the Lord of Providence. Beseech thou God not to deprive His servants from the liberal effusions of the Lord of creation in the Day of Resurrection. A man's life in this world is even as a breeze that wafteth in through one door and leaveth by another. In this day, it behooveth the loved ones of the Desire of the world, those who have quaffed from the ocean of true understanding and fixed their gaze on the horizon of mercy, to strive with utmost love and joy and through wisdom and utterance to enlighten the wayward and awaken the heedless. Say: O friends! Today is the dawn of the day of justice. Strive ye to become the daysprings of goodly deeds and acquire an upright and saintly character. In these days, man hath been accorded the means of attaining that which is conducive to everlasting life. The honourable Asad, upon him rest My glory, is with Us and hath presented thy missive. Praised be God that the fragrance of service and steadfastness wafteth therefrom. In this day, one must cling unto that which diffuseth the sweet-smelling savours of justice, equity, and goodly deeds, and act wholly for the sake of God, the Lord of creation and the Ordainer in the Promised Day. This holy injunction hath been sent down by the All-Wise, the All-Knowing. To this truth beareth witness every one of the Divine Books. He hath commanded all to observe piety and uprightness, and to avoid wickedness and oppression.

Blessed is the city whose inhabitants have not been deterred by worldly distractions from the light of godliness, trustworthiness, and virtue. This sublime statement is as the most luminous daystar shining resplendent from the horizon of the Divine Tablets. Well is it with him who discerneth and observeth it, and woe betide the heedless. [34]

2.1 Passing of Bahá'u'lláh

The ascension of the Ancient Beauty[35] in 1892 affected Naṣru'lláh severely and brought him into a state of despair and hopelessness. It was a Tablet from 'Abdu'l-Bahá which brought life back to his heart

---

[34] Provisional translation authorised by The Universal House of Justice.

[35] A title of Bahá'u'lláh

through illustrating the continuity of the Cause of God. In that Tablet the Centre of the Covenant tells Siyyid Naṣru'lláh that He has not received any news from him for a long time. 'Abdu'l-Bahá compares Siyyid Naṣru'lláh to a nightingale that has stopped singing in the divine garden and mentions His concern. Further, he is encouraged to open his mouth and sing in such a way that the spiritual world can reverberate with his melodies. 'Abdu'l-Bahá called Siyyid Naṣru'lláh His beloved and urges him to speak up and to stand up in God's servitude.

According to Rúhu'lláh Mihrabkhání:

After reading this Tablet from 'Abdu'l-Bahá, he was refreshed and he became aware of his own status and purpose. He kept in mind Bahá'u'lláh's advice from a Tablet revealed in his honour, which says, "Good for those servants whose wealth and property do not deprive them in the Day of God", and then he became one of those who sacrificed his life and wealth for the service of the Cause until the end of his life.[36]

Being protected by 'Abdu'l-Bahá's shadow, Naṣru'lláh rose above his limitations and became consistently an example of service. Following Bahá'u'lláh's ascension, Naṣru'lláh subsequently attained 'Abdu'l-Bahá's presence in 'Akká.

2.2 Guidance from 'Abdu'l-Bahá

'Abdu'l-Bahá revealed several Tablets to Naṣru'lláh advising him of various matters. In those Tablets, 'Abdu'l-Bahá speaks highly of Naṣru'lláh's station of servitude. This is one of the Tablets [37]praising his steadfastness:

Baku

Jináb-i-Áqá Siyyid Naṣru'lláh, may the Glory of God be upon him!

---

[36]Rúhu'lláh Mihrabkhání. *Khándán-i Sádát-i-Khams.* Darmstadt, Mu'assassih-'i `Asr-i Jadid, 1994.

[37]*Bahá'í Reference Library.* Writings and Talks of 'Abdu'l-Bahá. Available from: https://www.bahai.org/library/authoritative-texts/abdul-baha/additional-tablets-extracts-talks/852331323/852331323.pdf

He is God

O thou who hast held fast unto the unbreakable Handle![38] Render thanks unto God that thou hast quaffed from the cup of steadfastness and constancy and clung unto the sure handle of perseverance. Thou hast been inebriated with the wine of true knowledge; thou hast proceeded from the habitation of ruin to the abode of prosperity. Wherefore, seize the chalice of the Covenant, exhilarate the friends with the wine of the Divine Testament, and frustrate the purpose of those who waver. Tear off the robe of stillness, drink deep from the pure chalice, and hasten to embrace the true Friend. By the grace and bounty of God, souls have been raised that stand immovable as a mountain of iron in the Covenant and are as firm and strong as an impregnable foundation. They are like unto a steel barrier in the face of the Gog of vacillation, a strong wall before the Magog of confusion, a shelter amidst the whirlwind of sedition, and a safeguard against the tempest of trials. I fain would hope that through the bounties and bestowals of the Ancient Beauty—may My soul be a sacrifice for His faithful lovers—this exquisite robe may befittingly adorn the figure of that servant of the Abhá Beauty, and thou mayest be so firm and steadfast that all the friends in that land may too become steadfast and firm.

The Glory of God rest upon thee and upon all them that have held fast unto the Covenant!

With regard to the late King's assassin, His Excellency the Prime Minister [39] informed all the consuls in the surrounding regions that, after careful investigation and inquiry, it had become clear that the contemptible assassin [40] was an anti-

---

[38] Cf. Qur'án 2:256.

[39] 'Alí-Aṣghar Khán

[40] Following the assassination of Náṣiri'd-Dín Sháh on 1 May 1896, it was assumed, in the atmosphere of all-pervasive fear, and in light of the previous attempt on the life of the Sháh in 1852, that his murderer, Mírzá Riḍáy-i-Kirmání, was a Bábí. Only later did the government acknowledge the fact that Mírzá Riḍá was an adherent of Siyyid Jamálu'd-Dín-i-Afghání, a political activist and an enemy of the Cause.

monarchist and an atheist who had no affiliation with other groups. Indeed, the establishment of the truth of the matter was due to the competence, discernment, capacity, fairmindedness, and justice of the Prime Minister. Praised be God that the truth of this treason and the partisanship of that arrogant outcast were made clear and evident. This is for no other reason save the confirmations of the Kingdom. All the friends of God must pray continuously, by day and by night, for the glory of His Majesty, the new just king, [41] and should also value the fairness and justice of the Prime Minister and pray for his well-being.

The Glory of God rest upon thee.

Ibn-i-Abhar—upon him be the effulgent Glory of God— highly praised the steadfastness and constancy shown by thee and by all the friends in that land. Blessed, doubly blessed, are ye, O servants of the All-Merciful!

Deliver thou the enclosed letters. Among them is a letter to Nabíl-i-Musáfir, that is, Ḥájí Muḥammad-Báqir-i-Hamadání, which must be delivered to his son Ḥájí Muḥammad-Taqí, who hath returned from the Holy Land. Be sure to deliver it.

Three main themes can be found in those Tablets are : Firmness in the Covenant, general advice to the Bahá'ís about not getting involved in politics and praising him for being such a wonderful Bahá'í. At a time when Bahá'í literature was sparce such guidance was very valuable for Naṣru'lláh's Bahá'í activities.

2.2.1 Firmness in the Covenant

In several tablets 'Abdu'l-Bahá reminded and praised Siyyid Naṣru'lláh for his firmness in the Covenant and testified that the Sádát-i-Khams (the five brothers) tried the best to serve the Faith. Siyyid Naṣru'lláh resolutely adhered to 'Abdu'l-Bahá's leadership following Bahá'u'lláh's ascension in 1892. 'Abdu'l-Bahá testifies in those Tablets that Siyyid Naṣru'lláh certainly has drunk from the cup of steadfastness in His Covenant. He is compared to a mountain in the Cause of God and encouraged to be a river of eternal life for his loved

---

[41] Muẓaffari'd-Dín Sháh

ones and a flame of fire to His enemies. He also stated that the light of the Covenant covers the whole world and those who are steadfast have attained great happiness. Siyyid Naṣru'lláh is further reminded that in the Cause there is no place for the weak ones. To those who are not steadfast, 'Abdu'l-Bahá advised them to rely on God so that they can pass the test.[42]

2.2.2 Advice on Politics

'Abdu'l-Bahá also expounded and elucidated the political crises that Iran was experiencing. In clear terms, Siyyid Naṣru'lláh was counselled that the teachings of Bahá'u'lláh were the only remedy for Iran otherwise the country would continue to experience its current perturbations. Without the Bahá'í teachings, Siyyid Naṣru'lláh was told, the poison in people's liver could not be cured. Hence, the situation of danger and frustration could not be eliminated. 'Abdu'l-Bahá refers to the Iranian people as being asleep and all their lives being spent on material aspirations. He reiterates that nothing but the healing from the divine doctor can have a positive effect.

Also, 'Abdu'l-Bahá advised that the believers should not get involved in politics in order to remain safe, despite all the internal tumult. When people observed the Bahá'í Teachings they realised their benign influence.

'Abdu'l-Bahá reminded Siyyid Naṣru'lláh that Iranian people found nothing in politics and their minds became empty-handed when they looked into the religious establishment. Iran attempted everything in terms of politics and they received nothing then they turned to their religious beliefs finding themselves still wanting. Abdu'l-Bahá reiterated to Siyyid Naṣru'lláh that Bahá'u'lláh's teachings are the only divine remedy for Iran's illnesses.

In a Tablet, 'Abdu'l-Bahá told him the story of Mr Brian, the American Foreign minister, who upon his return to America gave talks and declared to the newspaper that Asia can only settle when Bahá'í teachings are followed. Siyyid Naṣru'lláh was also told that disunity is a global problem, not only in Iran but also in Europe, which could be

---

[42]Rúhu'lláh Mihrabkhání. *Khándán-i Sádát-i-Khams.* Darmstadt, Mu'assassih-'i `Asr-i Jadid, 1994.

described as birth pains. Hence the principles of Bahá'u'lláh because were the only solution to prevent wars.

Siyyid Naṣru'lláh is told that Bahá'u'lláh Himself had predicted all the current ordeals and 'Abdu'l-Bahá expressed His hopes that the First World War is transformed into peace so all of humanity attains everlasting unity and happiness.

2.2.3 Tributes to Siyyid Naṣru'lláh

In many of His Tablets, 'Abdu'l-Bahá pays tribute to Siyyid Naṣru'lláh's special attributes. In one of them, the Centre of the Covenant compares Siyyid Naṣru'lláh along with two other distinguished believers, Hájí Mullá Reza and Mírzá 'Azizu'lláh Khan-i-Varqá, to the stars of heaven. He says that those souls are the three shining stars of the Constellation of Taer. He also refers to them as falcons of the heavens of certitude.[43]

In one Tablet 'Abdu'l-Bahá advises Siyyid Naṣru'lláh that in Tehran as well as in the rest of the world people are ready to receive Bahá'u'lláh's message. He also praised Siyyid Naṣru'lláh for teaching the Faith and said that this is a task that everyone can do, that is, spending one's life in the service to Bahá'u'lláh. 'Abdu'l-Bahá counsels him to be happy and thankful for such a bounty.[44]

In another Tablet 'Abdu'l-Bahá tells him that his crowning achievement is having guided the greatest men of the country. Such was 'Abdu'l-Bahá's love for Siyyid Naṣru'lláh that He would have written a letter to him every day were it not for the tests that He was going through. The mere fact of mentioning Siyyid Naṣru'lláh's name, 'Abdu'l-Bahá says, would move the ocean of kindness and produce waves.[45]

In those Tablets, 'Abdu'l-Bahá promises that the fame of the services of Sádát-i-Khams will endure for centuries to come and will

---

[43]Rúhu'lláh Mihrabkhání. *Khándán-i Sádát-i-Khams.* Darmstadt, Mu'assassih-'i 'Asr-i Jadid, 1994.

[44]Rúhu'lláh Mihrabkhání. *Khándán-i Sádát-i-Khams.* Darmstadt, Mu'assassih-'i 'Asr-i Jadid, 1994.

[45]Rúhu'lláh Mihrabkhání. *Khándán-i Sádát-i-Khams.* Darmstadt, Mu'assassih-'i 'Asr-i Jadid, 1994.

spread in the heavens. 'Abdu'l-Bahá even compared them to stars shining forever promising that the blessings of Bahá'u'lláh will shine on that family forever. He also said that He prays for his protection and mercy every second and that He misses Siyyid Naṣru'lláh, that although he is far from 'Abdu'l-Bahá still he is in His heart and that nothing prevents 'Abdu'l-Bahá from remembering him.[46]

3. Service

Siyyid Naṣru'lláh's remarkable services to the Faith took place in the fields of teaching particularly to prominent people, protection of the Bahá'ís and defense of the Faith, service within the Bahá'í community and contribution to the Fund.

3.1 Teaching the Faith

As seen in the previous section, teaching the Faith was a recurrent theme in 'Abdu'l-Bahá's Tablets to Siyyid Naṣru'lláh. But it was teaching the Faith to prominent people that yielded Siyyid Naṣru'lláh his best fruits. Around the first decade of the 20th century he managed to transfer his business and residence from Baku to Tehran. Because of his wealth and reputation for his professionalism, Siyyid Naṣru'lláh managed to access the highest levels of Iranian society to protect the Faith. Being a Russian citizen added to his influence, giving him special additional legal protection from persecutions.

3.2 Teaching the Faith to Prominent People

Siyyid Naṣru'lláh successfully formed relationships with prominent people both to teach them the Faith and to engage them in times of persecution. We do not know much about his work in this field because those missions were not always recorded for his own protection, the safeguarding of the Faith and his contacts in the government. Because of such sensitivities, much of what Siyyid Naṣru'lláh did for the Cause of Bahá'u'lláh was known to Him alone.

Some of those stories, however, have been left for posterity to testify this kind of service for which he was so praised by 'Abdu'l-Bahá. Akin to the biblical Joseph of Arimathea, Siyyid Naṣru'lláh put

---

[46] Rúhu'lláh Mihrabkhání. *Khándán-i Sádát-i-Khams*. Darmstadt, Mu'assassih-'i 'Asr-i Jadid, 1994.

his wealth to serve the interests of the Faith when it was most needed. According to Rúhu'lláh Mihrabkhání:

> But one of the most important services of Jináb-i-Báqirof in Iran was the teaching of the Faith to people of highest authority in Iran. Those who have studied the history of religion are well aware that the true enemies of the Cause of God in every religion have been the clerics and not the government officials. Read the stories of Zoroastrianism, Judaism, Christianity and Islam and that becomes clear to you. Whenever the government has risen against another religion, they have been influenced by the clergy or have been forced by them. Otherwise the clerics would have instigated the public against the government. There are many evidences that show this in the history of the new Cause. As a result, one of the things that Bahá'ís tried to achieve was to enlighten the minds of the government officials. So that those who govern the people, if they have pure hearts, and hold it against divine light or be at least open to the teachings of the Bahá'í Faith, then they could understand that the Bahá'ís are not the enemies of the state, and that their focus is on people's hearts, which is the real place for governance, not politics. This is because wicked clerics have always tried to make the officials believe that the Bahá'ís are trying to change everything and take control of the government and abolish all social norms and religious rituals.
>
> At the time of 'Abdu'l-Bahá, because there were political revolutions going on in Iran, and people wanted change, the clergy used that state of confusion in Iran to brainwash and spread lies in the minds of the population and the government against the Bahá'ís. Some tried to represent Bahá'ís as constitutionalists to those in favour of dictatorship while others tried to represent th Bahá'ís as in favour of dictatorship to constitutionalists. These enemies spreading these ideas in their papers and propaganda.
>
> When Jináb-i-Báqirof left Baku to Tehran, due to his inherent capacity, generosity and hospitality and his business and luxurious life, he could come into contact with the circles of great people in the country and taught some of them and

cleared their thoughts, so that they became aware of the truth and the purity of the Bahá'í Faith. Because he used extreme prudence and secrecy in teaching these people, not much is known about these endeavours. But from the Tablets that 'Abdu'l-Bahá wrote in his honour we know that the Centre of the Covenant was constantly guiding him in his efforts to teach people of capacity, and that 'Abdu'l-Bahá constantly encouraged and guided him to do this and occasionally sent a Tablet to those people of capacity through him and asked those in power to protect the oppressed people.[47]

Talking about his great-uncle's relationship with the Prime Minister of Iran, Mas'ud Khamsi wrote:

In 1919 when Jináb-i-Muhammad Partovi was returning from his pilgrimage to the Holy Land, he was invited by Siyyid Naṣru'lláh Báqirof to meet him at his business premises. At the appointed hour, Jináb-i-Báqirof together with Jináb-i-Partovi got into his famous personal carriage to a destination unknown to Jináb-i-Partovi. After passing many streets and alleys, the carriage stopped in front of an ordinary door. The door opened after they knocked once as if they were expected. They went to the so-called Andaruni (inside) division. They went from a door at the back to the front of the house, which was the so-called Biruni (outside) division. There the Prime Minister of Iran [48] greeted the guests and entered the hall. Jináb-i-Báqirof introduced Mr Partovi to the Prime Minister and said that Jináb-i-Partovi had just recently arrived from meeting the holy presence of 'Abdu'l-Bahá, the Greatest Branch of the Tree of God. The Prime Minister expressed his happiness and bliss from having visited Him and at the table constantly asked him questions about how 'Abdu'l-Bahá was and how things were there and what the news was. [49]

---

[47] Rúhu'lláh Mihrabkhání. *Khándán-i Sádát-i-Khams*. Darmstadt, Mu'assassih-'i `Asr-i Jadid, 1994.

[48] Vossug Ed Dowleh. He was Prime Minister between 8 August 1918 and 3 July 1920.

[49] Rúhu'lláh Mihrabkhání. *Khándán-i Sádát-i-Khams*. Darmstadt, Mu'assassih-'i `Asr-i Jadid, 1994.

3.3 Defending the Bahá'ís

Siyyid Naṣru'lláh also used his influence in the government to safeguard the Bahá'ís who were in danger by the clergy's harassment. In many circumstances he used his influence to assist the friends, overly or covertly, in an environment where the believers had no legal protection at all, epitomizing what 'Abdu'l-Bahá' said, "Service to the friends is service to the Kingdom of God..."[50]

Jináb-i-Fazel Mazandarani in his book *History of the Manifestation of Truth*, cited by Rúhu'lláh Mihrabkhání, wrote the following:

> At those times when the enemies wanted to harm the Bahá'ís, no one could do anything to Mr Báqirof or his property or his wealth, or prevent the support that he gave to the oppressed. Among these situations, one was the rescue of Jináb-i-Fazel Mazandarani himself. When he was in Iraq, he was accused of instigating the public and he was arrested with his companion 'Abdu'l-Husayn Ardistani. They were under chains with fetters at the consulate and were delivered to the border control of Iran. Jináb-i-Báqirof approached the government and both of them were not only not harmed but also freed. Another time was his support of the Bahá'ís of Tehran when their houses and their businesses were attacked and robbed.[51]

Mas'ud Khamsi also wrote of Siyyid Naṣru'lláh:

> When there was an attack on the businesses and properties of the Bahá'ís in Tehran, Mr Naṣru'lláh Báqirof went to visit the Prime Minister Aminu'l-Mulk and officially requested the arrest of those who had done such things and to bring them to justice. He said if the Prime Minister did not immediately respond positively to his request then he would send a telegram to the court of the Czar of Russia, stating that the Bahá'í people were being oppressed and that the government of Iran was not helping, and that he would ask the Czar of Russia to send a couple of warships to Bandar-i-Anzali, so that Mr Báqirof and

---

[50]'Abdu'l-Bahá. *Selections from the Writings of 'Abdu'l-Bahá*. Bahá'í World Centre, 1982, p. 27.

[51]Rúhu'lláh Mihrabkhání. *Khándán-i Sádát-i-Khams*. Darmstadt, Mu'assassih-'i `Asr-i Jadid, 1994.

all the Bahá'ís of Iran could leave Iran and go to Russia.

The Prime Minister Aminu'l-Mulk knew Mr Báqirof and he knew that his business with Russia was doing extremely good, and if he didn't comply then Iran would lose its prestige in the eyes of Russia, and so he asked Mr Báqirof to wait and assured him that he would act in this case. As it is written in history, this is the first time that the troublemakers were arrested, taken to court and punished. One of them lost his hand for robbery, according to the Islamic Law.[52]

Another story told by Mas'ud Khamsi reflects Siyyid Naṣru'lláh's ability to protect the Bahá'ís:

> Mr Hojabr Sultan was one of the faithful and famous Bahá'ís from Mazindaran. The clergy and the government of Mazindaran plotted together and arrested him. They were plotting to hang him in the name of Bábi and Bahá'í to use this excuse to kill him and take his properties and divide it among each other. When the news reached Mr Naṣru'lláh Báqirof, who was in Tehran, he immediately organised some documents that showed that Mr Hojabr Sultan actually had business with Báqirof. Therefore, whatever property he had, any harm to him would cause damage to the property and financial loss of the Báqirof family. He sent this to the Consul of Russia. So the Embassy immediately forwarded this document to the foreign ministry of the government of Iran and asked them for an immediate release of Mr Hojabr Sultan, and said that if he was executed or imprisoned for a long time, the demand of Mr Naṣru'lláh, a Russian citizen, will be trampled and the Russian government will officially demand compensation from the Iranian government. As a result Mr Hojabr was released within a week. Such events occurred several times to different people.[53]

---

[52] Rúhu'lláh Mihrabkhání. *Khándán-i Sádát-i-Khams*. Darmstadt, Mu'assassih-'i 'Asr-i Jadid, 1994.

[53] Rúhu'lláh Mihrabkhání. *Khándán-i Sádát-i-Khams*. Darmstadt, Mu'assassih-'i 'Asr-i Jadid, 1994.

That Siyyid Naṣru'lláh protected the Bahá'ís did not mean that he was immune from being attacked for being a Bahá'í.

On the 1st May 1896 Násir'd-Dín Sháh, the all-powerful and most cruel Iranian monarch, was assassinated on the eve of the day when the nation was going to commemorate publicly his 50th year ascension to the throne. Already the Blessed Beauty had predicted his fall when the monarch would soon become "an object-lesson for the world".[54]

Bahá'ís were blamed resulting on a wave of persecutions around the country. It is known for example that Rúhu'lláh (the child-martyr) and his father Varqá were killed for this reason in Tehran. The following incident occurred in Baku soon after the Shah was assassinated giving insight into the believers' suffering. In the book *Bihjatu'l-Sudur* by Mírzá Haydar 'Alí Isfahání, cited in Zuhur al-Haqh, we read:

> The suspicions and accusations [of Násir'd-Dín Sháh's recent assassination] fell upon the Bábís. They could not find the difference between Bábís and Bahá'ís. Therefore, the Bahá'ís became frightened and stopped their gatherings. The Prime Minister prevented the view that the Bahá'ís were behind the attack from becoming a popular view. He issued a decree to the governors of all provinces that the murderer of the Shah was Mírzá Reza Kirmani, who is one of the followers of Siyyid Afghani [the intellectual author of the crime]. And therefore the governors should restore public order and release anyone from attacking this group [Bábís and Bahá'ís]. Despite this order, in some of the provinces, people who were prejudiced and enemies of the Faith started to accuse and instigate people to arise and kill and to take the properties of the Bahá'ís.

> As an example, Áqá Siyyid Naṣru'lláh Báqirof, who had a business in Baku, was walking by the seaside with his nephew Áqá Siyyid Ahmad, when a large group of people started chasing them and swearing at them. They managed to reach their place of business and the people followed them there, and it did not take long until the number reached 3,000 people,

---

[54] Shoghi Effendi. *The Promised Day Is Come.* Wilmette, US Bahá'í Publishing Trust, 1980, p. 65.

and were getting ready to attack when suddenly the police arrived and took Siyyid Naṣru'lláh and his nephew safely to their residence, and the group of 3,000 people dispersed. Then the Prime Minister sent the message to Muzaffar-i-din Mírzá, the oldest son of the Shah and the Heir Prince and the governor of Adherbayjan. The Prime Minister[55] sent the news to Muzaffar-i-din Shah to quickly go to Tehran and sit on the throne. Then the Prime Minister executed Mírzá Reza Kirmani, who was the murderer of the Shah, and therefore the talk about Bahá'ís slowly began to subside, and then felicity and tranquillity came back to the people.[56]

Martha Root offered more details of the incident:

One day they told me an incident of their good father this Agha Seyed Nasroullah Bakeroff [Siyyid Naṣru'lláh]. They said that at the time of Nasiro'd-Din Shah's [Násir'd-Dín Sháh] death by an assassin, their father was in Baku. The Muhammadans, very prejudiced, attacked him and said: "You killed the Shah!" Everything that ever happened was blamed upon the Bahá'ís. Fifty policemen came and took the father to the police court. The Chief of Police shook hands with Mr Bakeroff and said: "I know you Bahá'ís are the best people in the world and would not kill anybody! For your own safety, however, I imprison you here for two days, for if I free you the Muhammadans will put you to death". Thus his life was saved.[57]

Rúhu'lláh Mihrabkhání confirms the story showing how well the local authorities regarded Siyyid Naṣru'lláh:

One of the stories that Rúhu'lláh Khamsi writes details a memory of one of the servants, Mírzá Khalil, who was a good and active Bahá'í. When there was commotion in the city, Reza Khan, on behalf of the government, sent police/guards

---

[55]The heir to the throne.
[56]Fazel Mazandarini. Zuhúru'l-Haqq (The Manifestation of Truth). Tehran, vol 7, 1944, p. 94.
[57]Martha Root. Pilgrimage through Persia. Part 3: Qazvin and Tihran. *Star of the West* 21, 6 (September 1930), p. 177.

to protect Siyyid Naṣru'lláh and his family. This is something that this servant saw very often. Reza Khan himself at that time was a top officer, and he was sending some officers to protect Báqirof. Reza Khan Savad Kouhi, who became the Mír-Panj, general, and then the King of Iran, founder of the Pahlavi dynasty.

... No one dared to be against him. When revolts arose against the Bahá'ís, the government of Iran sent security to protect Báqirof's property and house.[58]

Siyyid Naṣru'lláh was also generous in helping Bahá'ís who required financial support, occasionally at 'Abdu'l-Bahá's request, as well as helping to quell disunity and other problems that sometimes arose among the Bahá'ís.

3.4 The Central Assembly of Tehran

It is noteworthy that Siyyid Naṣru'lláh also became a member of the Central Assembly of Tehran which was the precursor of the National Spiritual Assembly of the Bahá'ís of Iran elected in 1934.[59] This Central Assembly of Tehran reported directly to 'Abdu'l-Bahá. This was a long process of administrative growth starting in 1897 when 'Abdu'l-Bahá gave instructions to a Hand of the Cause, returning from the Holy Land, for the formation of a Tehran-based council in charge of the affairs of the Bahá'í Faith in Iran. Previously, a number of believers wanted to put in practice Bahá'u'lláh's precept in the Kitáb-i-Aqdas about setting up a local House of Justice and therefore informally created their own consultation body which was somehow kept secret for protection reasons, even for the Bahá'í community, although the group did not last long.[60]

In the Most Holy Book, revealed around 1873, the Blessed Beauty had written:

> The Lord hath ordained that in every city a House of Justice be established wherein shall gather counsellors to the number

---

[58] Rúhu'lláh Mihrabkhání. *Khándán-i Sádát-i-Khams*. Darmstadt, Mu'assassih-'i `Asr-i Jadid, 1994.

[59] Bahá'í News, August 1934.

[60] Moojan Momen. *The Bahá'í Communities of Iran*. George Ronald, 2015.

of Bahá, and should it exceed this number it doth not matter ... It is incumbent upon them to take counsel together and to have regard for the interests of the servants of God, for His sake, even as they regard their own interests, and to choose that which is meet and seemly. Thus hath the Lord your God commanded you.[61]

By the time of His ascension in 1892 Baha'u'llah had appointed four individuals as Hands of the Cause of God. They represented the only formal administrative structure of the Bahá'í Faith in Iran at that time. The aforementioned Tehran's "Assembly of Consultation" created later by 'Abdu'l- Bahá in 1897 was composed by the four Hands of the Cause and five other members appointed by the Hands. In 1899 this body became the Central Assembly of Tehran also charged with the propagation and protection of the Faith throughout Iran, whose members began to be elected around 1913.[62] Soon other Iranian communities in the country followed suit and formed their own local Bahá'í councils using the Tehran pattern. There were over thirty of these nascent local spiritual assemblies in Iran by the time 'Abdu'l- Bahá passed away in 1921.[63]

3.5 Diplomatic Missions

Siyyid Naṣru'lláh was also 'Abdu'l-Bahá's representative to foreign diplomats in Iran, particularly to the Russian and British ambassadors who, at that time, exerted a strong influence on the Iranian government as the two major world powers.

In a letter to Siyyid Naṣru'lláh and his brother Siyyid Asadu'lláh, 'Abdu'l-Bahá tells that He has heard that the Russian ambassador has been supporting the Bahá'ís and therefore He asks the two brothers to send His appreciation for such an expression of justice and His prayers for the government of Russia. 'Abdu'l-Bahá also requests them to advise the ambassador that Bahá'ís are lovers of flowers, irrespective of the garden, as Bahá'u'lláh has taught us to be free of any prejudice towards a country, race, language or religion. In that

---

[61]Bahá'u'lláh. *The Kitáb-i-Aqdas*. Bahá'í World Centre, 1992, p. 29.
[62]Moojan Momen. *The Bahá'í Communities of Iran*. George Ronald, 2015.
[63]Bahá'í World Centre. *Century of Light*. Haifa, 2001.

Tablet, He quotes the Ancient Beauty's words:

> That one indeed is a man who, today, dedicateth himself to the service of the entire human race... It is not for him to pride himself who loveth his own country, but rather for him who loveth the whole world. The earth is but one country, and mankind its citizens. [64]

During the 1920s Iran's political disarray accelerated marking the final years of the Qajar dynasty to the point that in 1923 the Ahmad Shah, the last monarch, went into exile to France not to come back ever again, virtually abandoning the crown. The central power was very weak particularly for managing the provinces. In addition, the two antagonistic world powers at the time, England and Russia, were increasingly interfering in the government, dictating internal policies, even occupying parts of the Iranian territory, each pursuing their own interests and post First World War imperialist ambitions.

In May 1920 Haji 'Arab, a devoted believer was martyred and event which was followed by an intensification of the persecution against the Bahá'ís. Haji 'Arab had been killed in May 1920 in Sultánabád (now Iráq) at the instigation of the local clergy who invented the story that he had burnt a Koran. A report of the resident British Vice-Consul informed:

> On the 8th of the month, a Babee entered a mosque and burnt a Khoran. Rumour then said that the man was captured almost in the act and taken before the Governor who set him free on the payment of a bribe said to tbe T's 4000. The priest and populace then became very incensed and demanded that the man should be handed over to them; a demonstration was made two days after before the Governor's house. In fear, however, the Governor closed his gates which the crowd then burst open; he made his escape by the back entrance to the Nazmiah, not without having several missiles thrown at him. The rabble then proceeded to destroy his household possessions and did considerable damage, the Governor's estimate being T's 1000. Up to the 15th, the Bazaars were all

---

[64] Bahá'u'lláh. *Gleanings from the Writings of Bahá'u'lláh*. US Bahá'í Publishing Trust, p. 346, 1990.

closed and so remained until the arrival of the Gendarmerie company from Malayir. Ultimately the Babee was captured and brought into town by the Gendarmerie, found guilty and hanged in the Maidan on the 21st. At one time the situation was most serious, large numbers of people collecting in the Maidan and demonstrating against the Governor; on one occasion several blank shots had to be fired before they dispersed...[65]

Siyyid Naṣru'lláh made a representation on behalf of 'Abdu'l-Bahá to Mr Herman Norman, the British Ambassador in Tehran, so that he could interpose his good offices to protect the Bahá'í community. Moojan Momen wrote:

> However, it must be noted that there was no question of 'Abdu'l-Bahá having asked the British Government to undertake the protection of the Bahá'ís in Persia. Indeed, the Bahá'ís of Persia were at no time taken under the protection of any foreign power in the same way as the Christian, Zoroastrian and other minority groups were. In 'Abdu'l-Bahá's letter to Lord Curzon relating to Haji 'Arab's martyrdom there is the following sentence specifically disclaiming any such desire: "Our object is not this that His Majesty's Government should undertake any formal protection but rather to incite the Persian Government to undertake the protection of the Bahá'ís and to shield them from the evil of the oppressors. Such a measure would lead to the strength and grandeur of Persia itself".

Later in the year of 1920, 'Abdu'l-Bahá opened, for the first time, direct communications with Mr Norman, the British Ambassador in Tihran. 'Abdu'l-Bahá's first letter, undated, was delivered to Mr Norman on 8 November by Siyyid Nasru'llah Báqirof. In this letter 'Abdu'l-Bahá assures Mr Norman of prayers for the success of his endeavours towards the betterment of Iran, and appoints Báqirof as intermediary for any messages that Norman may wish to send to 'Abdu'l-Bahá.

Norman sent a suitable reply, through Báqirof, dated 9 November 1920.

---

[65] Moojan Momen. *The Bábi and Bahá'í Religions - 1844-1944.* George Ronald Oxford, pp. 445, 1981.

'Abdu'l-Bahá's second letter to Mr Norman was dated 29 October 1920. On 5 February 1921, Báqirof wrote to Norman asking for an appointment in order to deliver the letter personally. Norman's comment on this was: 'It's ridiculous that the letter cannot be sent round by a servant like any other, but as this appears to be impossible, he can bring it at 10 a.m. next Tuesday, Feb 8, if that will suit him.'

'Abdu'l-Bahá's letter was translated thus by Col. T. W. Haig: 'I trust in Almighty that you will be successful in your services to the just govt of G.B. and in supporting the oppressed people who are the well-wishers of the human kind. Agha Seyed Nasrullah Bagheroff [Siyyid Naṣru'lláh] who enjoys my confidence is at Tehran. He will inform you of the circumstances of the murder of Haji Arab. You should believe what he tells you. I always pray for the just govt of G.B. and wish you success. Please accept the assurances of my highest respect.'

Norman appended the following note to 'Abdu'l-Bahá's letter: 'I think we might send a polite reply, thanking him for his letter, wishing him health, success and prosperity and promising to do all that I can in an unofficial way and so far as the very limited means at my disposal allow, to help his adherents here. He will no doubt make his desires known to me through Seyyed Noosrullah. In any case I always act on information received through our Consuls. I will sign the letter, which should be sent to Seyyed Naṣru'lláh for transmission. H.C.N. Feb. 9, 1921.' Norman's letter was eventually dispatched dated 14 February 1921.

'Abdu'l-Bahá's third letter to Norman is addressed to 'His Excellency, the Well-wisher of the Persians' and dated 17 January 1921. The following is Kamal Báqiroff's[66] translation:

> The answer of the letter which was a brilliant proof as to your equitable affections was the cause of extreme thankfulness and gratitude, and this great resolution and high intention will ever be the cause of cheerfulness and gladness among the Bahais and will never be forgotten.

---

[66]Siyyid Naṣru'lláh's son.

This justice-dispensing is in fact the call of eternity and in the annals of these well-wishers will decorate an important page. Jenabe Bagheroff and his friends are so very grateful to you that made me extremely happy too, and all have highly praised your efforts and I shall ever with earnestness, to [at] His threshold, as His protection succour and bounty. With highest respect [I] write you this letter and beg your approval.

In a note appended to this letter and dated 15 May 1921, Norman writes: 'I should like to send a polite reply in Persian through Bagherov, saying how much pleasure it has given me to receive this letter and assuring Abdul Baha that I shall never relax my efforts on behalf of his followers and always give an attentive hearing to any representation that they make to me.'[67]

The Haji 'Arab's episode was reported by the *Times of London* bringing some publicity to the Bahá'í Faith: "The Bahais, or followers of Bahai'ullah [sic], and his predecessor the Bab, who are a kind of Oriental Quakers, spring from Islam, and profess a universal quietist religion, which has brought them converts in Western Europe, and especially in America, have added another to their long list of martyrs...."[68]

The next year Siyyid Naṣru'lláh made a similar representation this time when a believer named Mirzá Ya'qúb was attacked on the street and shot at midday on 24 January 1921. The murder took place in the city of Kirmanshah, southern Iran. A Bahá'í delegation on behalf of the Tehran Central Assembly composed by Siyyid Naṣru'lláh and another believer approached Sir Walter Smart, the British Consular official in the capital. Consequently, Mr Norman, the British Ambassador, instructed that a telegram be sent to his local representative: "You should impress on [Kirmanshah's] Gov. Gen. my abhorrence of this wanton crime and urge him to arrest and punish the murderer

---

[67] Moojan Momen. *The Bábi and Bahá'í Religions - 1844-1944*. George Ronald Oxford, pp. 346-347, 1981.

[68] Moojan Momen. *The Bábi and Bahá'í Religions - 1844-1944*. George Ronald Oxford, pp. 446, 1981.

forthwith"[69].

We also saw Mr Norman engaged with Siyyid Naṣru'lláh and another representative of the Tehran Central Assembly, when a mob attacked and destroyed in June 1920 the tombs of the King and the Beloved of Martyrs in Isfahan, at the instigation of the Muslim priests. The King and the Beloved of Martyrs were two famous Bahá'ís who were beheaded in 1879 for their beliefs.[70] Upon receiving the Tehran Central Assembly's complaint, the Ambassador telegraphed the British Consul on that city to address the Governor in order to restore the graves. Indeed, Mr Norman was a good man.

3.6 Communications between Iran and the Holy Land

In addition to those diplomatic roles, Siyyid Naṣru'lláh managed 'Abdu'l-Bahá's correspondence between Haifa and the Bahá'ís of Iran protected by the safety that his Russian citizenship afforded him. While in Baku he was also the postal contact between 'Abdu'l-Bahá and the friends in that city.

The First World War ended in November 1918 with the signing of the Armistice of Compiègne. The December edition of Star of the West published the "First Tablet revealed for Bahais of Persia since opening of doors of Holy Land", having Siyyid Naṣru'lláh as its recipient. Two months before the British forces composed mainly by Indian soldiers had successfully fought the Battle of Haifa marking the liberation of Palestine from the Turkish yoke and precipitating the end of the war. As a result, 'Abdu'l-Bahá was rescued from His fifty-year captivity and from Jamal Pasha, the Turkish commander-in-chief, who threatened to crucify Him on Mount Carmel and destroy all Bahá'í shrines at the end of the war. Soon after His rescue, General Edmund Allenby cabled the Foreign Office in London requesting to "notify the world that Abdul Baha is safe".[71] During the war pilgrimages to the Holy Land were suspended and the postal service with Iran was almost paralysed for political and transportation reasons. The Tablet reads

---

[69] Moojan Momen. *The Bábi and Bahá'í Religions - 1844-1944*. George Ronald Oxford, p. 447, 1981.

[70] Adib Taherzadeh. *The Revelation of Bahá'u'lláh, vol. IV*. George Ronald Oxford, 1987.

[71] Shoghi Effendi. *God Passes by*. Wilmette, US Bahá'í Publishing Trust, 1979, p. 306.

as follows:

> To his honor Agha Sayad Nasrollah Bakeroff.—Upon him Be BAHA'O'LLAH-EL-ABHA.
>
> HE IS GOD!
>
> O thou who art firm in the Covenant!
>
> It was a long time since the thread of correspondence had been entirely broken, and the hearts were affected with sorrow and agitation. Now, praise be to God, that in these days, through divine favor, the black clouds are dispersed and the light of composure and tranquillity has enlightened this region; the tyrannous government is done away with and followed by a just administration. All the people are delivered from the most great hardship and the most difficult affliction. In this huge tempest and violent revolution, in which all nations of the world were caught and were involved in dire calamity, cities were destroyed, people were slaughtered, properties were pillaged and taken as booty, the cries and lamentations of the helpless ones were raised from every prominent spot and the tears falling from the eyes of the orphans like a flowing torrent in all the low countries—under all these conditions, praise be to God, that through the favor and bounty of the Blessed Perfection and because the believers of Cod have lived in accord with the lordly teachings, they have been protected and guarded. Not even a single particle of dust settled on the face of a believer. Verily, this is a most great miracle which cannot be denied except by every stiff-necked transgressor! It has meanwhile be come evident and manifest that the holy teachings of His Highness BAHA'O'LLAH are the cause of the comfort and illumination of the world of humanity. In the blessed Tablets (of BAHA'O'LLAH) the justice and the administrative sagacity of the Imperial government of England have been repeatedly dwelt upon, and now it has become clear that, in reality, the inhabitants of this country, after untold sufferings, have attained to composure and security.
>
> This is the first letter that I write to Persia. God willing, I shall write others afterwards. Convey with the utmost longing to

each and all the believers of God the wonderful Abha greeting, and give us the glad-tidings of the health and safety of all the believers. Although the tempest and the hurricane were intense and violent, yet, praise be to God, the Ark of Salvation reached the heaven of security, while protected and guarded. Announce greeting and salutation on behalf of Abdul-Baha with the utmost joy and fragrance "to the hands of the Cause of God," his honor Ameen[72] and likewise the rulers of firmness and steadfastness in the Covenant and Testament.

Upon thee be Baha-el-Abha!
(Signed) Abdul-Baha Abbas [73]

3.7 Contributions to the Funds

Siyyid Naṣru'lláh generously contributed to the Funds of the Faith and to important projects such as the building of the Shrine of the Báb and the renovation of the House of Bahá'u'lláh in Baghdad. Likewise, he significantly contributed to 'Abdu'l-Bahá's travels to the West. This story is told by Rúhu'lláh Mihrabkhání:

> While 'Abdu'l-Bahá wanted to travel to Europe and America, the Bahá'ís of America collected some money for this travel and sent it but 'Abdu'l-Bahá refused to accept it. 'Abdu'l-Bahá then through Mr [Siyyid Naṣru'lláh] Báqirof sent the message to Abu'l-Hasan Amín, Amínu'lláh, the trustee of Huqúqu'lláh[74], to arrange for 40,000 tumans, which was sufficient for the travel, to be sent by telegram because 'Abdu'l-Bahá thought this trip was in behalf of the Bahá'ís of Iran. So Haji Amin the same night contacted those Bahá'ís that could afford that much money and informed them about the message of 'Abdu'l-Bahá. So the Bahá'ís started to sacrifice and gathered that money. As Mr Balyuzi has written, a great part of the money was provided

---

[72]Hájí Amín (1831-1928), appointed by Bahá'u'lláh as the Trustee (Amin) of The Huqúq'u'lláh (The "Right of God"). The Huqúqu'lláh (In Arabic, "Right of God") is an ordenance enunciated by Bahá'u'lláh in the Kitáb-i-Aqdas. It is a voluntary payment offered to the Center of the Cause based on 19% of personal income after necessary expenses are deducted. The funds are used for socio-economic projects or for philanthropic purposes.

[73]*Star of the West*, Vol. IX Massa'ul 1, 74 (December 12, 1918), no. 15.

[74]See footnote 85 regarding the Law of Huqúq'u'lláh.

by Mr Báqirof.

Jináb-i-Rúhu'lláh Khamsi narrates that when the sum was ready it was decided that Jináb-i-Haji Amin would go and send this by telegraph to 'Abdu'l-Bahá. Then they found his hesitation to go and send the telegram. When they asked for the cause, they realised that he did not have the money to send the telegram. Siyyid Naṣru'lláh took off his cloak and gave it to him and asked him to go and sell it to pay for the telegram.

The second [Siyyid Naṣru'lláh's] son was Amínu'lláh[75]. After the passing of his older brother, Mír Abdullah, he became the oldest son. He was involved in helping his father in the business and after the passing of his father he and Mír Habib, the youngest son of Siyyid Naṣru'lláh, inherited a wealthy residence, but as Mr Báqirof had stated, in his will wished that 90,000 Tumans of his wealth should be given as Huqúqu'lláh. Amínu'lláh, did not delay the payment and with Mír Habib's consent, left the house to Haji Amin and this house later became the school [76] for the education of girls.[77]

4. Relationship with 'Abdul-Bahá

We know that at least once Siyyid Naṣru'lláh visited 'Abdu'l-Bahá from Baku. He attempted another pilgrimage from Tehran but it could not materialise because of conditions surrounding 'Abdu'l-Bahá's environment.

Naṣru'lláh was devastated with the passing of 'Abdu'l-Bahá in November 1921. Rúhu'lláh Mihrabkhání wrote:

> Jenab-i-Báqirof was still living when 'Abdu'l-Bahá passed away and this servant of God, who was trained by the hand of the Centre of the Covenant, started to serve Shoghi Effendi. In his book, *Memories of Nine Years in 'Akká*, Jináb-i-Dr-Youness Khan-Afroukhteh, quotes a sentence from Áqá Siyyid Naṣru'lláh

---

[75] Amínu'lláh Khamsi became later on a member of the National Spiritual Assembly of Iran for several years. He was born in Baku in 1890 and passed away in Tehran in 1948.

[76] The Tarbiyat School for Girls in Tehran was established in 1911.

[77] Rúhu'lláh Mihrabkhání. *Khándán-i Sádát-i-Khams.* Darmstadt, Mu'assassih-'i `Asr-i Jadid, 1994.

when Shoghi Effendi started his Guardianship, which is a historical sentence and shows his spiritual maturity. This is exactly what Jináb-i-Dr-Youness Khan-Afroukhteh wrote on page 395 of his book: "As soon as the ascension of 'Abdu'l-Bahá occurred the news reached the Spiritual Assembly of Tehran. The Book of Covenant was read in the spiritual assembly of Tehran, at the end of the reading of the Book of Covenant, Jináb-i-Báqirof stood up and said without any reservation: "Praised be God, the Faith has become young". Hearing this I remembered a poet who expressed his joy on one hand and his sorrow on the other in a single verse, when a dying king was passing the crown to the next king. The verse goes like this: "Why not grieving? Why not laughing? As the sea subsided, a gem showed up".[78]

5. Passing and Significance

Siyyid Naṣru'lláh died four years later in 1924. Mr Mihrabkhání wrote about the incidents surrounding his passing:

> Jináb-i-Báqirof did not have the opportunity to serve Shoghi Effendi, because in 1923 he passed to the Abhá Kingdom and joined 'Abdu'l-Bahá, for whom he had sacrificed all his life, and his remains were earthed in Golestan-i-Javid in Tehran, in Amirabad. Shortly after that, Jináb-i-Hájí Amín who was his faithful friend also joined him, and the descendants of Jináb-i-Báqirof requested the descendants of Haji Amin that these two blessed souls, as they were united in this life, in the next life should also be next to each other. Therefore, the body of Hájí Amín also was buried next to Jináb-i-Báqirof. When Amirabad became part of Greater Tehran, the government ordered to build a new Bahá'í cemetery on the south of Tehran, therefore the descendants of Mr Báqirof removed the two bodies and transferred them to the new Bahá'í cemetery, and they were buried within a meter of each other.[79]

---

[78] Rúhu'lláh Mihrabkhání. *Khándán-i Sádát-i-Khams*. Darmstadt, Mu'assassih-'i 'Asr-i Jadid, 1994.

[79] Rúhu'lláh Mihrabkhání. *Khándán-i Sádát-i-Khams*. Darmstadt, Mu'assassih-'i 'Asr-i Jadid, 1994.

After the passing of Jináb-i-Báqirof, the following telegram was sent on behalf of Shoghi Effendi to his family:

> Compulsory silence delayed me to give my condolences in regard to your irreplaceable loss. That blessed soul who ascended to the Lord is resting forever in the arms of the Eternal Beloved. Shoghi [80]

Likewise, the Greatest Holy Leaf, 'Abdu'l-Bahá's sister, sent the following communication to Siyyid Naṣru'lláh's family:

> The servants and handmaidens of the Holy Threshold of the Abhá Beauty: The dreadful news of the passing of the blessed soul of Hazrat-i-Áqá Siyyid Naṣru'lláh Báqirof to the Abhá Kingdom was received by these downhearted souls, and this new calamity and descended disaster was added to the sorrows and pains of this mortal being, and in the hearts of the Holy Leaves. However, after the advent of the greatest calamity and the immense tragedy of the passing of the beloved 'Abdu'l-Bahá, it is explicable that for the nightingales in the rose garden of faithfulness, living in this mortal cage is like being in a prison cell so tight and small. The holy souls in every breath of their lives beseech to take their flights to the realm of the Almighty, and wish to flee from this world of dust, like a desolate drop supplicating its union with the sea, and a bird aspiring to take its flight to the celestial nest. Therefore, this departed soul certainly reached the ultimate goal of those who are near to God, and achieved the greatest desire of the sincere ones, and was blessed with the everlasting joy, and eternal bliss. That exalted soul during his earthly life was relentless in his rendering service, in his servitude, and in his sacrifices in the path of the celestial light. 'Abdu'l-Bahá gave a special attention to that precious soul, and often indicated His gratification for his conduct, behaviour, and demeanour, as his deeds were endowed with sincerity and purity of motive, and his heart was like a garden attributable to the love of God, and like a glowing candle in all the gatherings.

---

[80] Rúhu'lláh Mihrabkhání. *Khándán-i Sádát-i-Khams*. Darmstadt, Mu'assassih-'i 'Asr-i Jadid, 1994.

The hope of this mortal soul from the threshold of the Blessed Beauty is that those saplings of the Abhá Paradise, and the survivors of that reservoir of faithfulness be brought with the divine glad tidings, and be joyful and happy from the Lord's Beneficence. May they find solace from the dewdrops of the effusions of the Celestial Bounties, and find consolation from the outpouring of magnanimity, and may walk the footsteps of that honourable man, and dwell in that abode, and be wayfarers in that path, so that the gates of triumph, felicity, divine assistance, and salvation be wide open from every direction for that family, and their lineage for eternity. Praise be to God, that those saplings of the garden of the love of God, for many years, being in the nearness to the splendour Spot, with utmost joy and happiness were nurtured in the shadow of the Blessed ('Abdu'l-Bahá), and were in every moment subject of the beneficence of the Beloved, and his grace and kindness. Now is the time to manifest the results of those blessings and favours, which will no doubt, be made manifest. All the members of the Blessed family share the sorrows of those mourners and with their poignant hearts offer their condolences. May glory and praise be upon you. [81]

---

[81] Rúhu'lláh Mihrabkhání. *Khándán-i Sádát-i-Khams*. Darmstadt, Mu'assassih-'i `Asr-i Jadid, 1994.

Figure 11: 'Abdu'l-Bahá in Budapest. Siyyid Ahmad is second from the left.

Figure 12: 'Abdu'l-Bahá in Stuttgart. Courtesy: Bahá'í Media.

Figure 13: The Grand Hotel of Tehran in the 1900s.

Figure 14: Shahpoor Avenue, Rasht, 1934.
Source: Shahre Farang.

Figure 15: Reza Shah in 1941.
Source: Wikimedia Commons

Figure 16: Siyyid Ahmad's family. Mas'ud Khamsi is standing behind his father Siyyid Ahmad on the left side.
Source: Khándán-i Sádát-i-Khams.

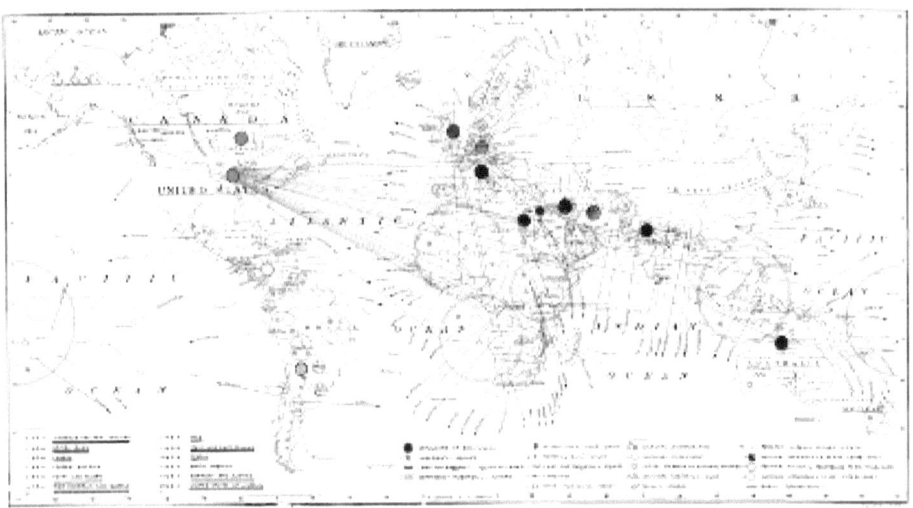

Figure 17: Shoghi Effendi's map at the beginnning of the Ten Year Crusade.

Figure 18: Khonsar nowadays.
Courtesy: Nasser Sadeghi, CC BY-SA 3.0

Figure 19: Jane and Mas'ud Khamsi wedding.
Source: Bahá'í Peruvian National Archives.

Figure 20: Jane and Mas'ud at the 1953 Kampala Conference.
Source: Bahá'í Peruvian National Archives.

PART 3:
Siyyid Ahmad Khamsi-Báqirof (c1880-1950)

1. Family Life

Another distinguished member of the Sádát-Khams was Siyyid Ahmad who will always be remembered for his love, devotion and service to 'Abdu'l-Bahá. A reputable businessman because of his integrity and trustworthiness, he was highly regarded among the higher circles of the Iranian society. Such a position gave him the background to protect the Bahá'í community and advance the process of developing the new institutions. Siyyid Ahmad had the inestimable privilege to accompany 'Abdu'l-Bahá to His travels in Europe in 1913.

We do not know exactly the year of his birth although it appears to be around the 1880's in Rasht. As stated previously his father Siyyid Reza was one of the five brothers who passed away in 1881 about two years after he had become a Bahá'í. Siyyid Ahmad was mostly raised by Siyyid Naṣru'lláh.

According to Mas'ud Khamsi "My father was brought up in Russia [Baku] by his aunts and uncles, he lost his father when he was very little..."[82] It appears that Siyyid Ahmad was raised and introduced to the commercial world mostly by his uncle Siyyid Naṣru'lláh who became a kind of father for him.

According to Rúhu'lláh Mihrabkhání, "Siyyid Ahmad grew older in Badkubeh [Baku] and as his uncles expanded their business to cover Iran and Russia, he came to Iran and stayed in Rasht ... Siyyid Ahmad [later] moved from Rasht to Tehran and stayed there because of the expansion of his job. He was still rendering services to the Cause of God in addition to dealing with economic and commercial issues ... Siyyid Ahmad shone like a star in the heaven of the Cause of God and

---

[82] *Pioneering and Services of Mas'ud Khamsi,* unpublished manuscript.

managed to render many services to the Cause".[83]

Dr Iraj Ayman, who knew the family in Tehran, later related:

> The Báqirof family was a very extended family. There were some members who were not Bahá'ís and some who were Bahá'ís. And they had a very sizeable rice plantation in Rasht and producing a very special type of rice, which was very special and expensive in Iran. So, they were coming and going. They were both residents in Tehran and Rasht. It was not that sometimes they were always in Rasht and later on move to Tehran. It was all the time both places. There were a number of non-Bahá'ís members also, some of them I knew.[84]

Little Mas'ud was also an ocular witness of many of the ancient Persian ceremonies held mostly by peasants. Mas'ud said that as a child, he and his father enjoyed participating in those festivities from Zoroastrian origin in their land estates where large harvests were collected by the servants. Dancing around a big fire, singing ceremonious songs, sacrificing lambs and wearing traditional clothes were some of the features of those festivals.

2. Homayoun Khánum

Siyyid Ahmad married Homayoun Khánum in Baku and had six children. Paying tribute to his wife, Rúhu'lláh Mihrabkhání wrote:

> Siyyid Ahmad married Miss Homayoun, the daughter of his uncle Siyyid Mahmúd from Sádát-i-Khams [the five brothers]. The Bahá'í history of Iran has mostly been about men and not women due to the cultural environment of the country. Women were often denied from doing important jobs. But it is obvious that next to a lion there is a lioness that encourages and infuses enthusiasm in the men to render spiritual services to the Cause of God.
>
> Miss Homayoun was one of these lionesses, encouraging her husband to render services to the Cause of God. Because of

---

[83]Rúhu'lláh Mihrabkhání. *Khándán-i Sádát-i-Khams*. Darmstadt, Mu'assassih-'i `Asr-i Jadid, 1994.

[84]Personal communication to the author.

this, Siyyid Ahmad's house was more like a caravanserai and was always full of guests. Whenever his friends or strangers travelled to Rasht, they knew the door of this house was open to them. Ms Homayoun herself did most of the job to look after the guests and did not leave it to their maids and servants. She fed them, provided them with somewhere to sleep, and did for everyone, whether rich or poor, giving them loving kindness and friendship.

Sometimes there were great guests too. Among them were Miss Martha Root and Mrs Ransom-Kehler.[85] These two spent some of their time there and this nest of kindness was adorned with their presence, while the door of the house was still open as some friends as well as strangers kept coming and going. At the time of the departure of Martha Root, the entire members of the Spiritual Assembly accompanied her to Qazvín [which is the main city where she wanted to live].

The virtues of Ms Homayoun were not limited to kindness to the guests, and she also had a strong interest in helping the poor and those who were in need and weak in the society of Rasht. At the time of Muharram, or other important Muslim days such as Safar, she sent food for the prisoners. In the winter, she visited the poor and those who were in need in the city and got them kerosene [used as a fuel], clothes and also coal, and also gave them lots of kindness and encouragement flowing from her own spiritual kindness.

From the union of Siyyid Ahmad and Homayoun Khánum six children were left, four daughters and two sons, all of whom were the spiritual inheritors of their father's virtues and services. As for the girls, Miss Laga married Mírzá Muhammad-i-Khan-i-Partovi, who was a brave and knowledgeable preacher of the Faith and was the centre of the teaching services in different parts of Russia and Iran.

The second daughter was Miss Bahireh. She married Jináb-

---

[85] Miss Martha Root (1872-1939) and Mrs Keith Ransom-Kehler (1876-1933) were two valiant American women who visited Baha'I communities in Iran. They were both posthumously appointed Hands of the Cause by Shoghi Effendi.

i-Habib Sabet [1922-2013], who was a famous businessman in Iran. This person dedicated all his life and wealth to the service to the Cause along with his wife, who also rendered much service to the Cause during and after her husband's life.

The other daughter was Mulik Khánum. She married Shoghi Ghadimi. He was a great and devoted servant of the Faith in Ishqabad.

The last daughter was Soraya Khánum [1921-1997]. She married Azíz Yazdí [1909-2004] and they pioneered together to Kenya in Africa. Her husband Jináb-i-Yazdí was appointed a Continental Counselor by the Universal House of Justice. In recent years [written in 1973] he has been a member of the Teaching Centre located in the Holy Land [Haifa][86][87], rendering international services and at present they live in Canada. [88]

Siyyid Ahmad also had two sons: Mahmúd [1918-2003] and Mas'ud, who were steadfast and devoted to the Cause. In particular, as Rúhu'lláh Mihrabkhání said, "Mas'ud Khamsi was the light of the family".[89]

According to Mas'ud Khamsi: "My parents were open-minded and quite modern for those days, this is why during our childhood and youth we had freedom of actions, but one thing was obligatory and imposed on us and that was to attend the Bahá'í classes on Fridays, without any excuse."

When Reza Shah, the new monarch, created birth certificates and identification cards in the second half of the 1920s Siyyid Ahmad adopted the surname Khamsi like most of the members of the family. Apparently, the new Shah did not want people to acquire foreign surnames in their identification cards. Hence, Siyyid Ahmad was known as Siyyid Ahmad Khamsi or sometimes Siyyid Ahmad Khamsi

---

[86] Mr Yazdí passed away in 2004.

[87] *Bahá'í World News Service,* 9 April 2004. Available at: https://news.bahai.org/story/297/

[88] Rúhu'lláh Mihrabkhání. *Khándán-i Sádát-i-Khams.* Darmstadt, Mu'assassih-'i `Asr-i Jadid, 1994.

[89] Rúhu'lláh Mihrabkhání. *Khándán-i Sádát-i-Khams.* Darmstadt, Mu'assassih-'i `Asr-i Jadid, 1994.

Báqirof. He also had to surrender his Russian citizenship to become a national of Iran. By then Baku was totally in Communist hands and most prominent people, either intellectuals or entrepreneurs, had been executed, put in jail or exiled to Siberia.

4. Spiritual Dimensions of his Business

Both Bahá'ís and non-Bahá'ís knew Siyyid Ahmad for his integrity in conducting business. There are certain stories that illustrate his fame as a man of honesty, righteousness, competence and trustworthiness. He was most likely the richest active Bahá'í believer in the city of Rasht.

4.1 Trustworthiness: The Inheritance

Referring to his honourable reputation among the community, Rúhu'lláh Mihrabkhání wrote:

> Siyyid Ahmad was known to everyone in Rasht as a Bahá'í but his importance and credibility and reputation as an honest, trustworthy and generous figure, which attracted most people, did not allow his foes among the clerics to oppose him. Some of them even respected him and had faith in him and what he did. This came to the fore when Hosseyn Lakani, the Imam Jomeh[90] of Rasht who was very rich and had many wives and many children, appointed him as the executor of his will to divide his belongings among the heirs, something which Siyyid Ahmad did with competence and honesty after the Imam passed away, making him more famous among people throughout Gilan and especially those in Rasht and further inspiring their praise.[91]

4.2 Competency: The Government Finances

Siyyid Ahmad was designated director of the Treasury Department in Gilan by Arthur Millspaugh. He was a former advisor to the US State Department Office of Foreign Trade and during 1922-1926 and in 1942-1945 was invited by the Iranian Government to re-organise the

---

[90]The Imam Jomeh used to be a high level clergyman running the collective Friday prayers.
[91]Rúhu'lláh Mihrabkhání. *Khándán-i Sádát-i-Khams.* Darmstadt, Mu'assassih-'i `Asr-i Jadid, 1994.

country's finances that were at the point of collapsing. According to Rúhu'lláh Mihrabkhání:

> When Mr Millspaugh, an American councillor, was trying to solve the internal problems of Iran, he was looking for people who were capable, trustworthy and knowledgeable. He chose Siyyid-i-Ahmad-i-Khamsi as the director of the Rasht Revenue. This was a governmental institution at the time, which included ministries such as roads, health, tax, etc.

4.3 Socio-Economic Development: Tea Plantation Innovation

Siyyid Ahmad was the first person to introduce the cultivation of tea in Gilan at 'Abdu'l-Bahá's suggestion. Before this time, Iran relied heavily on importing tea but this agricultural innovation also brought practical benefits to the economy and inhabitants of the province. He began planting tea bushes in his properties in Lakan, a practice that was later adopted by other agriculturists from the area.

These tea plantation practices were shared with the broader community to the extent that it eventually became the largest crop of the province of Gilan. Mahmúd Khamsi, another son of Siyyid Ahmad, relates:

> My father, in Deh Bozorg [Great Village] in the southern part of Rasht by the name of Lakan, stretching many kilometres in width and length, planted the first tea that had been imported by one of his friends from China to Iran. So, the first plantations of tea happened in this village, Lakan, by Siyyid Ahmad. Later on, hundreds of hectares of tea orchards were initiated by Siyyid Ahmad and others. My father also sent some of the young leaves of the tea plantation, which he regularly used for his family, to 'Abdu'l-Bahá.

After receiving this tea, 'Abdu'l-Bahá revealed a Tablet in which He praises the tea and the crop. 'Abdu'l-Bahá says that this tea is acceptable and pleasant especially because it comes from a dear friend. He prays that more plantations will spread and therefore Iran will be independent from foreign tea.

In order to realise 'Abdu'l-Bahá's vision for an expansion of tea plantations, Siyyid Ahmad established an innovative training and research centre dedicated to enhance tea production in the village of Lakan.

The Báqirofs also had large rice plantations in the province of Gilan. According to Dr Iraj Ayman:

> ... every year they would offer some amount of rice to the World Centre starting from the time of the Guardian and continue until I was in Iran, the rest of the family they were making sure that every year they would send some amount of rice as a contribution.[92]

5. Trip to Europe

One of Siyyid Ahmad's greatest blessing was to be allowed to accompany 'Abdu'l-Bahá on His historical travels to Europe. 'Abdu'l-Bahá had arrived in December 1912 to Liverpool from His long journey to North America. The next month he travelled from London to Paris. The following section will describe that journey using personal accounts of people involved during that period.

5.1 Paris

'Abdu'l-Bahá spent several weeks in Paris before undertaking a trip to Germany, Austria and Hungary. Afterwards he returned to the Holy Land in June 1913.

During this second visit to Paris 'Abdu'l-Bahá did not have many public engagements but met with a number of believers who arrived from Iran to meet Him. There is a photograph of them with 'Abdu'l-Bahá at the Eiffel Tower with Siyyid Ahmad next to Him. However, from all of those believers Abdu'l-Bahá only chose Siyyid Ahmad to be added to His entourage coming from North America.

Mahmúd Zarqani, one of 'Abdu'l-Bahá's amanuenses who kept a diary of His travels to the West, wrote:

> It was not possible to hear or record the utterances and words of 'Abdu-l-Bahá except in the public gatherings and some utterances in His own house and also in a hotel He moved to. Jináb-i-Siyyid Ahmad had a residence in that hotel before 'Abdu'l-Bahá, where he beseeched 'Abdu'l-Bahá that while

---

[92] Personal communication to the author.

'Abdu'l-Bahá was residing in the hotel Jináb-i-Siyyid Ahmad would be doing all the service to 'Abdu'l-Bahá. 'Abdu'l-Bahá accepted this and said: "Sádát-i-Khams have always been the servants of the Cause of God". That was his first rendering of service to 'Abdu'l-Bahá at the time of his travel, which was accepted by 'Abdu'l-Bahá from an old friend from Iran. But aside from that 'Abdu'l-Bahá never accepted gifts or cash given in big conferences and sent from cities and American states, as mentioned earlier in the first volume. [93]

Mas'ud Khamsi, Siyyid Ahmad's son, wrote:

At the time when 'Abdu'l-Bahá was staying in Paris for His travels, Áqá Siyyid Ahmad was the cause of His meetings with very important governmental officials of Iran, such as General Mutamed Sepahsalar Rashti and General Tunekabani, and also the Iranian students from Gilan and Mazindaran, so these students when they got back to Iran remembered their meeting with 'Abdu'l-Bahá until the last days of their life, and were thankful to Siyyid Ahmad who arranged such a meeting between students and 'Abdu'l-Bahá and moreover attended Bahá'í meetings in his homes.[94]

According to Siyyid Ahmad's son:

One day he [Siyyid Ahmad] had fallen from a horse and had severe pain in his side, so he could not attend 'Abdu'l-Bahá's presence. So 'Abdu'l-Bahá sent a servant enquiring the reason of the absence of Siyyid Ahmad. When 'Abdu'l-Bahá knew the reason, He personally went to Siyyid Ahmad's room and rubbed where he had pain with hands of kindness and tenderness. The pain was gone immediately and Siyyid Ahmad stood up and started walking and the pain never came back.[95]

---

[93] Rúhu'lláh Mihrabkhání. *Khándán-i Sádát-i-Khams*. Darmstadt, Mu'assassih-'i `Asr-i Jadid, 1994.

[94] Rúhu'lláh Mihrabkhání. *Khándán-i Sádát-i-Khams*. Darmstadt, Mu'assassih-'i `Asr-i Jadid, 1994.

[95] Rúhu'lláh Mihrabkhání. *Khándán-i Sádát-i-Khams*. Darmstadt, Mu'assassih-'i `Asr-i Jadid, 1994.

In the hotel in Rue Lauriston where He was staying, 'Abdu'l-Bahá celebrated the Feast of Naw-Rúz with the friends. He had a number of guests for a luncheon that day. Mahmúd Zarqani mentioned:

> 21st March 1913 was a glorious day of success, the Festival of Naw Ruz, a day of joy, where 'Abdu'l-Bahá asked those who were accompanying Him to attend His presence and especially Siyyid Ahmad Baqiroff, Áqá Siyyid Asadu'lláh, and me (Zarqani), and He showered us with His blessings and kindness.[96]

According to Mas'ud Khamsi "Jináb-i-Siyyid Asadu'lláh prepared the Haftsin[97] and Samovar and Iranian cup in the presence of 'Abdu'l-Bahá, causing much joy and contentment to 'Abdu'l-Bahá, the Most Mighty Branch."[98] An Iranian Bahá'í student recorded the details of that special Naw-Rúz where three different celebrations were held in just one day to everyone's delight:

> In the second half of March 1913, we received an invitation letter from the Iranian Embassy for the day of Naw-Rúz. On Friday, March 21st, Mírzá Habíbu'lláh Khán Sahíhí and I left for Paris and headed for rue Saint-Didier where Dr. Muhammad Khán resided. The concierge accompanied us to a hotel located at 97 Lauriston Street. We met at the restaurant of the hotel with Ágha Mírzá Ahmad Sohrab and Ághá Mírzá Ahmad Bagherov having coffee. In the meantime, 'Abdu'l-Bahá had come downstairs and had taken a seat in a private room adorned with a central table on which New Year's specialties were arranged such as oriental nuts and various Iranian and Western confectionary and sweets. It was in this room that we had the honour of finding ourselves in the presence of 'Abdu'l-Bahá. Ághá Mírzá Ahmad Bagherov was sitting across from 'Abdu'l-Bahá. The Master wished us a happy new year and allowed us to take a seat. With his own hands, he offered

---

[96]Rúhu'lláh Mihrabkhání. *Khándán-i Sádát-i-Khams.* Darmstadt, Mu'assassih-'i 'Asr-i Jadid, 1994.
[97]Symbolic table arrangement set up in Persian homes to celebrate the New Year.
[98]Rúhu'lláh Mihrabkhání. *Khándán-i Sádát-i-Khams.* Darmstadt, Mu'assassih-'i 'Asr-i Jadid, 1994.

us sweets and said: "Iranians eat, Westerners only taste. You are all Iranians. You should eat". We obeyed with no hesitation. Meanwhile, Ághá Mírzá Mahmúd Zarqání and Dr. Muhammad Khán entered. After a few moments, 'Abdu'l-Bahá left the room, leaving the task of hosting in the hands of Jinábi Zarqání. Then, Mírzá Jalál, Ághá Mírza 'Alí Adib (Jinábi Adíb'son) and Ághá Mírzá Asadu'lláh arrived.

We got up as we had to go to the embassy, but near the door of the hotel, we met Mírzá Husayn Qazvíní (non-Bahá'í), who had come to pay his respects to 'Abdu'l-Bahá and informed us that the reception at the embassy would take place only in the afternoon. We could not ask for anything better and we joined the friends again. Mírzá Mahmúd Morshedzádih and Issá Sádiq, who were students in Versailles at the School of Pedagogy, also arrived. At that moment, the Master came back and we all followed him to the reception room. 'Abdu'l-Bahá inquired about the health of all the newcomers and wished them a happy new year. He then spoke of the feast of Naw-Rúz and Ághá Mírzá Ahmad Sohrab translated as there were, in attendance, some English and French friends as well as a distinguished non-Bahá'í young man who had heard the name of 'Abdu'l-Bahá, had read in the papers the news of his arrival in Paris and had asked permission to be introduced. Everyone, Bahá'ís and non-Bahá'ís, had their eyes on 'Abdu'l-Bahá and heard his words with delight. Shortly before noon, the Westerners asked permission to withdraw. 'Abdu'l-Bahá entered the dining room. Four of us were about to take our leave, when 'Abdu'l-Bahá invited us to stay. We were nine people around the table: 'Abdu'l-Bahá, Entezámu's-Saltanih, Dr. Muhammad Khán, Achraf, Issá Sádiq, Mírzá Husayn Qazvíní, Mírzá Mahmúd Morshedzádih, Ágha Mírzá Jalál and Ágha Mírzá Habibu'lláh Khán Sahíhí.

'Abdu'l-Bahá talked about Persian and Western food and also about traditions and customs in both cultures. After lunch, Ágha Mirza Sohrab presented to 'Abdu'l-Bahá two bouquets of flowers offered on the occasion of Naw-Rúz by an English lady friend who had been present in the morning. 'Abdu'l-Bahá accepted them and then retired to rest.

In the afternoon, we went to the Embassy of Iran. Iranian Bahá'ís, whether they were passing or residing in Paris, had the obligation, according to the instructions of 'Abdu'l-Bahá, to attend at the embassy. All arrived gradually. The students stayed longer than the others in order to present their problems to the Minister Plenipotentiary Montazu's Saltanih. It was at that moment that 'Abdu'l-Bahá, accompanied by Mr Dreyfus, entered the great hall of the embassy. The minister invited all the students to introduce themselves to 'Abdu'l-Bahá. We took a spot around the big hall — we were about thirty people. 'Abdu'l-Bahá extended his solicitude and kindness to all, congratulated them on the new year, and praised them for their efforts in acquiring science and knowledge. He spoke in detail about the historical background of Arab and European cultures and said that the latter owed much to the former. He described the transfer of the knowledge and sciences from the Arabs to the Europeans through the Spaniards. He added: "You too must learn from Europeans and acquire the qualities and knowledge they have so as to offer them as gifts to Iran. I will pray for you to succeed". The entire audience listened silently in the greatest concentration and respect. After the last of 'Abdu'l-Bahá's explanations, the minister invited him to another room for tea. After a quarter of an hour, the Master returned and we had the honour to see him again before his departure with Mr. Dreyfus.

However, before leaving Mr. Dreyfus announced to the Bahá'í students that on that same evening, a meeting would be held at his home. And so, after having dined at a restaurant, we came to Mr. Dreyfus home. There was a large audience — Iranian and Western Bahá'ís. 'Abdu'l-Bahá was giving explanations about Naw-Rúz. He went through the history of the creation of this festival, from ancient times to Baha'u'llah's era, and described the traditions and customs of the Iranians – dressing in new clothes, eating and drinking sweet things, and rejoicing. Finally, he compared the feast of Naw-Rúz to the divine revelation and the inauguration of a new era. He recalled the customs of the ancient kings of planning and founding new buildings, charities and institutions on this day. He expressed the necessity of founding, on such a blessed day, charitable institutions, of laying the foundations of assemblies for peace, so that the memory of the feast may remain, and that one may be able in the future to recall that such work is the result of such year's Naw-Rúz feast. 'Abdu'l-Bahá spoke in Persian and Mr. Dreyfus would translate. When the Master finished his speech, he shook the hand of each person present and left the room. [99]

5.2 Stuttgart

The Bahá'í friends in Stuttgart had invited 'Abdu'l-Bahá to come but, as He was not feeling well, they had to wait until He had recovered. Finally, 'Abdu'l-Bahá with Siyyid Ahmad in His entourage left Paris for Stuttgart on 30 March 1913. It is interesting to note that 'Abdu'l-Bahá told them to discard their Eastern garments and use Western clothes withholding the use of oriental headgear. The train to Stuttgart in Germany's southwest, 630 km away from Paris, arrived early in the evening of 1st April 1913 and the Master stayed in the Hotel Maquardt which was one of the best in the city and close to the train station. The friends in Stuttgart were not advised of 'Abdu'l-Bahá's coming as per His wishes because He did not want it to have any newspaper publicity.

According to Hasan Balyuzi:

Then He let His attendants telephone to some of the Bahá'ís and inform them of His arrival. Much surprised, these Bahá'ís hurried to His hotel. 'Abdu'l-Bahá explained that He had wanted His arrival to be a complete surprise. He loved the Bahá'ís of Stuttgart, He said, and had spoken often of the sterling qualities of German Bahá'ís, of their sincerity and steadfastness; therefore the Faith would gain great strength in their midst.

Bahá'ís streamed into the hotel the next morning. It was planned

---

[99] Achraf Achraf. Souvenir du jeune A. Ashraf, Étudiant Baha'i Iranien à Paris. *Payám-i- Bahá'í*, Juli 1981.

that 'Abdu'l-Bahá would meet them at His hotel in the mornings, and at other times He would go out to meetings at their homes or elsewhere. That evening, as 'Abdu'l-Bahá's car drew up before the house where a meeting had been arranged, the cry of 'Ya Bahá'u'l-Abhá' went up from a large number gathered outside. The next day, 'Abdu'l-Bahá remarked that the hotelier might leave his hotel and seek refuge elsewhere, because of such numbers pouring in. Indeed the staff of the hotel were shaken and astonished to see so many of their countrymen pay such attention and respect to an Easterner who, as it seemed, had come from nowhere. One of the Bahá'ís asked 'Abdu'l-Bahá what to say when people enquired who He was. Tell them, He said, that He was a person calling men to the Kingdom of God, a promoter of the Faith of Bahá'u'lláh, a herald of peace and reconciliation, and an advocate of the oneness of humanity.

A clergyman of Stuttgart had been greatly impressed by *Some Answered Questions*, and requested 'Abdu'l-Bahá's permission to translate the book into German. This permission was given to him; but to his next request to be permitted to communicate these teachings to the Kaiser, 'Abdu'l-Bahá replied that it was not advisable, because the Emperor was proud and would not deign to listen.

In the evening of April 3rd, 'Abdu'l-Bahá addressed a large audience in the upper hall of the City (Burger) Museum. Sohrab's English translation of 'Abdu'l-Bahá's talk was, in turn, rendered into German by Herr Eckstein. 'Abdu'l-Bahá said:

> I came from a distant land. I have travelled twenty thousand miles until I came to you in Stuttgart. Forty years I was a prisoner. I was young when I was put into prison and my hair was white when the prison doors opened. After all these long years of the sufferings of prison life I willingly took upon myself all the hardships of a long journey. Now I am here in order to be united with you, in order to meet you. My purpose is that perchance you may illumine the world of humanity; that all men may unite in perfect love and friendship; that religious prejudices, national prejudices, race distinctions, all may be completely abandoned. The religions of today consist of dogmas. Because these dogmas

differ from each other, discord and even hatred is manifest. Religion must be the basis of all good fellowship. Think of the turmoil that today exists in the Balkans; how much blood is shed; how many thousands of mothers have lost their sons, how many children have become orphans, and how many buildings, villages, and cities have been destroyed! The Balkan states have become a volcano. All this ruin originates from the prejudices created by the different dogmas, called forth by superstitions and race prejudices. The essence of the religion of God is love, and the Holy Books bear testimony to that, for the essence of the religion of God is the light of the world of humanity; but mankind today has forgotten what constitutes true religion. Each nation and each people today hold to some definite dogma ... These traditions and these dogmas are like the husks surrounding the kernel. We must release the kernel from the husk. The world of humanity is in the dark. Our aim is to illumine mankind ... It is our hope that this darkness may be dispelled and that the rays of the Sun of Reality will shine again ... This century is the century of light. This period is the period of science. This cycle is the cycle of reality. This age is the age of progress and freedom of thought. This day is the greatest day of the Lord ... This time is the time in which all is resurrected into new life. Therefore, I desire that all may be united in harmony. Strive and work so that the standard of the world of human Oneness may be raised among men, so that the lights of universal peace may shine and the East and the West embrace, and the material world become a mirror of the Kingdom of God, that eternal light may shine forth and that the day [may] break which will not be followed by night ... [100]

'Abdu'l-Bahá's visit to Esslingen was particularly moving and impressive. Anna Koestlin had organized a meeting (which was more like a festival) on behalf of the children whom she taught. Alma Knobloch wrote to her sister Pauline (Mrs Joseph Hannen) in America:

---

[100] Hasan Balyuzi. *'Abdu'l-Bahá*. George Ronald Oxford, 1972, p. 381.

We have had some wonderful meetings; the one in Esslingen surpassed them all. It was the children's meeting, last Friday, April 4th, 1913, in the afternoon. They had secured a very pretty hall, which was most beautifully decorated with greens, plants and flowers, with large and small tables near the walls and round tables in the centre. About fifty children and eighty adults were present. In a smaller room adjoining the hall the children had been assembled holding flowers in their hands, forming two lines for 'Abdu'l-Bahá to pass through. It looked most beautiful as 'Abdu'l-Bahá came upstairs. He passed through a short hall and looked so pleased and delighted to see the dear children.[101]

The children presented their flowers to 'Abdu'l-Bahá and He gave them boxes of chocolates and sweets. Later He spoke to them all — children and adults, young and old — and a photograph was taken outside the hall, 'Abdu'l-Bahá seated in their midst. The following day at His hotel He spoke with great joy of the previous day's gathering at Esslingen.

On April 5th, 'Abdu'l-Bahá spoke at a number of meetings. In the evening He addressed the Esperanto Society whose president, Professor Christaller, offered Him a warm welcome. The day ended with dinner at the home of Herr Eckstein. Other Bahá'ís whose homes 'Abdu'l-Bahá visited, where meetings were held, included Consul and Frau Schwarz, Herr and Frau Schweizer, and Herr and Frau Herrigel. The Schweizers lived in the town of Zuffenhausen.

The first meeting of the day on Sunday, April 6th, was at the Hotel Marquardt. So many were there and so many tarried behind, once the meeting was over, that 'Abdu'l-Bahá teased them, saying that they would be forcing the owner of the hotel to run away. In the afternoon, 'Abdu'l-Bahá was driven in the Black Forest. Bahá'ís had gathered at the park in Wagenburg. As there were too many to photograph together, several group photographs were taken with 'Abdu'l-Bahá in the centre of each. In the evening, there was a public meeting at

---

[101] Hasan Balyuzi. *'Abdu'l-Bahá*. George Ronald Oxford, p. 1972, p. 382.

the Obere Museum, and once more the attendance was high. 'Abdu'l-Bahá and His attendants had dinner that night at the home which Miss Knobloch shared with Fraulein Doring. 'Abdu'l-Bahá intended to leave for Budapest on April 7th, but was persuaded by Consul Schwarz to visit Bad Mergentheim, approximately sixty miles distant from Stuttgart, where the Consul owned the hotel and the mineral bath. 'Abdu'l-Bahá said at Bad Mergentheim that since He had left Persia He had never until then heard so many nightingales singing in such beautiful surroundings. However, He would not stay more than one night. For years a monument to commemorate 'Abdu'l-Bahá's visit, consisting of a metal plaque of His profile mounted on stone, stood in parkland in Bad Mergentheim. It was removed when the Nazis came to power. As far as can be ascertained, it was melted down.

'Abdu'l-Bahá returned to Stuttgart the next day and had luncheon at the home of Consul and Frau Schwarz. All day the Bahá'ís streamed in to visit Him until His train left for Budapest at 8 p.m.[102]

The next destination after Stuttgart was Budapest, Hungary's capital, which was 750 km away. The entourage left Stuttgart on 8 April at 8 pm reaching Vienna twelve hours later and arriving in Vienna at 8 am on 9 April. To reach Budapest one needs to change trains in Vienna, Austria's capital, which was sitting in the middle of the two cities. Reza Khamsi-Báqirof and other Iranian friends were waiting for him on the Vienna train platforms to greet 'Abdu'l-Bahá. Reza Khamsi-Báqirof, as seen in the first part of the book, was Siyyid Ahmad's first cousin and had settled in Vienna with his family in 1911. Reza Khamsi Báqirof had already been with 'Abdu'l-Bahá in Paris in the previous weeks.

5.3 Budapest

They arrived in Vienna on 9th April 1913. 'Abdu'l-Bahá was already feeling weak with a chest condition starting to develop. In Budapest there were not Bahá'ís but rather a "welcoming committee" waiting

---

[102] Hasan Balyuzi. *'Abdu'l-Bahá*. George Ronald Oxford, 1972, pp. 380-384.

for them.

According to Shoghi Effendi:

... whilst in Budapest He granted an interview to the President of the University, met on a number of occasions the famous Orientalist Prof. Arminius Vambery, addressed the Theosophical Society, and was visited by the President of the Turanian, and representatives of the Turkish Societies, army officers, several members of Parliament, and a deputation of Young Turks, led by Prof. Julius Germanus, who accorded Him a hearty welcome to the city. "During this time," is the written testimony of Dr. Rusztem Vambery, "His ('Abdu'l-Bahá) room in the Dunapalota Hotel became a veritable mecca for all those whom the mysticism of the East and the wisdom of its Master attracted into its magic circle. Among His visitors were Count Albert Apponyi, Prelate Alexander Giesswein, Professor Ignatius Goldziher, the Orientalist of world-wide renown, Professor Robert A. Nadler, the famous Budapest painter, and leader of the Hungarian Theosophical Society.[103]

5.4 Vienna

Already sick, 'Abdu'l-Bahá travelled back the 250 km between Budapest to Vienna on 18 April reaching Vienna in the same evening. Among His activities, He addressed a gathering of Theosophists but most of the time He was unwell and under the care of doctors recommending rest. The following stories about 'Abdu'l-Bahá's sojourn in Vienna have been extracted from the book *Die Geschichte der Österreichischen Bahá'í Gemeinde* (The History of the Austrian Bahá'í Community).

5.4.1 'Abdu'l-Bahá and the Turkish Ambassador

The next morning (April 19) 'Abdu'l-Bahá visited the Ottoman ambassador in Vienna. This ambassador had asked his consul in Budapest to visit 'Abdu'l-Bahá and inform him of His departure from the Hungarian metropolis. 'Abdu'l-Bahá was accompanied by Siyyid Ahmad Khamsi, who was also in Budapest accompanying the Master. Even though the

---

[103]Shoghi Effendi. *God Passes By.* Wilmette, US Bahá'í Publishing Trust, 1979, p. 287.

ambassador was a fanatical Muslim, he was pleased to learn about 'Abdu'l-Bahá's trip to America and expressed regret for the suffering 'Abdu'l-Bahá had endured in the prison city of 'Akká. He showered his guest with expressions of gratitude and insisted that He should stay for lunch.[104]

5.4.2 'Abdu'l-Bahá's Generosity

[One day] 'Abdu'l-Bahá decided to take a walk. An annual festival was being held in Vienna at the time called the "Vienna Flower Day", where women and young girls in their most beautiful dresses and with daffodils and azaleas in their arms offered these flowers to passers-by who met them. The proceeds from the donations thus collected were intended for the ill, but especially sick children and their families. Flowers were also offered to 'Abdu'l-Bahá and His companions, and He gave donations again and again. He then arrived at a park in the Inner City, where children were playing. He took them in His arms and gave everyone some money. When they returned to the hotel, 'Abdu'l-Bahá had emptied his own pockets, and everything that His companions had carried on them had, likewise, been given away. "Today people have bankrupted us," He said with a smile. [105]

5.4.3 'Abdu'l-Bahá's Detachment

In the evening of the same day, He spoke at the invitation of the Theosophical Society in their centre at the residence of the Likaneder family in the first district of Vienna, Johannesgasse 2. In front of a large audience, he explained the inner reality of man and the progress of the soul. Mírzá Mahmúd Zarqani reported that "the hearts of the audience were deeply moved, and after the speech, they swarmed around him like moths". One would never have thought that such a meeting could be organized for Him in Vienna and that one could find people there who loved Him so much and held Him in such esteem.

---

[104] Alex Käfer. *Die Geschichte der Österreichischen Bahá'í Gemeinde.* Horizonte Verlag, 2005, p. 27.

[105] Alex Käfer. *Die Geschichte der Österreichischen Bahá'í Gemeinde.* Horizonte Verlag, 2005, p. 28.

'Abdu'l-Bahá was still suffering from the consequences of the flu that He had contracted in Budapest. Nevertheless, He climbed 120 steps to the fourth floor of the building to reach the auditorium, since the building was new and did not have an elevator yet. [106]

5.4.4 'Abdu'l-Bahá and the Khamsi Family

At that time, the Khamsi Baqiroff family lived in the third district of Vienna, 5 Baumannstrasse, door 5. 'Abdu'l-Bahá partook of a modest meal at the home of this devoted family. Mrs. Khamsi-Baqiroff had prepared a Persian dish, and 'Abdu'l-Bahá insisted on having the entire family with Him at the table. He then rested on a sofa where the children massaged His tired muscles a little while he talked to them. Ms. Khamsi-Baqiroff received permission to bring Persian food to the Grand Hotel, "but only small chicken," 'Abdu'l-Bahá reported to have emphasised. He also asked her to wash His headgear for Him, even though she found it to be perfectly clean. Moreover, He asked her to repair the brown velvet hem of his coat ('Aba), and all the friends came to collect pieces of the hem that fell off during the repair.[107]

5.4.5 Attending 'Abdu'l-Bahá

According to his son Mas'ud Khamsi:
One of the glorious achievements of Siyyid Ahmad was when 'Abdu'l-Bahá was down with the flu and was not attending the European bath, so he prepared the bathroom in the Persian style and personally took 'Abdu'l-Bahá to wash His body and then after that, with the permission of 'Abdu'l-Bahá, he kept all His clothes, soap and rubber (kise) as a blessing. In 1940, all these blessed things were sent to the International Archives for better protection.[108]

---

[106] Alex Käfer. *Die Geschichte der Österreichischen Bahá'í Gemeinde.* Horizonte Verlag, 2005, p. 28.

[107] Alex Käfer. *Die Geschichte der Österreichischen Bahá'í Gemeinde.* Horizonte Verlag, 2005, p. 27.

[108] Rúhu'lláh Mihrabkhání. *Khándán-i Sádát-i-Khams.* Darmstadt, Mu'assassih-'i `Asr-i Jadid, 1994.

5.5 Second Visit to Stuttgart

The entourage travelled back to Stuttgart on 24 April 1913 arriving there in the morning of the following day always accompanied by Siyyid Ahmad. Detailing 'Abdu'l-Bahá's activities in that city, Hasan Balyuzi wrote:

> During this second visit to Stuttgart, which also lasted a week, He was mostly unwell. The cold contracted in Budapest had persisted and was now affecting His chest. The Bahá'ís of Stuttgart had arranged and advertised a meeting for the evening of the 25th at the Burger Museum. In the afternoon the condition of His chest worsened, causing great concern. Physicians told Him that He should not go out, and should use His voice as little as possible. His attendants, whom He had sent on to the meeting, felt that the large and eager assemblage there would be disappointed and dismayed should they be deprived of meeting 'Abdu'l-Bahá. They returned to the hotel with a plan which they thought would both safeguard 'Abdu'l-Bahá's health and make it possible for the people to meet Him. A saloon car, well-protected from the elements, would take 'Abdu'l-Bahá to the Museum where, in a room apart from the main hall, people could be allowed into His presence. As soon as they presented this plan to 'Abdu'l-Bahá and told Him of the eagerness and disappointment of the audience, He arose. Physicians had made Him stay indoors, He said; but His health was for the purpose of serving the Faith. While Wilhelm Herrigel was giving a talk in His stead, He walked into the hall, to the utmost delight and surprise of the audience, and using His full voice delivered a discourse on the need of world peace and the power that can guarantee it. The talk over, 'Abdu'l-Bahá was about to leave and return quickly to His hotel, when a voice was heard, wailing. He stopped and asked His attendants to make enquiries. It was found that a lady who had tried to reach 'Abdu'l-Bahá, and had been kept back by the press of the crowd, was weeping. 'Abdu'l-Bahá stayed to speak to her words of great kindness. The next day, to questions about His health, He answered that the previous night's venture, although considered very risky, had proved

the right medicine for Him.

The war in the Balkans was mentioned in conversation that day. 'Abdu'l-Bahá advised the Bahá'ís to talk of their own war against materialism and ignorance; the Balkan war led to death, their war to life; that war led to disaster, their war always to glory and victory. Christ waged this war on the Cross and triumphed over all. A man from Switzerland was among His visitors. To him He said that His stay in Switzerland had been too short and He had not met many people there, but He could feel that they were people of great capabilities, and when the Cause reached them, it would find devoted advocates.

On April 27th a number of children were brought to the hotel. The sight of children always gave 'Abdu'l-Bahá great joy. He said that He particularly loved children because they were nearer to the Kingdom of God. Later, the parents of one child told Him how, when asked to pray for the Master's health, the child had replied that He would go away if He recovered; 'we don't want him to go away'. 'Abdu'l-Bahá was greatly touched.

Although He had felt better, and had gone out of doors and to meetings as well, physicians warned Him, on April 29th, not to attend meetings or tax His voice. Should He follow their advice, He would be able to travel to Paris within three days.

On the morning of May 1st 'Abdu'l-Bahá met the Bahá'ís of Stuttgart in groups. He spoke very tenderly to them. To one group He said that He wished to converse with them but His chest was not helpful; He would always anticipate their good news. To another, He spoke of the two ways in which people say farewell; for some, memories gradually fade away (out of sight, out of mind), but others keep their memories ever fresh. There were Bahá'ís whom He had not seen for years; He was in Europe, they were in Persia, but they were always in His mind and close to Him. To a third group He said that, although His time in Stuttgart was limited, He hoped that the harvest would prove limitless.

Then He left for Paris. That morning He had been speaking to Bahá'ís at His hotel all the while, assuring them of His love and admiration.[109]

The entourage stayed in Stuttgart until 1 May on their way back to Paris after a memorable one-month trip.

6. Services to the Cause of God

Siyyid Ahmad's services to the Bahá'í Faith were very comprehensive and encompassed a variety of tasks. For example, he was instrumental in identifying and documenting Bahá'í Holy places in Iran, a mission that the Guardian had given to the National Spiritual Assembly. For Shoghi Effendi the documentation, purchase and conservation of those sacred buildings on Persian soil was a matter of great importance since the rapid modernisation and urbanisation of the country were destroying heritage buildings. In 1936 the beloved Guardian had instructed the National Spiritual Assembly of Iran to create a committee for the Holy Places in Iran while the House of Baha'u'llah in Tehran was finally purchased in 1942.[110]

It is noteworthy that around one decade before Shoghi Effendi had asked Effie Baker (1880-1868), an Australian believer, to travel throughout Iran and photograph historical places associated with the Bábí and Bahá'í history. It is because of her activities undertaken while travelling on rugged roads and often on mule, covered with a chador,[111] that we keep a graphic memory of those places which have now disappeared.

As we are going to see in this section Siyyid Ahmad helped many Bahá'ís and non-Bahá'ís who were under oppression, even when he himself was the target of attacks. At times, for his own security, he had to carry a gun. According to Rúhu'lláh Mihrabkhání:

> Siyyid Ahmad also had important relationship with the important people of the city, those who were in high positions, and they also respected him. His house was extremely rich and glamorous and was the place that these people frequented.

---

[109] Hasan Balyuzi. *'Abdu'l-Bahá*. George Ronald Oxford, 1972, pp. 390-391.

[110] Robert Stauffer. *History of the House of Bahá'u'lláh in Tihran*. Iran, 1978. Available at: https://bahai-library.com/stauffer_history_house_bahaullah

[111] A chador is a head covering cloth for women in Middle Eastern countries.

Therefore, he used these relationships to help the poor and those who were oppressed, Bahá'í or non-Bahá'í. [112]

His son Mas'ud Khamsi recalled that "On another occasion and other Tablets, He ['Abdu'l-Bahá] recommended my father to make friends with the Russian Consul in the city of Rasht, where my father lived."[113]

6.1 Helping Non-Bahá'ís

Timurtash was the governor of the province of Gilan during 1919-1920. He was known to be very cruel and brutal. He ordered the execution of a group of people which included a priest who was a friend of Siyyid Ahmad named Shariat Madar. According to Rúhu'lláh Mihrabkhání

> Allegedly at the time when Timurtash was the governor of Gilan [1919-1920], some of the people of the province were not happy with his misbehaviour and there was an uprising. As a result, he ordered the execution of some people among which were some religious leaders.
>
> Siyyid Ahmad had developed a friendship with some of these religious leaders and knew that they were innocent. Before these people were hanged, Siyyid Ahmad sent some of his servants who were working in a village near Rasht, called Eynak, to take these people who were going to be executed from the authorities and to bring them to the village of Eynak and eventually set them free. [114]

6.2 Protecting the Bahá'ís

In various circumstances Siyyid Ahmad was a champion against the oppression of the Bahá'í Faith. Two stories are shared below to illustrate his courage and bravery.

---

[112] Rúhu'lláh Mihrabkhání. Khándán-i Sádát-i-Khams. Darmstadt, Mu'assassih-'i `Asr-i Jadid, 1994.

[113] *Pioneering and Services of Mas'ud Khamsi,* unpublished manuscript.

[114] Rúhu'lláh Mihrabkhání. *Khándán-i Sádát-i-Khams.* Darmstadt, Mu'assassih-'i `Asr-i Jadid, 1994.

6.2.1 Safekeeping the Remains of Áqá 'Alí

Rúhu'lláh Mihrabkhání wrote:

> Another thing he [Siyyid Ahmad] did was the burial of the remains of Áqá 'Alí, a survivor of Shaykh Tabarsi. Evil-doers dragged the body of Áqá 'Alí with a rope through the street. But Áqá Siyyid Ahmad managed to get the holy remains of Áqá 'Alí and buried him next to the Imam Zadeh Vali, which was a pilgrimage place for the public. He then instructed a Muslim woman to be the custodian of the Imam Zadeh so that the Bahá'ís could go there as pilgrims [because he was one of the people who was taken in the Shaykh Tabarsi siege incident][115] without any fear. And then later on, when the Bahá'í cemetery was bought and built, the holy body of Áqá 'Alí was transferred to the Bahá'í cemetery. [116]

6.2.2 Habib Sabet's Story

Habib Sabet was Siyyid Ahmad's son-in-law married to his daughter Bahereh in 1929. As it is broadly known, Iran was the land of corruption where government transactions and procedures were arranged through bribery and kickbacks. Habib's story reveals how he as a Bahá'í stood firm against unfairness and how Siyyid Ahmad managed to release him from an unjust arrest:

> In those days, the only other factory in Iran was the sugar plant of "Kahrizak". This was controlled by the Ministry of Arts and Crafts under a Secretary of State named "Motazem-Saltaneh Farokh". By orders of Reza Shah, The Great, it was his duty to keep this factory going despite many problems. Sugar in those days was not in powder or cubes but in the form of a loaf or cone. In order to dry the loaves as they came out of the molds, it was necessary to place them in wooden racks, which were needed by the hundreds. These shelves or racks, which had to be uniform and sturdy, were beyond the possibilities of traditional carpenters who refused to build them anyway.

---

[115] The uprising took place between October 1848 and May 1849.

[116] Rúhu'lláh Mihrabkhání. *Khándán-i Sádát-i-Khams.* Darmstadt, Mu'assassih-'i `Asr-i Jadid, 1994.

The Ministry, which had a limited budget and a stingy Director, accepted our offer to produce these racks. The main condition was that they be delivered complete, installed and accepted by the inspectors. We fulfilled our part of the contract but the Ministry didn't pay. We waited for a while, but still they didn't pay. We had done our best but now we were in a financial pinch. The workers who had not been paid for some time quit their jobs. The lumber sellers came to the factory many times to collect their money. The situation became desperate. I decided to go and see the Minister Mr Farokh. His secretary would not let me in his office. I said, "I'll stay here until he comes out, I won't move unless I am paid. I'll even sleep here!" Finally, Mr Minister allowed me in. I didn't know if I could sit down. So, standing, I asked him very politely to issue the payment order, explaining in the meanwhile the deplorable situation at the factory. Contrary to my expectations, without the slightest regret or understanding, he ordered me out of the room. He said, "Whenever we have money, we'll pay you". I said, "If you didn't have the funds, why did you order?" He replied, "Don't be insolent," and with that he ordered his secretary to kick me out. But before leaving, I said, "Maybe the reason you don't pay me is because I am an honest person, and haven't tried to bribe anyone". Mr Farokh became very angry and insulted and said he would have the police arrest me.

Next morning, an officer from the Central Police Department, which was headed by Colonel Mohamed Hossein Ayrom, came to arrest me, in return for the work I had done and service rendered in making those shelves. I was in jail for two months. After that period, my father-in-law, Sayyed Ahmed [Ahmad] Khamsi, through his good friend the Minister of Justice, Mr 'Alí Akbar Davar, who had reorganized the Department of Justice and the Courts, interceded and I was called into the office of Colonel Ayrom. All of this, only after the matter had been brought to the attention of Reza Shah himself. The Colonel ordered some tea and sweets and started to appease me, saying that in reality he had nothing to do with the reason for my arrest. It was orders. After some time, the Department of

Arts and Crafts paid 3 000 Tomans, but I'll never forget that incident.[117]

6.2.3 Being Persecuted

Habib Sabet recounted this story showing Siyyid Ahmad being the subject of assassination and his absolute serenity and forbearance in the face of danger:

> In Rasht the clergy, just like in the rest of Iran, showed severe opposition to the Cause and the followers of the Faith. In the time of revolution and Mírzá Kuchik Khan's governance[118] one of the clerics who had joined Kuchik Khan's movement tried to cause trouble for the Bahá'ís and even martyr them, especially the famous and active Bahá'ís. In one instance, he sent two of Mírzá Kuchik Khan's soldiers with guns to the house of a Bahá'í, Ibthaj ul-Mulk, where they kidnapped him, grabbed him and took him to the forest where he was handed in to the cleric and fusilladed.
>
> A few days later, again two other armed soldiers went to the store of Siyyid-i-Ahmad-i-Khamsi himself and told him that the Shaykh, one of the clerics, had instructed them to take him to the forest where that cleric was. Siyyid Ahmad was completely aware of the martyrdom of his friend Ibthaj ul-Mulk and knew about the plot, so he told the soldiers that he had to inform his wife and family, but they didn't let him and forced him to get on the horse carriage. One of the soldiers sat next to him, while the other soldier sat in the front beside the driver of the carriage. Along the way before they got to the forest to hand Áqá Ahmad to the Shaykh, the soldier who was sitting in the front told his friend who was sitting next to Siyyid Ahmad, "Let's swap places because I am tired".
>
> Then the soldier sitting next to Áqáy-i-Khamsi [Siyyid Ahmad],

---

[117]Habib Sabet. *Memoirs*, pp 94-95, 1989. Available online from: https://archive.org/stream/HabibSabetMem/HabibSabetMem_djvu.txt

[118]Mírzá Kuchik Khan was the leader of an uprising against the government which took place from 1914 till 1921. The uprising became known as the "Jungle Movement" because it developed in the forests of Gilan province as a guerilla group.

asked Siyyid Ahmad if he saw the bullets fastened around the soldier's waist, and told him that he would use all the bullets to the end if he had to save Siyyid Ahmad's life. Jináb-i-Khamsi Siyyid Ahmad was surprised. He asked for the reason and the soldier replied:

"Some time ago I had some money. I wanted to leave it with someone whom I could trust. Everyone told me to go and leave the money with a Bahá'í called Siyyid Ahmad. So I came and left my money with you, I lent it to you. Then I went on a trip for pilgrimage. After I came back, I visited you to get my money back. You opened the safe. There were so many bags in the safe full of silver and cash and everything, and you returned the money plus the interest [without asking any questions]. I would never forget your kindness and this truthfulness of you. Today I have to repay you and save your life. Do you know Mírzá Kuchik Khan?"

To which Jináb-i-Khamsi replied, "Yes. He knows me very well as well" The soldier then said, "So I am at peace now".

The carriage went on until it came close to the house [where they were supposed to stop]. The soldier told his friend to wait there and to look after the prisoner. He said he would use one of the carriage horses to go somewhere and will come back. He took one of the horses and rode to Mírzá Kuchik Khan himself, and recounted the complete story of the cleric's intention, that he had arrested Siyyid Ahmad-i-Khamsi, and explained the situation as it was. Mírzá Kuchik Khán became very distressed from hearing such a story and said that this cleric wouldn't leave them alone. Then he issued an order to the soldier and said, "take Siyyid Ahmad to his residence in Rasht with absolute respect".[119]

7. Teaching the Faith

Siyyid Ahmad was actively involved supporting the spread of the Faith in the province of Rasht. He also supported the development of

---

[119] Rúhu'lláh Mihrabkhání. *Khándán-i Sádát-i-Khams.* Darmstadt, Mu'assassih-'i `Asr-i Jadid, 1994.

Bahá'í administration in the area. In the biography about the Hand of the Cause 'Alí-Akbar Furútan we read:

> In the year 1930, after sixteen years in Russia where he had lived since he was nine years old, Mr Furútan returned to Iran as a young, educated man. Travelling from 'Ishqábad by bus and train he went to Baku, where he boarded a boat for Anzali (Bandar-i-Pahlavi), Gilan. The Local Spiritual Assembly of 'Ishqábad had informed some friends in Anzali who had visited 'Ishqábad in previous years about his arrival and a few of them came to meet him. They took him to the home of one of the Bahá'ís and arranged meetings for him with friends. He stayed in Anzali for a few days before leaving for Rasht. The Local Spiritual Assembly had also alerted Mírzá Ahmad Khamsí Báqirov, who had been with 'Abdu'l-Bahá during His visit to Paris, about the capacities of this young man. He welcomed him and invited him to stay at his home. The friends in Rasht took advantage of his visit to arrange meetings, firesides and youth and moral education classes.
>
> The Bahá'í News of Iran, Akhbar-i-Amrí, reported his first activity in Gilan: "Following the decision of its fifth Regional Convention, the Local Assembly sent Messrs. Áqá Siyyid Ahmad Báqirov and Mírzá "Alí-Akbar Furútan to Siakol and Langarud to support the process of the Bahá'í elections in those regions". This was the first of many reports that would follow throughout the years. [120]

Because of his contacts with non-Bahá'ís at firesides he became known as an educator visiting their town, and the weekly newspaper Parvarish asked him for articles on education. He wrote several articles, which were published on the front page under his own byline; this was quite an achievement for a Bahá'í in Iran in those days.

Siyyid Ahmad passed away in 1950 in Rasht in the field of service. He was travel teaching within the province of Gilan along with the famous Bahá'í Jináb-i Fadil of Mazandaran and fell sick. It was left to

---

[120] Írán Furútan Muhájir. *Hand of the Cause of God Furútan*. Wilmette, US Baha'i Publishing Trust, p. 60, 2018.

his youngest son Mas'ud Khamsi to advance further the work that Siyyid Naṣru'lláh and Siyyid Ahmad had initiated and realize the promise that both Bahá'u'lláh and 'Abdu'l-Bahá had given about the glory of the Khamsi-Báqirof family.

Haifa, Israel
September 11, 1957

Mr. Massoud Khamsi,
Teheran, Iran.

Dear Baha'i Brother:
    Your loving letter of August 11th was duly received and its contents were presented to the Beloved Guardian.

    The Guardian has directed me to write you that the question of pioneering is a matter of the individual conscience and if an individual wishes to go pioneering, no one has a right to interfere or decide for him. Thus if you and your dear wife wish to go pioneering there is nothing to stop you from doing so. In fact, the Friends should all arise to assist you in every way possible so that new areas may be brought under the influence of the Light of Divine Guidance.

    With every good wish to you and your dear wife, I am

Faithfully yours,

Leroy Ioas

Figure 21: Shoghi Effendi's letter to Mas'ud Khamsi

SIYYID AHMAD KHAMSI-BÁQIROF (C1880-1950)

Figure 22: Last photograph of Shoghi Effendi.
Source: Bahá'í Media

Figure 23: Pioneering in Argentina 1959.
With Ahmad and Dorothy Khamsi.
Source: Bahá'í Peruvian National Archives.

Figure 24: Travel teaching in the Andes.
Courtesy: Bahá'í News, December 1961

Figure 25: Addressing the Bahá'í World Congress in London in 1963.
Source: Bahá'í Peruvian National Archives.

Figure 26: With indigenous believers in Bolivia.
Source: Bahá'í Peruvian National Archives.

Figure 27: Discussing teaching plans with Hand of the
Cause Dr Muhajir in Bolivia.
Courtesy: Stephen Pulley.

Figure 28: With Hand of the Cause Mr Faizi in Lima.
Source: Bahá'í Peruvian National Archives.

Figure 29: In Tehran before departing for Peru.
Source: Bahá'í Peruvian National Archives.

Figure 30: At the Green Light Expedition.
Source: The American Bahá'í Archives.

PART 4:
Mas'ud Khamsi
(1922-2013)

Mas'ud Khamsi was Siyyid's Ahmad youngest son and Siyyid Naṣru'lláh's grandnephew. Although under the shadow of these two illustrious predecessors Mas'ud Khamsi shone with his own light and attained blessings and victories by his own merits. He will be remembered for bringing the Faith to the indigenous masses of South America.

Whereas Siyyid Naṣru'lláh attained the presence of Bahá'u'lláh and 'Abdu'l-Bahá and Siyyid Ahmad met Abdu'l-Bahá, it was for Mas'ud Khamsi to encounter the Beloved Guardian of the Cause, Shoghi Effendi, rendering remarkable services not only in Iran but internationally. It is noteworthy that Mas'ud means *fortunate*, *blessed* and *successful* in Persian and so were his services to the Cause of God.

1. Childhood and Youth in Iran

Mas'ud came to this world the year after the ascension of 'Abdu'l-Bahá. His passport shows that he was born on 21 April 1922 only because at the moment of filling in his application form he did not remember the actual birthday choosing instead the first day of the Festival of Riḍván as his auspicious spiritual naissance. His great-uncle Siyyid Naṣru'lláh passed away two years later.

1.1 Childhood

Talking about his childhood, Mas'ud said:

> My parents were open-minded and quite modern for those days, this is why during our childhood and youth we had freedom of actions, but one thing was obligatory and imposed on us and that was to attend Bahá'í classes on Fridays, without

any excuse.[121]

His children's class teacher was once the Hand of the Cause of God 'Alí-Akbar Furútan who put great emphasis on cleanliness such as having one's nails cut, hair well cut and combed, and impeccable. "He taught us how to be a true Bahá'í", once he recalled.[122]

Since he was a child, Mas'ud was encouraged by his father to save his savings in the Nownahálán [123] Bahá'í Company. Those savings, according to Mas'ud Khamsi "my father immediately gave [them] to the Bahá'í company (Nownahalan) for children's savings and bought shares for my siblings and myself. Unfortunately, during Khomeni's regime these shares as well as those acquired by my wife and I for our children were seized, but I know that someday we will undoubtedly recover them". [124]

1.2 The Tuman

One of the most treasured objects of Mr Khamsi was the receipt of the contribution he made as a child to the construction of the Mashriqu'l-Adhkár of Chicago. Shoghi Effendi had been requesting the Bahá'ís of Iran to assist in the erection of Temple. His Bahá'í class teacher in Rasht, Mr Abbas Yabrom, had told the children about this need and encouraged them to send their savings. As a result Mas'ud sent the equivalent of one tuman to the Holy Land. The reward was receiving a receipt signed by the Guardian which Mas'ud called his *tuman*.[125]

Wherever he went, Mas'ud used to show to the friends his tuman remembering the need to contribute to the Fund. He used to say that it did not matter how much we contribute now for the Temple, as it

---

[121] *Pioneering and Services of Mas'ud Khamsi,* unpublished manuscript.

[122] *Pioneering and Services of Mas'ud Khamsi,* unpublished manuscript.

[123] The Nownahálán company (literally "saplings") was a Bahá'í children's thrift fund created under 'Abdu'l-Bahá's approval and blessing in 1917. Established as a non-profit and charitable institution, in 1967 it was composed by 9,000 shareholders with assets amounted to $1,700,000 which were all confiscated by the Islamic revolution. Many Iranian pioneers living overseas relied on the income generated by their savings.

[124] *Pioneering and Services of Mas'ud Khamsi,* unpublished manuscript.

[125] According to Moojan Momen by 1910 an unskilled labourer's earning was three tumans a month.

is not possible to add one more stone to the building. Somebody even offered one million dollars for the receipt but he rejected the offer because he said that document was for his grandchildren and great grandchildren.

"His favorite line in official Bahá'í gatherings", Shapoor Monadjem wrote, "was to take out a venerable receipt, signed by Shoghi Effendi himself, for a payment he had made to the Bahá'í Fund in the 1950s. He would show this little piece of paper to the audience with raised hand and glory in the fact that such an ordinary act of such little value should receive such an honour from the Scion of God. Mr Khamsi always would vibrate when he related this story as if wanting to show how our human balance in measuring acts of service is out of compass with their true worth as judged from on high. As modest and seemingly routine our contributions as true believers may be, they become, somehow, prodigious".[126]

About fifty years later, Mas'ud met Mr Yabrom by chance at a conference in the Bahá'í Centre of San Francisco. Once Mas'ud had delivered the keynote and the meeting ended, Mr Yabrom approached Mas'ud on the stage. Both recognised each other. Mas'ud said "Abbas Yabrom!" and he responded, "My student!" They hugged each other affectionately in an exchange of great emotions. Suddenly Mas'ud brought the famous tuman from his pocket and showed the Guardian's receipt to his teacher and said: "Mr Yabrom, at the children's classes in Rasht you told us that the Guardian and the World Centre needed contributions. I obeyed, sent my contribution and here is the receipt signed by the Guardian. I want you to see it after fifty years".[127]

1.3 Youth Activities in Iran

Mas'ud was a dedicated believer since his early youth. Dr Shapour Rassekh, a former Counselor and member of the National Spiritual Assembly of the Bahá'ís of Iran, said:

> In my generation, Mas'ud was the most outstanding person. He sacrificed his whole life for the Faith of God. Therefore, all of us we feel proud of him...He was the glory of the Khamsi

---

[126] Personal communication to the author.
[127] Story told by Moojan Matin.

family ... I witnessed his love for serving the Faith and his detachment from earthly belongings. He was an outstanding and distinguished young man... He was one of a few active youths who spoke English.[128]

In turn, 'Alí Nakhjavání, former member of the Universal House of Justice, commented:

> I was a couple of years older than dearly loved Mas'ud when I first met him in Tehran during the early years of the forties of the last century. He was not only a devoted youth, but also a dedicated lover of the Cause, intent upon doing his best to promote its best interests ... He was indeed outstanding in the unique qualities which he possessed from his youthful years in Iran.
>
> Mas'ud was the embodiment of purity of heart, of true detachment, of unquestioned loyalty to the Cause, and of valiant courage, reminiscent of the selfless champions of the heroic age of God's Holy Cause.[129]

Dr Iraj Ayman, former Counselor and member of the National Spiritual Assembly of the Bahá'ís of Iran, wrote about Mas'ud's early services:

> When I started to meet him he was almost a teenager accompanying his father to come to our home every week. He was 16 years old or something like that, because he was coming sometimes together with his elder brother Mahmúd who was of course a Bahá'í youth. So that is how it started. It was in Tehran. Mas'ud was a young Bahá'í. I was meeting him as an active member because in Iran we had a Bahá'í youth organisation which was very much similar to the normal organisation administration in the Bahá'í community that was only for young people. So there was a national committee, a local committee and many sub-committees, all sort of activities, and Mas'ud was one of those active members. But what made

---

[128] Personal communication to the author.
[129] Personal communication to the author.

him stand out from the others was that he spoke the English language fluently and that gave him an opportunity to associate with the non-Iranian people in Iran and that ended up with his acquaintance with his future wife and they were in friendly relationship for a while and finally they married. So, I remember that and because Mas'ud was contacting his parents living in Iran and was a member of a [teaching] committee which was set up to develop closest relationship between Bahá'ís and non-Bahá'í people from other countries who happened to be living in Iran. That was a special committee and he was a very active member. [130]

Since his youth, Mas'ud was very active in the Faith. For example, he was on the National Youth Committee of Iran together with Dr Rahmatu'lláh Muhájir, who would later be a Hand of the Cause of God. When he was young he was appointed to the National Youth Committee. The National Assembly also appointed an adult to this same Youth Committee. Then Mas'ud wondered whether it was wise to have an older member on the Youth Committee. He wrote a letter to the Guardian regarding this person who was much older than the youth. Apparently, the Guardian answered with a letter to the National Assembly in which he indicated that it would be a good idea to perhaps establish a 25 year-old age limit for young people. [131]

'Alí Nakhjavání provided information about another important facet of Mas'ud Khamsi's services:

> He asked the permission and blessing of his parents to go alone to villages in the vicinity of Tehran where Bahá'í farmers resided, in order to encourage them, help their children in Bahá'í classes, and assist in any way he could to improve the condition of their villages. I was deeply impressed at the time as I witnessed his courage, his detachment and his entire reliance upon divine assistance.[132]

---

[130] Story told by Dr Iraj Ayman.
[131] Story told by Kiko Sanchez.
[132] Personal communication to the author.

1.4 Schooling

Mas'ud finished his studies in Firooz Bahram School of Tehran. This was a place where many Bahá'í children used to go particularly after the closure of the Tarbiyat Bahá'í school in 1934 by Reza Shah. Firooz Bahman was, and still is, a prestigious educational establishment owned by Zoroastrian citizens. Education consisted of six years of primary education, three years of middle school education and three years of high school education. It is interesting to note that he, along with other Bahá'í students, was a classmate of Hassan Ali Mansour who eventually would become the prime minister of Iran. In the years to come Mas'ud, supported by Bahá'í institutions of Iran, cultivated further that relationship with Hassan Ali Mansour as a way to secure means to protect the Faith. According to Dr Iraj Ayman:

> Because [Hasan Ali Mansour] had some Bahá'í classmates like Mas'ud, he developed very positive attitudes towards the Bahá'í Faith and when he became prime minister he mentioned that one of his intentions is to arrange for the formal recognition of the Bahá'í Faith and the Bahá'í community in Iran. And that angered the mullahs because they heard about this intention and they were much against such a move. [Hassan Ali] Mansour was that type of a person.[133] The first thing he did was to organise a council for economic studies, because he had studied economics, and invited me also to join that group, so I was almost meeting him every few days in that activity, but Mas'ud was not a member of that activity, but however he was friend with [Hassan Ali] Mansour.[134]

1.5 Homefront Pioneering

Mas'ud's homefront pioneering took place between 1941 and 1942 in the middle of the Second World War that was ravaging the whole globe. Those were tense political times in Iran. Around that time England and the Soviet Union had invaded the southern and northern Iran, respectively. In particular, the Russians occupied Rasht. Although Iran declared itself neutral in the conflict there were allegations of

---

[133] Prime Minister Mansur was assassinated by Islamic extremists in January 1965 aged 41 years old.

[134] Story told by Dr Iraj Ayman.

leaning towards German interests. Following the invasion, Reza Shah was forced to abdicate in favour of his son Muhammad Reza Pahlavi in September 1941. By that time Iran was drowned in a deep political crisis where food was scarce and riots and protests were ongoing.

According to Mas'ud:

> At the age of 19 between 1941 and 1942, Shoghi Effendi was asking the Persians through cables to leave the capital city (Tehran). I decided to move as a pioneer by myself to Khonsar, near Isfahan, a rough and dangerous city in the centre of Iran.[135]

As a consequence of the Guardian's call there was a fever everywhere to go overseas or homefront pioneering. According to Javidukht Khadem:

> The response of the Bahá'ís to the call for pioneers was truly impressive. They were so eager to please their Guardian, so eager to carry out his wishes! Everyone was talking about this. Everyone wanted to go, regardless of the hardships and sacrifices. Many families went immediately. Many youth, some still in their mid-teens, were longing to go ...[136]

Young Mas'ud chose a place that everyone feared to go. It was called the land of bears[137] not because there were bears, perhaps there were no bears, but because its inhabitants were very aggressive people. Mas'ud's mother became very concerned that he was very young and had just finished his school studies.

Nevertheless, he told his parents that he wanted to be a pioneer in this dreaded land. "You should not go," they said. He replied, "I am going to leave because the Guardian has said that I should not be listening to you. I want to be a pioneer and therefore I can decide for myself". And so he left and became a pioneer.

Mas'ud wanted to go to a difficult place because he said that he was not afraid of anything or anyone and because he was going to be

---

[135] *Pioneering and Services of Mas'ud Khamsi*, unpublished manuscript.

[136] Javidukht Khadem. *Zikrullah Khadem: The Itinerant Hand of the Cause of God.* Wilmette, Ill.: Bahá'í Publishing Trust, 1990.

[137] Khansar (Khonsar or Khwansar) is located in the province of Isfahan.

accompanied by the Blessed Beauty and nothing was going to happen to him. It was his father who made it happen although not without fear, because few people had been to those lands. Hence, Mas'ud, with his little suitcase and a bag in hand, left for his pioneering service to that place.

Being her youngest son, Mas'ud's mother was reluctant to let him go to Khonsar. Late one evening she went to wake up Mr Furutan because she knew the influence he had on Mas'ud. He had been his children's class teacher for many years and knew him as a young man. Mr Furutan could surely influence Mas'ud in the way that his mother was hoping for. Mas'ud's mother was able to wake Mr Furutan up (at around 1 am). She begged him to make Mas'ud desist from going to such a place. She did not want her son to die in a strange land. Mr Furutan said, "Do not worry, he will be very well protected. I am sorry that I cannot help you ... when a young man decides to undertake his pioneering service, nobody should stop him. No one should prevent it." Mas'ud's mother was dismayed because she could not prevent this trip and thus, her only option was to hide extra money and stitch it into his coat.[138]

Mas'ud lived through many powerful experiences in this place. However, he happily returned because he said that he had witnessed important changes in the Khonsar people thanks to the Bahá'í teachings. Mas'ud said it had been one of the most wonderful experiences that he had ever had in his life. He had pioneered to the land of the bears and would never forget his experiences and the activities he engaged in Khonsar:

> Following in my family's footsteps I became friends with a community leader and the Faith and the Bahá'ís were then completely protected, I even invited more pioneers from other cities such as Isfahan, Yazd and Kashan so the Local Spiritual Assembly of Khonsar was established, I took note also of stories of the martyr "Al Kar" (the deaf one) and took pictures of his grave site for the Persian Bahá'í national archives.[139]

---

[138] Story provided by Marta Tirado.
[139] *Pioneering and Services of Mas'ud Khamsi,* unpublished manuscript.

After one year he had to return to Tehran due to bad health and because of Khonsar's altitude.[140] He also had to complete his university studies to obtain a Bachelor in Linguistics.

1.6 University Studies

Mas'ud enrolled to study languages at Tehran University. He wanted to become a medical doctor because of the potential to serve the Faith. However, Mas'ud studied linguistics because it was the only career path that let him remain as a pioneer and go to University only for exams. He also did a six-month internship at the famous "Internat Schloss Plön" of Hamburg to practice and to learn more of the German language before graduation. That educational establishment was an exclusive place for children of the European royalty and prominent people.

There is a story of Mas'ud in Peru at an advanced age showcasing his knowledge of linguistics and literature:

> On one occasion at the Catholic University of Peru there was a lecture on Persian poetry. Mr Khamsi had been invited and we were lucky to go with him, Jane and other friends. There was some literature about the persecution of the Bahá'ís of Iran that Mr Khamsi authorized me to bring and distribute. When we arrived we were amazed that the Muslims seemed to feel that Mr Khamsi was their leader. We Bahá'ís realized at that moment just how much they respected him and all came together to greet him. However the story does not finish here. There was a Mulla[141] and, as it is known, they do not shake hands with women. Mama Olya Rouhi, one of the believers insisted to shake hands with the Mulla until he finally did. There were Peruvian poets reciting poems of famous Persian poets such as Omar Khayyam and Hafez. I was behind Mr Khamsi when he whispered in my ear, "that poet that they are referring to is a mundane poet". Mr Khamsi stood up and asked to go to the stage to talk about Persian poetry. Mr Khamsi began to speak so well about Persian poetry and reciting Persian verses that the professors who had the Persian poetry chair

---

[140]Khonsar was at 2,300 m above sea level.
[141]A Muslim priest.

looked at him with respect. Very few Bahá'ís knew about that facet of Mr Khamsi. He started talking about the great Persian poets so eloquently. I never imagined that Mr Khamsi had such eloquence for Persian poetry.[142]

1.7 Work in Tehran

After graduation Mas'ud began working in the family business. According to Ali Nakhjavani:

> My next recollection of Mas'ud Khamsi was when in Tehran he was among the brilliant youth who participated in Bahá'í gatherings. When he finished his studies, he was employed by his brother-in-law, Mr Habib Sabet, in the latter's business undertakings.[143]

According to Mas'ud

> My first job was in Tehran, first in a private business and then with a group who were partners of my sister Bahereh and brother-in-law Habib Sabet, at that time they lived in the United States.[144]

He once was a Director of the first television station in Iran established by Mr Sabet, his brother-in-law. Within the Bahá'í environment he was actively occupied with others gaining the goals of Shoghi Effendi's first 45-month Iranian National Plan which consisted of the consolidation of all Bahá'í local communities, the re-establishment of 62 dissolved Spiritual Assemblies, the formation of 22 new groups and the creation of 13 new centres throughout Iran.[145]

1.8 Mary Jane Snyder Khamsi

Mas'ud Khamsi married Mary Jane Snyder Khamsi, who was not a Bahá'í, in 1951, one or two years after his father Siyyid Ahmad passed away. She was born in Rochester, New York, in 1922. Dorothy Khamsi-

---

[142] Story told by Azam Matin.

[143] Personal communication to the author.

[144] *Pioneering and Services of Mas'ud Khamsi,* unpublished manuscript.

[145] The Bahá'í World Centre. *The Bahá'í World: A Biennial International Record, 1930-1932, Volume IV.* Wilmette, Bahá'í Publishing Trust, 1933, pp. 34-35.

Samandari, Mas'ud's daughter recalled the circumstances of their engagement:

> Mary Jane Snyder worked at the State Department in Washington, D.C. and was offered a 2-year job either in Japan or Iran to work at the US Embassy. She went by boat through the Suez Canal and in Tehran shared residence with an American couple. One early Sunday morning she answered the door and standing in the doorway was a handsome man in an elegant tweed suit, she said her heart jumped, he was there for business with the couple. He drove a Studerbaker. They dated for a while and Mother returned to the US as she came from the Presbyterian faith and a different culture, and no family in Iran, it wouldn't work, so they brokenheartedly said goodbye and she returned to the US. A few months after, my father with his mother's consent, requested she comes back to marry him.[146]

Receiving the marriage consent from his mother was not easy. When he announced his marriage with a North American lady, his mother was opposed to the idea. She said, "I am not giving you permission because she is not a Bahá'í. She will be a Bahá'í only to marry you. This is not going to be a good marriage". Mas'ud said that he kept praying for days until his mother finally issued the consent. It was a difficult time for both of them when they were getting to know each other.

Jane became a Bahá'í through Enoch Olinga, a dedicated African travel teacher and later a Hand of the Cause of God. From then onward she became a strong and dedicated believer. In Mas'ud words:

> She became a Bahá'í in Kampala, Uganda in 1953 during the Bahá'í Conference, and became my companion in service to the Blessed Beauty. Together we participated in several international Conferences planned by the beloved Guardian in preparation for the World Spiritual Crusade that began in 1953.[147]

---

[146] Personal communication to the author.

[147] *Pioneering and Services of Mas'ud Khamsi*, unpublished manuscript.

Jane was a radiant lady full of laughter and happiness while Mas'ud always had a great sense of humour. They both made a special couple. A personal assistant told the following story many years later:

> One day I was at Mr. Khamsi's house having tea with Jane and him. After working with him for almost four years I knew Mr. Khamsi very well, particularly what he was going to say next. Suddenly Mr. Khamsi covered his mouth with the right hand and I told him, "Mr. Khamsi, you have remembered a joke". "And how do you know?", he asked me to which I responded, "Mr. Khamsi, I have been working with you for so long!" "Ah, I'm going to tell you a joke," Mr. Khamsi said "but first I'll tell you what happened to me with Jane." He continued, "When my daughter Dorothy was born, I was in the United States at the hotel with Jane". I asked him "What is the joke?", "Wait a minute", he told me. "In that hotel there were no service for washing cloth diapers". He made me understood that at that time there were no disposable diapers like nowadays. Jane was laughing heartedly and I asked Mr Khamsi for the reason, "Mr. Khamsi, if nobody washed the diapers in the hotel, who then washed them?" He stared at Jane who kept laughing. "You guess", he asked me and I said "Was it Jane?". Jane said "No, because Bahá'u'lláh talks about equality of men and women". So I asked again, "Mr. Khamsi, who then washed the diapers?" "Very good question - I washed the diapers", said Mr Khamsi "And Jane?" I probed further. "That's also a very good question", he replied. "As my forehead was sweating, she was wiping it with a wet cloth!" [148]

A special tribute should be paid to Jane Khamsi as the person who stood beside Mas'ud in his historical services supporting him throughout the many years in the field of pioneering in foreign places. During extensive periods he was absent from home for national and international teaching trips, with the rearing of the children left to her without any extended family around to help except a few members of the local Bahá'í community. One must highlight her dedicated services on Local Spiritual Assemblies and national committees in Bolivia and

---

[148] Story told by Conrado Rodriguez.

Peru. Besides the public figure, there was a woman who made her own sacrifice, consolidating the family in the background. Dorothy Khamsi-Samandari recalled some of those commitments:

> My father would invite 100-200 people for picnics monthly, people would appear at the house unannounced (at meal time) pioneers and travel-teachers would pass through and so to save for the Fund they would stay in homes. Often deepenings and weddings also were held. This meant constantly cooking and washing etc., and often no privacy, then he (Mas'ud) would leave for a month or a few weeks again to summer schools or conferences leaving my Mom to arrange for herself with four needy kids.[149]

Some traveling teachers once wrote: "The Khamsi family's hospitality is one of the wonders of the South American continent ... Jane fed us so well to prepare us for the rest of our travels".[150]

There is a beautiful letter from Amatu'l-Bahá Rúhíyyih Khánum addressed to Mas'ud and Jane paying tribute to the Khamsi's dedication and devotion and wishing them well in their services to the Cause of Baha'u'llah:

Haifa 3 June 1967

Dear Mas'ud and Jane,

I am so very happy to have these times together with you and your lovely children – and so happy you are going back to South America. I know what you can do there and although it is not miracles it can be very close to miracles because of your spirit, your understanding, your faith and capacity as Bahá'ís. I also feel sure the four children, each in their own way, will be of service to the Cause there. This is one more of the wonderful blessings of being a Bahá'í – that no matter how old or young we are there is a special portion of service ready for each of us if we only open our hands and take it ...

Rúhíyyih

---

[149] Personal communication to the author.

[150] Boris Handal. *In Memoriam Mas'ud Khamsi (1922-2013)*. Unpublished.

When Jane passed away in December 2018, the Universal House of Justice wrote to the National Spiritual Assembly of the Baha'is of the United States celebrating her life: "Her many years of devoted service to the Cause of God, including her valued contributions here at the Bahá'í World Centre, are fondly remembered".[151]

2. Meeting the Guardian

A crucial event in Mas'ud's life was meeting the beloved Guardian during the days of Fast in 1953, one that transformed him forever and empowered his being to reach unimaginable, never thought, altitudes of service during his life particularly in South America. It was an unexpected opportunity that came to him while attending with Jane a Bahá'í Conference in Kampala, Uganda. For Jane, having known the Bahá'í Faith only in Iran, the conference allowed her to meet believers from various parts of the world and become a firm and dedicated believer in the years to come including outstanding pioneering services in Argentina, Bolivia and Peru.

At the request of Shoghi Effendi, four intercontinental conferences were held in 1953 to commemorate the 100th year of Bahá'u'lláh's Revelation and to celebrate the launch of the Ten Year Teaching Plan that was going to expand the Bahá'í Faith all over the globe. These were held in Uganda, the United States, Sweden and India.

All of these conferences had Hands of the Cause of God in attendance representing the Guardian. Bahá'ís from all over the world were called to attend these teaching conferences. In particular, it was the Guardian's desire that Iranian Bahá'ís would attend the Conference of Kampala and therefore Mas'ud decided to obey.

The intercontinental Bahá'í Conference in Uganda took place in Kampala from 12th to the 18th February 1953. Mas'ud and Jane participated travelling all the way from Iran. At the conference were present ten Hands of the Cause, namely, Musa Banani, Valiyu'lláh Varqá, Shu'á'u'lláh 'Alá'i, Mason Remey, Horace Holley, Tarazu'lláh Samandari, Dhikru'lláh Khadem, Leroy Ioas, Dorothy Baker and 'Alí-Akbar Furútan. At that time, mass conversion had already started in

---

[151]Letter from the Universal House of Justice to the National Spiritual Assembly of the Baha'is of the United States dated 24 December 2018.

Uganda which brought so much joy to the Guardian. This coincided with the teaching activities undertaken in Africa, and the acceptance of multitudes in the Cause, in such countries as Uganda, Kenya and the Congo. Shoghi Effendi's message to the attendants read an appreciation to the native people of Africa:

> I welcome with open arms the unexpectedly large number of the representatives of the pure-hearted and the spiritually receptive Negro race, so dearly loved by 'Abdu'l-Bahá, for whose conversion to His Father's Faith He so deeply yearned and whose interests He so ardently championed in the course of His memorable visit to the North American continent. I am reminded, on this historic occasion, of the significant words uttered by Bahá'u'lláh Himself, Who as attested by the Center of the Covenant, in His Writings, "compared the colored people to the black pupil of the eye," through which "the light of the spirit shineth forth."[152]

2.1 The Kampala Conference

At the conference two important events two place: Jane became a Bahá'í and Mas'ud received an opportunity to visit Shoghi Effendi in the Holy Land. Jane's declaration, after a few years of marriage, brought much happiness to Mas'ud and such a bond was blessed through many years of spiritual partnership in the Cause of Bahá'u'lláh. These two blessings Mas'ud had attributed to having obeyed the Guardian's wishes of Iranian Bahá'ís attending the Kampala conference.

As to the significance of visiting the Guardian, Mas'ud wrote:

> Mr Keivan, a teacher and a knowledgeable Bahá'í, knowing Shoghi Effendi's unique personality, realized that he would be the last Guardian. When he returned to Persia he encouraged many Bahá'ís to go immediately on pilgrimage so that they could personally meet Shoghi Effendi.[153]

---

[152] Shoghi Effendi. *Messages to the Bahá'í World: 1950–1957*. Wilmette, US Bahá'í Publishing Trust, 1971, p. 92.

[153] *Pioneering and Services of Mas'ud Khamsi*, unpublished manuscript.

2.2 Thinking of Going on Pilgrimage

If Siyyid Naṣru'lláh had attained the presence of Bahá'u'lláh and 'Abdu'l-Bahá in the Holy Land and Siyyid Ahmad had the same inestimable bounty in visiting 'Abdu'l-Bahá, it was Mas'ud's longing to meet the beloved Guardian Shoghi Effendi one day. Siyyid Nasru'llah and Siyyid Ahmad never had had the privilege of being in the presence of the Sign of God on earth. Mas'ud had, however, one hesitation:

> Every Bahá'í wanted to go to the World Centre and meet Shoghi Effendi, the head of the Bahá'í Faith. So I had of course that desire, but I had one reservation. I was afraid that if I was with Shoghi Effendi and if he asked me questions which I could not answer correctly, this would be a cause of shame for me because I was a Bahá'í of third generation and in Iran there were so many teachers yet I could not answer correctly. That was my reservation.[154]

The following lines reveal how God opened the pilgrimage door to Mas'ud:

> ... the Persians said, let's go on our way for pilgrimage and to visit Shoghi Effendi. So they wrote a letter to the Hand of the Cause, Mr Ioas, and Shoghi Effendi answered. He said those who have been before, do not come, and those new ones, come. And Mas'ud Khamsi was the first one on the list. So then there was nothing for me to run away. My name was already there.[155]

In the meantime, Jane flew to the United States via London to visit her family.

2.3 Travelling to Haifa from Kampala

Mas'ud's narrative continued his story when at 30 years of age he met Shoghi Effendi:

> So we decided to go because problems always seemed to

---

[154] *Interview with Mas'ud Khamsi.* Lima, Peru. The transcription has been edited for style purposes as the taping was of poor quality. Tape provided by Masud Samandari.

[155] *Interview with Mas'ud Khamsi.* Lima, Peru. Tape provided by Masud Samandari.

happen when going to Israel from Kampala. Our tickets were to Egypt and from Egypt, an Arabian country, and therefore you could not go to Israel. I went to Egypt and I bought tickets to go to Greece. When the plane landed in Cyprus, I got out and went to a hotel and went to the Israel embassy to get a visa. With all my enthusiasm despite being tired I got there. The Consul said to me, "I am not giving to Persians visa for Israel". I said, "I am Bahá'í". He said: "I don't care. Last night they destroyed another centre in Tehran. You take other planes to Israel".

I was very disappointed and came to the hotel and sent a cable to Shoghi Effendi, that I am here, that the Consul does not give me visa. And the next day I received a cable that "the consul is instructed to give you visa, refer again to him". So I went there. So the next day I could fly. Haifa has its own airport that I therefore I could fly there. And it was nice. It was night and I got a taxi. They were very nice to me at the airport, and the captain, he said, "are you going to the Bahá'í properties, for the Bahá'í house, Abbas Effendi's house?" They wanted even to get out all my suitcases with me and go to their own rooms. I said, no, I am going [to the Bahá'í properties] . Anyhow, I went to the Pilgrim house, caught a taxi to the Shrine of the Báb and all the Bahá'í people were there. It was very nice, and there was a room right at the entrance to the hall, so they gave me that. [156]

2.4 Meeting the Guardian

When I arrived at the Pilgrim House Dr Hakim[157] was there. He was very nice. Then early next morning Dr Hakim came and said, "Shoghi Effendi wants to see you". Persians and pilgrims had to wait to see Shoghi Effendi in the gardens until he came to meet them at the gardens. And he said, "Shoghi Effendi wants to see you". I had fear that Shoghi Effendi would ask me something that I don't know. I went with Dr Hakim to the

---

[156]*Interview with Mas'ud Khamsi.* Lima, Peru. The text has been edited. Tape provided by Masud Samandari.

[157]Dr Lutfu'lláh Hakím (1888-1968) was appointed by the Guardian to the first International Bahá'í Council in 1951. In 1963, he was elected to the first Universal House of Justice.

Master's House, and of course Rúhíyyih Khánum was living there with Shoghi Effendi. And I went to the entrance of the building. He told me, "Shoghi Effendi is in the salon waiting for you". So I opened the door, Shoghi Effendi was sitting in the lounge chair known as 'Abdu'l-Bahá's chair. So I came in, he got up and as a Persian, I bowed.

He greeted me in Farsi and we embraced each other, "Befarmaid moftakhar konid" (Please give us the honour of your presence). I was with tears on my face but when he put his hands around me, and pressed a little, all my fears were cast away. "Come", he said, "sit down and talk". As Shoghi Effendi knew my family, they were classmates with our cousins in Beirut and then in Oxford, so he asked me, "How is the family, how did you come? In the past the Persian friends had to come in a cart and horse and this and that, now you are coming in an airplane. So I have to go right now because the last group of Persians are going to 'Akká and Bahji, I will join them". So I went to 'Akká and Bahji ... I had to sleep there. They gave me the room that Shoghi Effendi was sleeping in. So I stayed, and had a good look at all the books.

I found that of all the books I had there was only one that Shoghi Effendi also had it. That was the book that was about the first ambassador of Spain in Iran writing about Iran. So, I looked at the book which was written History of Persia.[158] It was printed 1880. For sure he had to come to know about the Bahá'í Faith. The book depicts the very bad situation of the Persians. And we imagine that these laws and ordinances of the Bahá'í Faith are what Bahá'ís and everyone needs.

I slept late that night and in the morning with the Persians, I went to the Shrine. That morning I don't forget. That week was Esther [Jewish feast of Purim] [159] Esther was a Jewish princess, a queen of Iran in the time of the Xerxes, and Haman, the prime minister, acted exactly like Hitler ... Her uncle Mordercai found out that Haman planned to kill all the Jews so he informed the

---

[158] Adolfo Rivadeneyra. *Viaje al Interior de Persia*. Madrid, 1880.
[159] Purim celebration in 1953 fell on March 1.

queen, and the queen informed the king[160], and he immediately got the prime minister. Xerxes [the Persian king] ordered to punish all these [prime minister's] people, and he sent the soldiers to guard the Jews instead of killing them. So that is why Jews are very respectful of Esther and they have a feast in honour of Esther.

So I got to the gate of the garden, walked in the garden, and the gardener was there. He said, "Where have you been? Shoghi Effendi has been long time walking in the lane and was been waiting for you". I said, "I did not know. Nobody told me". I was enjoying seeing the [garden]. Anyhow, I ran to him and Shoghi Effendi said, "How it was?, how did you see the orchards and the Shrine of Bahá'u'lláh and this very beautiful garden of Bahji?"

When Shoghi Effendi was with me, he was telling me all the time about the future, the distant future, and the importance of pioneering. He was always mentioning Mr Banani. "Banani was rich in Iran and when he went to England, and heard about pioneering in Africa, he came to me and asked, 'Can I be of service'? I told him to go to Africa. So with the age and with not knowing the language he went to Africa". Shoghi Effendi was insisting about the importance and his desire for the Bahá'í friends to go pioneering. I understood what Shoghi Effendi wanted. He turned his look to me and he did not want to say it directly.[161]

According to Rúhu'lláh Mihrabkhání: "During those meetings with Shoghi Effendi, in two full days Shoghi Effendi talked about mass teaching and expressed its importance. The wisdom of his words became known years later and the related topics were applied in Bolivia among Indians".[162] In a similar manner, he once wrote:

---

[160] The plot to kill Jews was organised by the prime minister under false pretexts and obtained the king's approval. Esther explained the King about the prime minister's motives and as a result the sovereign ordered his hanging and the protection of the Jewish people.

[161] *Interview with Mas'ud Khamsi*. Lima, Peru. Tape provided by Masud Samandari.

[162] Rúhu'lláh Mihrabkhání. *Khándán-i Sádát-i-Khams*. Darmstadt, Mu'assassih-'i

On certain occasions, when I was on pilgrimage, I ran into the beloved Guardian. He told me that pilgrims should come to the Holy Land to visit the Holy Places mainly and not necessarily to see the Guardian. The beloved Guardian also let me know the pain he felt for his relatives who were Covenant breakers.[163]

The following are Mas'ud's stories recalled by believers about what happened during his pilgrimage:

On a certain occasion Mr Khamsi spoke of his meetings with the Guardian and became very excited. Tears fell down his face. It was very interesting listening to him. On one occasion, he said that the Guardian asked him to visit Mr Musa Banani, who was a pioneer in Africa because Mr Banani was a diabetic and Shoghi Effendi had received the news that he had already lost a leg and was losing his sight - he had already lost an eye. The Guardian entrusted him to tell Mr Banani that because of his health he was allowed to leave his pioneering post in Africa. Mr Khamsi told that story with tears. It was too much for him to see Mr Banani in such condition and to have to communicate to him the Guardian's wishes. Mr Banani replied, "With much respect for the Guardian, I'll leave my bones here. I will not leave my pioneering post". Mr Banani did not disobey but asked Mr Khamsi to tell the Guardian that he wanted to stay and die in Africa - and so it happened.[164], [165]

One day Mr. Khamsi began to relate the importance of the Covenant. He told us a story about when he was seated in front of the Guardian, in a meeting where Shoghi Effendi was talking about the development of the Faith worldwide. Suddenly tears appeared in his eyes with his face glowing in the night – it was shining. These were the feelings of a man who had so much love for Guardian. He was crying as he remembered the Guardian telling him about the Andes. He did not know why at

---

Asr-i Jadid, 1994.

[163] *Pioneering and Service of Mas'ud Khamsi*, unpublished manuscript.

[164] Story told by Omar Brdarevic.

[165] The Hand of the Cause of God Musa Banani passed away in Kampala, Uganda, in 1971 aged 85.

the time because he was in Africa. We could all clearly see his spiritual brilliance when he remembered and shared his love for his beloved Guardian. [166]

Once Mr Khamsi told us that he was accompanying the Guardian around the Shrine of the Báb and the Guardian suddenly stopped and pointed his finger towards the golden dome and said to him, "Even the dome is in danger", referring to the future attacks on the Faith. [167]

I remember that once when speaking about the Iranian government, he mentioned that Shoghi Effendi had said that as long as the current cowardly king is ruling, he would not go to Iran. He said that for a while there was speculation in Iran that Shoghi Effendi had come there to see the country and that he was hiding somewhere in the country. Mr Khamsi said that this was only a rumour as Shoghi Effendi had said that, "until this cowardly king is no longer ruling, I will not step in Iran". [168]

The most moving thing for me was his impressions about Shoghi Effendi during his four interviews with him. On one occasion, the Guardian literally had to be picked up after hours of prayer since his body had become completely numb. In another, after a prayer he saw how the Guardian's shoes were ripped at the heel for having taken them off and on constantly to pray.

The most moving thing for me was his impressions about Shoghi Effendi during his four interviews with him. On one occasion, the Guardian literally had to be picked up after hours of prayer since his body had become completely numb. In another, after a prayer he saw how the Guardian's shoes were ripped at the heel for having taken them off and on constantly to pray. [169]

As you may know, on that trip, Mas'ud was a few days alone with the Guardian. That is when he received "lessons on the

---

[166] Story told by Hector Núñez.
[167] Story told by Moojan Matin.
[168] Story told by Azam Matin.
[169] Story told by Grover Gonzales.

indigenous people" from the Guardian. Mas'ud had no idea why the Guardian was giving him those lessons. We now know why.[170]

It was a special moment indeed to have been present at a meeting with Mr. Khamsi, especially when he talked about his visit to the Guardian. We were gathered at the gazebo of his house in Lima, where he often had meetings with friends. On one occasion we were all seated and someone asked him about his visit with the Guardian. At that moment his condition of joy and smile suddenly changed to one of silence and he was completely immobile for a few moments. We all noticed an indescribable reverence present in the atmosphere as if time had suddenly stopped. He then bowed his head and cried two or three seconds but quickly composed and said, "What can I say of such a visit? I had arrived from Iran and was eager to see him. When I looked into his eyes, I could see the universe and eternity at the same time. At that meeting the Guardian spoke with us about the amazing plans and achievements that had been accomplished despite the severe repressions and persecutions in Iran. The Guardian told us that the forces are advancing - are marching without stopping - and that we must all participate and not lose our opportunity. He shared some stories, recently received from some distant countries and the success that the Faith had achieved in far away places. Then the Guardian turned to me and told me that I will start my international services soon. At that moment I knew that I was going to leave Iran and I was going to travel the world and be blessed with opportunities to serve my beloved Faith abroad and achieve international victories for the Faith".[171]

Mr Khamsi also had the opportunity to visit the beloved Guardian Shoghi Effendi in Haifa. He had heard many stories from pilgrims returning from visits to the Guardian and from hearing about the Guardian's magnetic personality. He thought the Baha'is were exaggerating, however, when he met Shoghi Effendi for the first time and was hugged by him, Mr Khamsi

---

[170]Story told by Mahmud Samandari.
[171]Story told by Farid Tebyani.

said he felt like he had been embraced by all the mothers of the world together. [172] One of the things that Shoghi Effendi gave Mr Khamsi as a personal gift was a pillow belonging to 'Abdu'l-Bahá. [173]

Meeting Shoghi Effendi was a turnaround event in Mas'ud's existence redefining him forever. It appeared like a solemn promise he had made to serve the Guardian till his last breath. Coming back to Tehran, spiritually charged, his mind was restless constantly thinking about Shoghi Effendi's conversations about pioneering, mass teaching and what are the new expectations he needs to shoulder. With two little children, a successful business career with international links, a comfortable life lived in opulence and navigating among the upper echelons of Tehran society, Mas'ud had to reconcile Shoghi Effendi's hopes with his current pattern of living, an undertaking that would undoubtedly have challenged the many assumptions he harboured about what it means to live a true Bahá'í life. This earnest longing to please the Guardian would have stemmed from Mas'ud's unyielding firmness in the Covenant, which was to characterise his entire life, seeing his faithfulness in obeying 'Abdu'l-Bahá's admonitions as being inextricably linked with his purpose in life:

> O ye the faithful loved ones of 'Abdu'l-Bahá! It is incumbent upon you to take the greatest care of Shoghi Effendi, the twig that hath branched from and the fruit given forth by the two hallowed and Divine Lote-Trees, that no dust of despondency and sorrow may stain his radiant nature, that day by day he may wax greater in happiness, in joy and spirituality, and may grow to become even as a fruitful tree.[174]

3. First Pioneering to South America

Pioneering always had an important place in the history and development of the Faith of God. Since the early days, and in the absence of professional clergy, the believers were called to spread

---

[172] Story told by Boris Handal.
[173] Story told by Marta Tirado.
[174] 'Abdu'l-Bahá. *The Will and Testament of 'Abdu'l-Bahá*. Wilmette, US Bahá'í Publishing Trust, 1990 reprint, p. 25.

to new territories and shared the new Teachings with their friends, neighbours and associates. Bahá'u'lláh referred to this service as "prince of all goodly deeds, and the ornament of every goodly act". [175] He also gave the following assurances to all that raise to serve Him:

> They that have forsaken their country for the purpose of teaching Our Cause — these shall the Faithful Spirit strengthen through its power. A company of Our chosen angels shall go forth with them, as bidden by Him Who is the Almighty, the All-Wise. How great the blessedness that awaiteth him that hath attained the honor of serving the Almighty! By My life! No act, however great, can compare with it, except such deeds as have been ordained by God, the All-Powerful, the Most Mighty. [176]

The Khamsi family's debut into the field of international pioneering came a few years later. A chain of events took Mas'ud and Jane to settle in South America in 1957, first to Argentina and then to Bolivia, four years after meeting Shoghi Effendi.

It was not an easy decision to make the move because impediments were raised along the way to which the Khamsi couple faced with determination and courage. At the end they succeeded in their decision and were able to render amazing victories to the Cause of Bahá'u'lláh in Argentina, Bolivia and Peru.

3.1 Planning to Pioneer to South America

It was 1953, a year in which Shoghi Effendi launched the world-embracing Ten Year Global Crusade. This global teaching campaign was aimed to bring the Faith to all corners of the globe culminating in 1963 with the election of the Universal House of Justice.

"The entire body of the avowed supporters of Bahá'u'lláh's all-conquering Faith", the beloved Guardian wrote in October 1952, "are now summoned to achieve in a single decade feats eclipsing in totality the achievements which in the course of the eleven preceding

---

[175] Bahá'u'lláh. *Gleanings from the Writings of Bahá'u'lláh*. Wilmette, US Bahá'í Publishing Trust, 1990, p. 346.

[176] Bahá'u'lláh. *Gleanings from the Writings of Bahá'u'lláh*. Wilmette, US Bahá'í Publishing Trust, 1990, p. 334.

decades illuminated the annals of Bahá'í pioneering".[177] Mas'ud had considered seriously Shoghi Effendi's exhortation particularly in light of his recent encounter with him.

It is noteworthy that Azíz Yazdí, Mas'ud's brother-in-law, pioneered to Kenya in December 1952. Two months later, Soraya Khamsi, Mas'ud's sister, joined his husband with the children. This was Mas'ud's plan to leave Iran:

> When I returned to Tehran in 1953, I continued my job in a private business and started to serve in the Bahá'í Administration, but the importance of pioneering was always on my mind, so my wife Jane and I together, decided to leave Persia. As I was involved in achieving some goals of the Ten Year Plan in Persia, most Bahá'í friends, even the friends who were not Bahá'ís, insisted on my staying in Persia, but finally through the Hand of the Cause of God Mr Leroy Ioas, we decided to write to Shoghi Effendi asking for guidance. In his answer, Shoghi Effendi told me that my wife and I should take the Torch of the Faith as far as possible. When I consulted the matter with the Hands of the Cause of God in Tehran, we decided to go pioneering in Latin America. The Faith had been recently introduced there through the Ten Year plan, established by Shoghi Effendi. Unfortunately, while we were getting ready to leave, Shoghi Effendi passed away in November of 1957.[178]

When asked in an interview whether Shoghi Effendi asked him to go to South America, Mas'ud replied:

> No, nothing. But I understood that I had to go. And he mentioned these places are open for pioneering and he mentioned especially the Indian Ocean, places like Jakarta in Indonesia, as well as other places. So when I went back to Iran, I had a house in Tehran, a big house, so I tried to sell the house and go pioneering ... where Shoghi Effendi likes it. So we went to Indonesia, as soon as after Dr Muhajir, who was

---

[177] Shoghi Effendi. *Messages to the Bahá'í World: 1950–1957.* Wilmette, US Bahá'í Publishing Trust, p. 41, 1971.

[178] *Pioneering and Services of Mas'ud Khamsi,* unpublished manuscript.

a month before me in Haifa, and heard the same thing from Shoghi Effendi, and… went to Jakarta.[179] This was the first time we were in Indonesia. So when I decided to go pioneering and there were many difficulties for me, from everybody … Assembly members were encouraging me to stay because I had a friendship with the prime minister Hassan Ali Mansur who was my classmate, and the plan of Shoghi Effendi was to get many of the senior persons in high positions acquainted with the Bahá'í religion. So I had to do, I had to stay in Iran to finish. Then I wrote a letter to Mr Ioas sharing that I wanted to go pioneering and everybody is against me, so he answered me that Shoghi Effendi said "pioneering is a personal affair, nobody can intervene. Contrary to what everybody has asked, you go pioneering". "And I suggest", Shoghi Effendi said, "you and your wife go the farthest and to a new place for the Faith". I sat down and discussed with the Hands of Iran, there were three to four Hands in Iran. They told me to go to the farthest place which was South America and it is new… So we prepared to go. Jane was pregnant, so I sent her to America and have the baby [Dorothy] [180] … We already had Ahmad.[181]

"In between we sent a letter to Shoghi Effendi that we are going but Shoghi Effendi passed away", Mas'ud said. "So that was the last letter that Shoghi Effendi wrote to us". Shoghi Effendi's passing on 4 November 1957 was a big loss for Mas'ud, particularly when his death was unexpected. Three weeks later Dorothy was born in Washington DC.

This is Shoghi Effendi's reply to Mas'ud:

Haifa, Israel
September 11, 1957

Mr Massoud Khamsi
Teheran, Iran

Dear Bahá'í Brother:

---

[179]Dr Muhajir went pioneering in 1954 to Indonesia
[180]Dorothy, born in Washington DC, November 1957.
[181]Ahmad, born in Tehran, January 1955.

Your loving letter of August 11th was duly received and its contents were presented to the Beloved Guardian.

The Guardian has directed me to write you that the questions of pioneering is a matter of the individual conscience and if an individual wishes to go pioneering, no one has a right to interfere or decide for him. Thus if you and your dear wife wish to go pioneering there is nothing to stop you from doing so. In fact, the Friends should arise to assist you in every way possible so that the new areas may be brought under the influence of the Light of Divine Guidance.

With every good wish to you and your dear wife, I am

Faithfully yours,
Leroy Ioas

It is of note, that it was an intrinsic part of the manner in which Shoghi Effendi accompanied the Bahá'í World that he did not instruct the friends how they should respond to the exigencies of the Divine Plan, rather calling their attention to their inescapable responsibility. In a letter written on his behalf to National Spiritual Assembly of the United States in July 1956 and published in *Bahá'í News*, a year when the Khamsis were seriously considering pioneering, the Guardian explains:

> The friends are not being forced to do anything either by the Guardian or by the National Assembly. However, the condition that the world is in is bringing many issues to a head. It would be perhaps impossible to find a nation or people not in a state of crisis today. The materialism, the lack of true religion and the consequent baser forces in human nature which are being released, have brought the whole world to the brink of probably the greatest crisis it has ever faced or will have to face. The Bahá'ís are a part of the world. They too feel the great pressures which are brought to bear upon all people today, whoever and wherever they may be. On the other hand, the Divine Plan, which is the direct method of working toward the establishment of peace and world order, has perforce reached an important and challenging point in its unfoldment; because of the desperate needs of the world, the Bahá'ís find themselves,

even though so limited in numbers, in financial strength and in prestige, called upon to fulfil a great responsibility. They must, at all times, remember that when the Guardian makes his appeals to the friends, he is only presenting the situation to them. Each one must evaluate what his own response can be and should be; nobody can do this for him. There is no other pressure than the pressure of historical circumstances. He fully realizes that the demands made upon the Bahá'ís are great, and that they often feel inadequate, tired and perhaps frightened in the face of the tasks that confront them. This is only natural. On the other hand, they must realize that the power of God can and will assist them; and that because they are privileged to have accepted the Manifestation of God for this Day, this very act has placed upon them a great moral responsibility toward their fellow-men. It is this moral responsibility to which the Guardian is constantly calling their attention, as he too cannot but obey the compelling force of circumstances and fulfil his paramount duty of calling to the attention of the believers their opportunity, their privileges, and their responsibilities. [182]

Determined to make his dream come true and to pursue his promise to the beloved Guardian, Mas'ud in consultation with Jane continued to look around the world "so that the new areas may be brought under the influence of the Light of Divine Guidance" as per Shoghi Effendi's guidance. According to Dr Iraj Ayman: "He wanted to go to somewhere that was rather new and no one, that nobody else has gone there".[183]

Mas'ud's narrative continues:

At that time, all of Latin America was administratively under the supervision of the National Spiritual Assembly of the Bahá'ís of the United States. Shoghi Effendi had recently divided South America into two areas; five countries to the south and five to the north. Buenos Aires, Argentina was the seat for the

---

[182] Letter written on behalf of the Guardian, to the National Spiritual Assembly of the United States, 19 July 1956. *Bahá'í News,* no. 307, p. 2, September, 1956.

[183] Personal communication to the author.

southern countries and Lima, Peru for the northern countries. When we consulted with the NSA of the United States about the countries who needed more pioneers they told us Argentina and Uruguay.

When I received Shoghi Effendi's reply, my wife Jane went to the United States to give birth there to my second child, therefore there was no doubt that we were definitively leaving Persia. I sold my belongings to arrange our future moving to America, after the birth of my daughter Dorothy, we set out for our destination that was planned to be Uruguay.[184]

In America, according to Mas'ud, "we waited [in US] until the baby was three months, because the aeroplane does not allow babies before three months. So I went to Africa, they asked us to consult with the assembly. They told us to go to Argentina or Uruguay".[185] As per above, during that period out of Iran, Mas'ud had attended the ceremony dedicated to the laying of the foundation stone for the House of Worship in Kampala on January 1958 led by Amatu'l-Bahá Rúhíyyih Khánum. It appears that at one time Africa was being considered as a possible pioneering place.

3.2 Settling in Argentina

Mas'ud explained how he subsequently settled in South America. From all the possible places considered, it appears that the Will of God had other directions. Although Africa and Uruguay were the initial potential destinations, Argentina and Bolivia were the places chosen by the Providence for the Khamsis in the end. By the 1950s South America was a little known region in the Western World with a reduced influx of foreign visitors, certainly a place fitting Shoghi Effendi's description of "new areas" that can "be brought under the influence of the Light of Divine Guidance".

We decided to go to Uruguay, and settle down in Argentina, in Buenos Aires. The Bahá'ís knew we were coming there; few Bahá'ís were Persians and few Argentinians. They were there [at the Buenos Aires airport]. And they said, "You don't

---

[184]*Interview with Mas'ud Khamsi*. Lima, Peru. Tape provided by Masud Samandari.
[185]*Interview with Mas'ud Khamsi*. Lima, Peru. Tape provided by Masud Samandari.

go to Uruguay, you go wherever we take you". So they took my suitcase and everything and we went along. That was my first time living in South America.

Since there were enough Bahá'ís in the capital city, Buenos Aires, we decided to live in Bahia Blanca [White Bay][186] just outside the capital. Some [Persian] Bahá'ís were in Brazil. Shoghi Effendi was not very happy with all the Bahá'ís going to Brazil so I stayed in Argentina, but not to live in Buenos Aires. Therefore I went to another city [Bahia Blanca], a pioneer post where there were no Bahá'ís at that time and ... we stayed there for a while...

Once we settled [in Bahia Blanca] we started to teach and make use of our new neighbour who was the owner of the only newspaper of the south of Argentina called "Estrella del Sur" (Star of the South) ... We published the first article on the Bahá'í Faith, as I did not know Spanish they copied the complete pamphlet "What is the Bahá'í Faith?"

When we were living in Buenos Aires, we participated in conventions and meetings of other countries such as Uruguay and Chile. We met Hand of the Cause of God Dr Grossman, who later in consultation with the Hands of the Cause of God at the Holy Land, asked us to go to Bolivia because they needed to teach the indigenous population. We accepted, but we had to wait until Bahia, our third child was born and was old enough to travel to La Paz. The United States Embassy in La Paz advised us that it would be dangerous for a new-born child [to travel].[187]

Jane did not want to go to Bolivia. She said, "I have a baby". We wrote a letter to the American Consul of Buenos Aires to give us some information. We don't know anything about Bolivia, so we got letters from an American lady and that American lady was very American. She wrote, "Don't come, it is so bad that your children will die there."[188]

---

[186] Bahia Blanca is a port city 650 km southwest of Buenos Aires and the 18th largest town in Argentina.

[187] La Paz, Bolivia's capital, is situated at 3 640 m above the sea level.

[188] *Interview with Mas'ud Khamsi.* Lima, Peru. Tape provided by Masud Samandari.

3.3 Settling in Bolivia

It is at this point of time that the Hand of the Cause of God Herman Grossman (1989-1968) steps into the Khamsis destiny. Traveling in 1959 and 1960 throughout South America as a Hand for the Western Hemisphere he was able to assist those nascent communities in their election of their national assemblies for the Ridvan 1963 when the Universal House of Justice was going to be elected. Mr Grossman had born in Argentina in 1899, a son of German Immigrants who returned to their motherland when he was about ten years old. Mas'ud recounts his settlement to La Paz, Bolivia, the most elevated capital city in the world.

> Dr Grossman, who was really wonderful, was born in the Argentina and spoke Spanish. So we went to Uruguay Convention and then to Chile Convention. Dr Grossman was seeing how I treated the Indian representatives. And I was putting them in my car and taking them to the city. I was always busy translating from English to them.
>
> We arrived in La Paz in 1959, and were warmly received by the Bahá'ís with much love, but we had problems with the altitude and lack of oxygen and had to stay in bed for some days to function and adapt. In Bolivia there were great opportunities to serve the Faith, for example in mass conversion, deepening of Bahá'ís and relations with prominent people and authorities such as the President, Ministers of State and local Governors. The Country was undeveloped and open to all progress and innovation. In 1961 we had our fourth child, Gary, born in La Paz, Bolivia. [189]

In 1960, Mas'ud was elected to the Spiritual Assembly of the Bahá'ís of Argentina, Bolivia, Chile, Paraguay and Uruguay. The next year, when independent National Assemblies were formed in each South American country, Mas'ud was elected to the National Assembly of Bolivia and to the Local Assembly of La Paz. By the end of that same year, Mas'ud was appointed as an Auxiliary Board member by Hands of the Cause Jalál Khazeh and Dhikru'lláh Khádem and had to resolve, in several countries, outbreaks of Covenant-breaking, following the

---

[189] *Pioneering and Services of Mas'ud Khamsi*, unpublished manuscript.

passing of the beloved Guardian.

More importantly, in Bolivia Mas'ud began working systematically on bringing large numbers in indigenous communities closer to Bahá'u'lláh's Revelation, finding great receptivity and success, hastening the process of entry by troops envisioned by the beloved Guardian. [190]

Entry by troops had sporadically started in Bolivia but it was through Mas'ud's accompaniment, concomitant with the spontaneous indigenous spirituality, that helped to make it more systematic and successful. According to Amatu'l-Bahá Rúhíyyih Khánum: "The first mass conversion in the Western hemisphere began in Bolivia, how much joy it brought to the heart of the Guardian. I remember how he announced it to the Bahá'í world and how thrilled we were".[191]

"Bolivia became soon, specially after the passing of the beloved Guardian", said Ali Nakhjavani, "the first country on Latin America to experience the process of teaching the masses. The Hands of the Cause in the Holy Land warmly encouraged and fully supported Mas'ud's exploits in that country".[192]

During all his pioneering life Mas'ud was faithful to 'Abdu'l-Bahá's command in the following paragraph of the *Tablets of the Divine Plan* which was generally known in Bahá'í circles as *The Promise:*

> Attach great importance to the indigenous population of America. For these souls may be likened unto the ancient inhabitants of the Arabian Peninsula, who, prior to the Mission of Muḥammad, were like unto savages. When the light of Muḥammad shone forth in their midst, however, they became so radiant as to illumine the world. Likewise, these Indians, should they be educated and guided, there can be no doubt that they will become so illumined as to enlighten the whole world.[193]

---

[190] Shoghi Effendi. *Citadel of Faith: Messages to America 1947-1957*. US Bahá'í Publishing Trust, 1980 reprint, p. 117.

[191] Amatu'l-Bahá Rúhíyyih Khánum. *The Green Light Expedition* (see appendix 1).

[192] Personal communication to the author.

[193] 'Abdu'l-Bahá. *Tablets of the Divine Plan*. US Bahá'í Publishing Trust, 1933, p. 33.

3.4 The Beginning of Mass Teaching in South America

The Faith was brought to the sub-continent by Leonora Armstrong, the Spiritual Mother of Latin America, when she settled in Brasil as a pioneer in 1921, following 'Abdu'l-Baha's call in the Tablets of the Divine Plan. [194]

The year prior the Hand of the Cause Martha Root had circumnavigated South America on a historic journey praised by 'Abdu'l-Baha:

> Praise be to God the Call of the Kingdom has been received in South America and the seeds of Guidance have been sown in those cities and regions. Certainly the heat of the Sun of Reality, the rain of the Eternal Bounty and the breeze of the Love of God will make them germinate: have confidence.[195]

Most of the initial expansion of the Bahá'í Faith commenced in urban centres. The Faith arrived in Bolivia in 1940 when Eleanor Adler, and American pioneer, settled in La Paz. The first Local Spiritual Assembly of La Paz was formed in 1945. All those nascent communities and communities were at that time under the jurisdiction of the National Spiritual Assembly of the United States. In 1951, a Regional Spiritual Assembly for the ten South American countries was formed and in 1957 it was subsequently split up into two other Regional Assemblies with five countries each. The goals of the Ten Year Crusade aimed that by 1963 each of these ten countries had their own National Spiritual Assembly in order to sustain the election of the Universal House of Justice for the first time. In order to achieve those national goals, it was necessary to increase the number of local spiritual assemblies that in turn elected their own National Spiritual Assembly by 1961.

After Ms Adler, gradually other pioneers came to Bolivia taking the Cause to other parts of the country. It took until 1956 when an Indigenous person became the first of an ethnic group to become a believer, one who in turn began teaching and enrolling his own people

---

[194] Boris Handal. *Eve Nicklin, She of the Brave Heart*. SC, CreateSpace, 2011.

[195] Kay Zinky. *Martha Root, Herald of the Kingdom*. New Delhi, India: Bahá'í Publishing Trust, 1983, p. 74.

with much success.[196]

It is noteworthy that mass teaching, when started in South America and other parts of the world, was a novelty within the Bahá'í communities, one that was not always understood and taken with a degree of reservation by some early believers. It was certainly a novel and impressive phenomenon for pioneers, local believers and institutions.

Large groups of new believers who could not read and write were rapidly and enthusiastically accepting the Faith in the next decades particularly in the rural and indigenous areas of Bolivia, Ecuador and Peru, three countries nested in the Andean mountains. Their lack of formal education was seen by some as a major impediment to register them officially as Bahá'ís and become a test for some who had been in the Faith for years.

And yet the Guardian had clarified a few months before his passing that the spark of faith is only the primal requirement to become a Bahá'í: "We cannot expect people who are illiterate (which is no reflection on their mental abilities or capacities) to have studied the Teachings, especially when so little literature is available in their own language in the first place..."[197] This often pervasive educational prejudice of the mind finds no basis in Bahá'u'lláh's Revelation: "The understanding of His words and the comprehension of the utterances of the Birds of Heaven are in no wise dependent upon human learning. They depend solely upon purity of heart, chastity of soul, and freedom of spirit".[198]

Traditionally, to become a Bahá'í, a protocol had to be followed where the applicant was to meet a Spiritual Assembly, either Local or National, and orally respond to a number of questions about the Faith to make sure that a solid knowledge about administration, laws, history and the Covenant had been grasped. However, mass teaching required only that a soul after listening about the Teachings, even in

---

[196] "Canton Huanuni Indian Assembly Formed In Bolivia". *Bahá'í News*. No. 323. February 1958, pp. 9–10.

[197] *The Compilation of Compilations: Prepared by The Universal House of Justice* (vol. 3). Maryborough, Victoria, Bahá'í Publications Australia, 2000, pp, 203-225.

[198] Baha'u'llah, *The Kitáb-i-Iqán*. US Bahá'í Publishing Trust, 1989, p. 210.

a public setting, accepted Bahá'u'lláh as the Manifestation of God for this age and had a general knowledge of the various dimensions of the Cause.

Explaining about the nature, process and urgency of having large numbers enrolling in the Faith, Shoghi Effendi had elaborated:

> This flow, moreover, will presage and hasten the advent of the day which, as prophesied by `Abdu'l-Bahá, will witness the entry by troops of peoples of divers nations and races into the Bahá'í world—a day which, viewed in its proper perspective, will be the prelude to that long-awaited hour when a mass conversion on the part of these same nations and races, and as a direct result of a chain of events, momentous and possibly catastrophic in nature and which cannot as yet be even dimly visualized, will suddenly revolutionize the fortunes of the Faith, derange the equilibrium of the world, and reinforce a thousandfold the numerical strength as well as the material power and the spiritual authority of the Faith of Bahá'u'lláh.[199]

"Those who declare themselves as Bahá'ís should become enchanted with the beauty of the Teachings, and touched by the love of Bahá'u'lláh," the Universal House of Justice had further advised in 1964, "The declarants need not know all the proofs, history, laws, and principles of the Faith but in the process of declaring themselves they must, in addition to catching the spark of faith, become basically informed about the Central Figures of the Faith, as well as the existence of laws they must follow and an administration they must obey".[200]

Talking about the commencement of mass teaching in Bolivia, Mas'ud recalled:

> When I met Andres Jachakollo one of the first Indigenous Bahá'ís and the others, I invited them to come to my home where deepening courses had started. Two very important events took place:

---

[199] Shoghi Effendi. *Citadel of Faith: Messages to America 1947-1957.* Wilmette, US Baha'i Publishing Trust, p. 117, 1953.

[200] The Universal House of Justice. *Wellspring of Guidance: Messages of the Universal House of Justice 1963-68.* Wilmette, US Bahá'í Publishing Trust, p. 32, 1969.

An older Indian who was not yet a Bahá'í came to know about the Faith. He came to attend the course, as he did not know the city he was hit by a car and was taken to a hospital. The police called me and told me: "An old peasant is at the hospital and has a paper with your name, your telephone and your address written on it". My interpreter Andres and I went immediately to see this Indian named Mr Mamani, when he saw us for the first time, he took my hand very strongly and started to cry saying: "Now, I am a Bahá'í, and if I die I want to be buried according to the Bahá'í laws". Fortunately after the accident he recuperated and could participate during the course at home and later greatly served the Faith.

After the course, I started my first trip to indigenous areas and became surprised upon arrival to a very small community in the department of Oruro, I heard children all together repeating words from their teacher. It was surprising that in such a small village there was a school. When I entered the classroom I recognized the teacher who was recently at my home for the first Bahá'í course where he had learned about Bahá'í teachings for children. He was a Bahá'í principal and when he returned to his community he gathered the neighbours and established this simple little school with children from his community.

I visited several places with Mr Athos Costas and Estanislao Alvarez as an Aymara [201] interpreter; the later became a Covenant breaker. Then I was informed about Toribio Miranda, a spiritual phenomenon that is important to know as he was a herald for the introduction of the Bahá'í Faith to the Indians in Bolivia. [202]

3.5 Teaching the Faith in Bolivia

Sabino Ortega, one of the first native indigenous Bahá'ís, has left an account of his teaching trips with Mas'ud as they together visited rural and remote Bahá'í communities:

The work pattern of Mr Khamsi as well as other pioneers

---

[201] A native language of Bolivia.
[202] *Pioneering and Services of Mas'ud Khamsi,* unpublished manuscript.

was to teach the faith in the rural areas every 15 to 20 days together with teams of indigenes teachers; usually walking for several hours before arriving to any given community. Upon returning from the field these teams of teachers were trained by pioneers who facilitated workshops and deepenings. The participants demonstrated their retention capacities and depth of understanding by taking verbal tests. After this they would plan for their next trip to the field. They were continually teaching or receiving training. Teaching the faith in this way was common in all the regions of the high plains (Altiplano) of Bolivia, such as, Oruro, La Paz, Potosi, Chuquisaca and Cochabamba.

Mr Khamsi usually travelled with a translator and sometimes was accompanied by someone who knew the terrain and the communities well. Although he taught with a translator, he eventually comprehended the native language. Sometimes he corrected the translator when he realized that his message was not clearly being communicated. At the same time other groups of teachers visited other communities.

Mr Khamsi's spiritual stature always inspired respect. For example, his teaching companions did not feel comfortable calling him by his first name Mas'ud, but rather always referred to him as Mr Khamsi. Equally, he inspired respect from local authorities.[203]

3.5.1 Genuine Love

In his narrative Sabino Ortega speaks of his dislike for the white man as a result of five centuries of Spaniard oppression and mistreatment against Indigenous people. However, such as negative disposition was overcome with the candid and sincere love that Bahá'í pioneers like Mas'ud and the other travel teachers displayed as they visit rural communities. The Universal House of Justice refers to these important dispositions in a letter dated 29 December 2015: "What is required from those involved, however, is long-term commitment and a yearning to become so familiar with the reality of a place that

---

[203] Personal communication to the author.

they integrate into local life and, eschewing any trace of prejudice or paternalism, form those bonds of true friendship that befit companions on a spiritual journey. The dynamic that develops in such settings creates a strong sense of collective will and movement".[204] According to Sabino:

> As a result of racial/cultural mistreatment that I received during my childhood and youth, I developed a strong prejudice against white people; I believed that all white people were bad. This caused a number of conscious and unconscious conflicts within me. Thanks to the pioneers such as my brothers Athos Costas, Mas'ud Khamsi and others that arrived in Bolivia, I was able to overcome this problem.[205]

Sabino Ortega distrusted white men and had some suspicions about Mas'ud Khamsi's intentions. In his words, "About Mas'ud Khamsi, I really wanted to know how honest he was". He says that they went out to the countryside and they were walking for days visiting the communities and he saw Mas'ud Khamsi sleeping where the peasants were sleeping, eating the food that the peasants ate, getting up in the hours of the farmers, and all. Consequently, Sabino became more and more convinced about Mas'ud's honesty. However, one thing that impressed him a lot was that one night, when they were getting ready to sleep, Mas'ud took off his boots and the stocking of one of his feet. Sabino saw that Mas'ud foot was with blood. Apparently, the boot had hurt him causing his foot to bleed. Sabino said that never during all those days that they walked together Mas'ud had complained about something. In fact, he was always very happy and very enthusiastic. This single one thing made Sabino change his whole perspective and understand that all these Baha'is were really sincere.[206] Sabino's personal discovery continues below:

> These pioneers mostly came from developed countries and particular origins that surrounded them with comfort. The latter most likely, contributed to the hardships they

---

[204]Letter of the Universal House of Justice dated 29 December 2015 addressed to the Conference of the Continental Boards of Counsellors.

[205]Personal communication to the author.

[206]Story told by Kiko Sanchez.

experienced in rural Bolivia traveling on foot and by jeep along dusty mountain pathways and roads high in the Andes; calling upon distant indigenous communities and isolated believers - but they never complained. I observed them closely and I saw that they did not grumble about the cold, hunger or other physical discomforts. Neither did they show disgust for anything; they did not flee from the harsh realities of the rural friends. They slept on the same floor and share the same meals together. They would always say, "We are going to get over this". And they never blamed the farmers for the troubles they encountered. They shared everything with the friends of the rural areas in a way that was simple and humble as if they were a part of the same social fabric. These positive attitudes, so fundamental to the faith, and their love for the farmers - so sincere – day by day changed my ways of thinking and being. Before I knew it I was transformed and was able to overcome my trauma. There was indeed so much love flowing from the pioneers - a love of all and total detachment from the world!

This manner of behaviour enabled us to understand that another prophecy of our people was unfolding without any need of explanation. By the pioneers' greetings and attitudes alone, upon their arrival at a given village was sufficient for the farmers to capture the Message. A tradition of the Quechua and Aymara peoples describes that a messenger of Wiracocha (an Andean Godhead) would arrive and bring dignity and love to the native people and would share these qualities with them.

It is said that Mr Khamsi returned from his first trip to the field, and asked his wife Jane if she could learn how to prepare the food that the farmers eat, such as, *chuño* (dehydrated potatoes), quinoa, and lawau (corn meal soup), so that he could accustom himself to this new diet.

Additionally, teams of indigenous teachers continually visited Mr Khamsi at his home to receive deepening in the faith. The above foods were always served at his house so that his guests would feel at home and enjoy this same food they were accustomed to. [207]

Sometimes Mas'ud used to travel teaching with his wife and children in their jeep. In the villages people invite visitors with the food they produce. The Khamsis went to a place where guinea pigs was the main product. In the Andes roasted guinea pigs are traditionally a delicacy offered to special guests. They look like little rabbits or big mice and are presented as a whole cooked animal on a dish along with potatoes. Jane Khamsi looked worried having never seen such, let alone eat them. She was shocked. Mas'ud turned to her and trying to alleviate the situation said with a smile: "Look, this is the most delicious I've ever seen. This is a very special animal and it cures all illnesses". The villagers laughed and cheered at the same time saying "How does he knows those things" to which Sabino replied, "He knows many things that I do not know myself". It was to gain greater trust with the community and Mas'ud delicately managed the situation explaining how difficult it was for his wife to see this. He then proceeded to eat and enjoy the meal. This was the way that Mas'ud showed gentleness to the indigenous people. So in each community that he arrived, what was offered was always eaten. [208]

3.5.2 Persecution

Bahá'u'lláh has said that "Adversity is the oil which feedeth the flame of this Lamp and by which its light is increased, did ye but know. Indeed, the repudiation of the froward serveth but to proclaim this Faith and to spread the Cause of God and His Revelation throughout the world".[209] It is therefore not surprising that such spiritual phenomenon took form when the Faith began to grow like wildfire in the Bolivian fields.

Sabino relates an incident that shows how opposition to the Faith always brings growth:

At the time there was little freedom to teach the faith. There was opposition from the priests. Similarly, there was opposition on

---

[207] Personal communication to the author.
[208] Story told by Sabino Ortega.
[209] Bahá'u'lláh. *The Summons of the Lord of Hosts*. Bahá'í World Centre, 2002 edition, p. 146.

behalf of political parties who raised false accusations about the Bahá'ís. We were characterized as being communists and denounced in varied ways. Things grew far worse as the Faith spread as we experienced entry by troops. At the time, homes of villagers who had become Baha'is were pillaged, women were raped, and houses burnt to the ground, and local food storages were deliberately contaminated.

Mr Khamsi was not entirely free of these persecutions. Once in Tarabuquillo, Chuquisaca he was arrested by farmers who had been enraged by calumny from a priest. They tied the jeep to a tree and took Mr Khamsi prisoner to Tarabuco, a distance of 60 km. There a priest accused him in front of local authorities claiming that he was speaking against the virgins and saints and was accused of other such false claims. Mr Khamsi responded: "We never spoke against anyone nor have we done harm to anyone". At this point the Sub-Prefect turned to the priest and said: "How can you accuse this person so humble and so honourable who has demonstrated his sincerity by his manner of speaking? There is no sign of any violence". Then, a Bahá'í farmer who was also taken prisoner with Mr Khamsi said: "This priest is not defending the Virgin Mary, he is defending the gifts of hens and eggs that he receives from new visitors to the village that he no longer receives". After some further back and forth dialogue among those present, the Sub-Prefect realized Mr Khamsi's innocence and he freed him immediately.

When they returned to the community where the jeep was tied to the tree, the majority of the dwellers there had become Bahá'ís as a result of the teaching work that Mr Meliton Saavedra had been doing at the time in this village. He had not been taken prisoner with the rest because he was an old man.[210]

3.5.4 Teaching Results

Certainly, Shoghi Effendi's hopes and expectations about the Andes, as communicated to Mas'ud during his pilgrimage in 1953 were

---
[210]Personal communication to the author.

becoming more apparent. In Sabino's words:

> Sometimes during one trip to the field lasting 15 to 20 days by Indigenous teaching teams, there would be up to 70 people entering the Faith. In this way the excitement of teaching grew in many rural regions of the country as a result of the efforts of pioneers together with the native teachers. At the end of the 10-year Crusade in 1963 the number of believers had multiplied 6 times and Local Spiritual Assemblies grew in these rural regions from 4 to 92.
>
> In time, the number of believers registered in Bolivia grew to 70,000 and Local Spiritual Assemblies to 1,200 throughout the country. Nevertheless there were many more people in the countryside that considered themselves Baha'is but had not yet been registered officially. In an official Bolivian Government Census, some 300,000 people identified themselves in rural areas as Bahá'ís. Truly, there were cases of communities were there were no Bahá'ís registered but the residents on their own initiative elected Local Spiritual Assemblies yearly.[211]

3.5.5 The Legacy of Teaching

Even twenty years later, the teaching spirit of those early Bahá'í teachers was intact in the communities through which they travelled. Sabino said:

> In 1979 Continental Counselor Raul Pavon came to Bolivia from his native country of Ecuador. We travelled together throughout the country in order to identify an appropriate location for starting Radio Bahá'í. Upon arriving on the shores of Lake Poopó we left the jeep in the shade under a tree. The vehicle had a sign painted on a door that said "Fe Baha'i". We walked through the mountains in search of the right place to install the radio station. When we got back a large group of people surrounding the jeep joyously greeted us saying: "Alláh'u'Abhá". We asked them how they knew this Bahá'í salutation. They responded: "Eighteen years ago Mr Khamsi visited us, taught us the Faith and left us with Bahá'í prayer

---

[211]Personal communication to the author.

books. We never forgot this". They showed us these old prayer books as they surrounded us where the jeep was located and explained that they always came to this same place to pray. This group was known as the Antiguos Caminantes (Ancient Walkers).

They continued explaining: "With Mr Khamsi's visit our traditions and prophecies were fulfilled". They continued: "When Wiracocha returns, white men will come from other regions and eat what we eat, sleep where we sleep, and treat us equal to themselves. Mr Khamsi ate everything that he was given and humbly as if he were a part of us, informed us of the Message of Bahá'u'lláh. We observed sincere love and gratitude coming from him. This is why we accept the Message because it coincides with our culture and traditions".

Hearing this from these believers, Raul Pavon commented: "It appears that they are more Bahá'ís than we are even though we continually engage in activities and deepening. They on the other hand, without having received another visit for 18 years remain firm in their love for Bahá'u'lláh". [212]

3.5.6 Sharing the Learning

A degree of emphasis was given in disseminating the mass teaching experiences learned from Bolivia to other countries as Mas'ud explained:

> When mass conversion was well developed in Bolivia the Regional and National Spiritual Assemblies, recently established, asked me to travel to Peru, Ecuador and Colombia to guide and help Mass Conversion. In Peru I travelled with Fidel Flores and the pioneer couple Lester and Mabel Long, who lived in Huancayo, Peru. In Ecuador I travelled with Raul Pavon, in Colombia with Habib Rezvani, in all these countries we visited the Indigenous and I helped them in teaching these people.[213]

---

[212] Personal communication to the author.

[213] *Pioneering and Services of Mas'ud Khamsi,* unpublished manuscript.

3.6 His Love for Bolivia

In 1963 Mas'ud and his family left Bolivia for Iran but returned to South America in 1969 to settle in Peru, the adjoining country. From Peru, he always kept visiting Bolivia, never losing interest for the growth of the Faith in this country. He regularly came to participate in teaching conferences and summer schools encouraging the friends to teach the Faith.

The Hand of the Cause Rahmatu'lláh Muhajir visited Bolivia years later accompanied by Mas'ud. Dr Muhajir used to say that Bolivia might be the first country to become Bahá'í. In his diary, Dr Muhajir left some impressions of his 1961 first trip:

> 14 April: We left at 5:00 am for Chalipampa. A small clean bus took us to Lallagua. On the way we passed the village of Huanuni. Mas'ud said that once they had come to this area in a truck, they heard sounds of gunfire and the truck turned back. The Bahá'ís, however, climbed down and continued on their way. The gunfire, had become fiercer, and they thought it prudent to hide in a corner. They walked in the rain till they reached the town-gate and the guard gave them shelter in the school. The rebels found the leader of their opponents in the church, dragged him out and shot him. Then they found the Bahá'ís but let them go. These are the conditions under which the friends in this region have to teach the Faith. We arrived at Lallagua at noon. After a rest we left for Chalipampa. We'd walked for half-an-hour when it started to rain. Large hailstones hit us. The hail was so fierce and the freezing cold so biting that we could not continue any further. I apologized to my companions and told them that I had only walked for two kilometres and was already in bad shape that I simply could not envisage having the strength to continue. Mas'ud and Carmelo decided to go on and I decided to return. I was shattered and despondent. I sat there and wept because I could not walk a few kilometres in the path of God. I just sat there and wept. The weather was getting colder and the rain was worsening. I thought about poor dear Mas'ud, who was walking in these conditions to fulfil my obligations. He can visit them any time. I sent someone to call him back, and for my sake he agreed. Carmelo will go there to

tell them why I could not go. We walked from six a.m. to seven p.m. and accomplished nothing. I have grown old. I have to take my ambitions to the Abha-Kingdom. My only hope is that Bahá'u'lláh will forgive my sins with a drop from the ocean of His mercy. When the friends heard that I could not visit them, a hundred of them went to the neighbouring village and Athos and Angelica went to be with them.

15 April: Mas'ud and I left, to return to La Paz early this morning. Mas'ud said that all their teaching trips are either in torrential rain or fierce wind. Often their vehicles break down. Once their bus had broken down, they had talked to the villagers. On their return trip they found that many of them wanted to become Bahá'í.[214]

Another Hand of the Cause to visit Bolivia was Mr Abul-Qásim Faizí in 1962. By then Mas'ud was an Auxiliary Board member residing in La Paz with his family. According to May Faizi-Moore:

One of his most memorable meetings in Bolivia was by the side of the road. As he and Mas'úd Khamsí were on their way to yet another centre they saw in the distance a group of people sitting in a field by the roadside. In their curiosity they slowed down and as they drove closer, men, women and children rose to their feet, one by one, and came forward in greeting, They were Bahá'ís from a village which was very difficult to reach. The community, not wanting to miss meeting Faizi, had decided to walk down to the road on which they knew he would be travelling, sit by the roadside and wait for him. They had brought bread, potatoes and eggs with them for lunch, which they shared with Faizi and his companion. After saying prayers together and asking Faizi many questions they bade him farewell and returned to their village. Faizi was so delighted with this gathering that he felt its enjoyment for months.[215]

---

[214] Írán Furútan Muhájir. *Dr. Muhájir: Hand of the Cause of God, Knight of Bahá'u'lláh.* London, The Bahá'í Publishing Trust, 1992, pp. 504-506.

[215] May Faizi Moore. *Faizi.* George Ronald Oxford, 2013, p.256.

Ethel Wilcott McAllaster, a pioneer in Bolivia in 1959 with her ten-year old daughter Sally, remembered some anecdotes revealing the cultural challenges that arose while teaching Indigenous people:

> Masud Khamsi would come with as many as 30 Indians for meetings. They would sleep in my balcony. He had to teach them how to use the bathroom. They will eat by my large round table. My dining room touched the neighbour's who happened to be a teacher in the local school and he could not understand why I could I have these Indians actually sit and eat with us.

> So hot, so cold was the weather that you did not wear sun dresses or back-lift ones like we do. One day I put on one and everyone wanted to feel my back, especially the children. They thought it was funny. I told Mr. Khamsi about it. He was stern and asked if I didn't have another dress. He told me not to do that nor to wear shorts or anything that would cause people to look down on me since I represented the Faith. I try always to remember that no matter where I live.[216]

3.7 Returning to Iran

During his time in Bolivia both Mas'ud and Jane also served in different administrative capacities. Jane served on the Local Spiritual Assembly of La Paz while Mas'ud additionally served on the Regional Spiritual Assembly of the Bahá'ís of Argentina, Bolivia, Chile, Paraguay, and Uruguay (1960-1961) and later on the first National Spiritual Assembly of the Bahá'ís of Bolivia (1961) as its inaugural chairman. In 1962 he became an Auxiliary Board member for the protection of the Faith reporting to the Hands for the Western Hemisphere, Jalal Khazeh and Zikru'llah Khadem, replacing Mildred Mottahedeh who had been elected a member of the International Bahá'í Council in 1961 and went to live in the Holy Land accordingly. [217],[218]

Those were interesting times towards the election of the Universal House of Justice held in Ridvan 1963. The International Bahá'í Council

---

[216] Sally McAllaster, personal communication to the author.

[217] Bahá'í World Centre. *The Ministry of the Custodians 1957–1963*. Haifa, Israel, Universal House of Justice, 1992.

[218] *Bahá'í News*, February 1962.

was established by Shoghi Effendi in 1951 as an appointed body of nine believers an event that was announced by himself with these words:

> Proclaim National Assemblies of East and West weighty epoch-making decision of formation of first International Bahá'í Council, forerunner of supreme administrative institution destined to emerge in fullness of time within precincts beneath shadow of World Spiritual Center of Faith already established in twin cities of 'Akká and Haifa... [219]

After the passing of the beloved Guardian in 1957 the Hands of the Cause decided that, from 1961, the members were going to be elected through through the direct suffrage of the existing National Spiritual Assemblies around the world. The International Bahá'í Council ceased to exist with the election of the Universal House of Justice in 1963. The first National Spiritual of Bolivia was formed in Ridvan 1961.

By the end of the Ten Year Crusade in 1963 in a matter of about six years nearly 100 Spiritual Assemblies had been formed in the indigenous areas of Bolivia, including the enrolling of 8,000 new believers,[220] faithful to Shoghi Effendi's advice in July 1957 to the National Spiritual Assembly of Argentina, Chile, Uruguay, Paraguay and Bolivia's message that "One of the most worthy objectives of your Assembly must be the establishment of all-Indian Spiritual Assemblies".[221]

After his six dedicated years in South America the Khamsis had decided to come back to Iran. This was due to a combination of an insufficient flow of income and family sickness. Jane got sick with typhoid fever and had to go to a hospital in the United States. In addition to these difficulties, the government did not give Mas'ud work permission and he was living only on his savings. It was not an

---

[219] Shoghi Effendi. *Messages to the Bahá'í World – 1950–1957*. Wilmette, US Bahá'í Publishing Trust, 1971 edition, p. 7.

[220] Bahá'í World Centre. *The Bahá'í World: 1954-1963, Volume XIII*. Haifa, Israel: Bahá'í World Centre, 1970, p. 269.

[221] *The Compilation of Compilations: Prepared by The Universal House of Justice (vol. 3)*. Maryborough, Victoria, Bahá'í Publications Australia, 2000, pp. 203-225.

easy decision to make:

> Jane, in the hotel she could not move, and she was falling down because of the altitude. La Paz is 4 000 metre altitude. Jane had eyes problems, cataract. So we decided to go back to Iran. And that was the time when the House of Justice was elected for the first time.[222]

In 1963, Mr Khamsi participated in the first election of the Universal House of Justice in Haifa as a member of the National Spiritual Assembly of the Bahá'ís of Bolivia. From Haifa in company of other National Assembly colleagues including Andres Jachakollo they attended the first Bahá'í World Congress[223], the "Most Great Jubilee" in London to celebrate the centenary of the Declaration of Bahá'u'lláh in Riḍván Garden in April 1863.

The election of the Universal House of Justice was a major milestone in the history of the Bahá'í Faith, the culminating point of the Ten Year Crusade a global effort that had taken the Faith to all corners of the world.[224] It was a further memorable event because it was taking place ten years after Mas'ud had met Shoghi Effendi and promised himself to serve his Guardian as best he could. Now, the honour was for him to participate in the election of the inaugural Universal House of the Justice and to be in their presence, the new centre of the Cause, the "… august body to whom all believers must turn".[225]

Approximately 6 000 believers from all over the world attended the London celebration. Present were the newly elected members of the first Universal House of Justice and the Hands of the Cause of God. In Mas'ud's words:

> That was the time when the House of Justice for the first time

---

[222] *Interview with Mas'ud Khamsi.* Lima, Peru. Tape provided by Masud Samandari.

[223] The first Bahá'í World Congress was held in the Albert Hall, London, during 28 April and 2 May 1963.

[224] Fatheazam, Shahbaz. *The Last Refuge: Fifty Years of the Universal House of Justice.* Evanston, IL: Irfan Publication Occasional Papers, 2015.

[225] Bahá'í World Centre. *Messages from the Universal House of Justice 1963-1986.* Compiled by Geoffrey W. Marks. Wilmette, Illinois: Bahá'í Publishing Trust, 1996, p. v.

was elected. So I went to the Jubilee with Andres Jachakollo, a member of the Assembly. I was also member of the Assembly. So we came back [from Haifa] to London for the famous conference. The House of Justice was elected at that time and I went back to Iran.[226]

Mas'ud spoke to the audience about his mass teaching experiences in Bolivia. Andres Jachakollo also talked about his teaching work among the indigenous people of the Andes as the description below explains:

> Bahá'ís remember when Andres, dressed in indigenous clothing, rose at the World Congress and with a powerful voice said, "Why have we come? We have come to remember the centenary of the declaration of Bahá'u'lláh calling for the unity of all nations and all races". Andres' stentorian voice echoed through the Albert Hall, and his words were received with great applause.[227]

4. Return to Iran (1963-1969)

After their two pioneering posts in South America, the Khamsis moved for six years to Tehran with Mas'ud being very successful in a commercial and industrial career working with his brother-in-law Habib Sabet. Iran at that time was experiencing a rapid and sustainable economic boom due to the growing prices of oil for which the country was one of the major world producers.

Service to the Cause was always Mas'ud's main focus of attention, a priority now further empowered by the inspiration he had gained in South America, a continent difficult to forget and always in his mind with the best memories.

4.1 Activities in Iran after returning from Bolivia

In Iran, Mas'ud pursued his Bahá'í activities with the same zeal, enthusiasm, steadfastness and devotion:

---

[226] *Interview with Mas'ud Khamsi.* Lima, Peru. Tape provided by Masud Samandari.

[227] Bahá'í World Centre. *The Ministry of the Custodians: 1957-1963.* Haifa, Bahá'í World Centre, 1997, p. 189.

> The experience with [Bolivian] Indians gave me the chance to visit the Persian tribes of Bovir Ahmadi and Lors. I was surprised at how easy it was to teach them and had great opportunity because at that time there were not Mullas (Muslim priests) among them. Unfortunately soon after, I learned that the Muya'ddin Islam with the support of the government obliged the tribes to receive the priests, to preach and teach them prejudice.[228]

According to Dr Iraj Ayman, Mas'ud kept himself busy teaching also in the urban environment to all types of people:

> When he returned to Tehran he was appointed as a member of a committee especially for contacting, forming a relationship with non-Iranian Bahá'ís and other non-Iranians that National Assembly wanted some kind of contact with them. They organised some public meetings for non-Bahá'ís but in English language. So, they were non-Bahá'í foreigners in Iran who were attending and Mas'ud was very much active in organising those meetings and contacting these Bahá'ís and non-Bahá'ís because he was so fluent in English language and his wife had become a Bahá'í.[229]

Shapoor Monajem recalls Mas'ud's hospitality for South American visitors to Tehran:

> I can't ever be forgetful of the most precious gift of my life given to me and some other friends, members of the National Assembly of Brasil in 1968, who were taken and guided from his home in Tehran to an unforgettable surprise pilgrimage of the House of the Blessed beauty in that city.[230]

Prosperous as his life became in Iran, Mas'ud's heart was in South America. In October 1967 he visited Panama. According to him, at the laying of the foundation stone of the Mother Temple of Latin America by Hand of the Cause Rúhíyyih Khánum in Panama City, "I met up with

---

[228]*Pioneering and Services of Mas'ud Khamsi*, unpublished manuscript.
[229]Personal communication to the author.
[230]Story told by Shapoor Monadjem.

Amatu'l-Bahá Rúhíyyih Khánum again and she requested I accompany her and her cousin Joan Shute on a trip to Bolivia. In her own words she wanted to 'make sure that there are so many Bahá'ís and that the development of the Faith in Bolivia is a reality'. At that time we visited the president of Bolivia and the Minister of Education, who came with us to a Bahá'í Conference and he said in his own words that it was the first time he spoke Quechua, the language for the Indians - in a conference".[231]

Dr Ouladi, later a pioneer in Bolivia, wanted to pioneer to South America and therefore went to visit Mas'ud at his home in Tehran.

I once heard from Mr Khamsi that he had been a pioneer to Bolivia and had returned to Iran. We met at his marvelous home in Tehran and soon I discovered he was a Continental Counselor who had returned to Iran from Peru. Mr Khamsi lived in a very beautiful and grand residence. To gain admittance, I had to go through different people who worked for him. Mr Khamsi received me with open arms and spoke to me about Bolivia and about teaching. He also talked about going back to Bolivia to continue his teaching work there. He had everything he could possibly need in Iran but was not satisfied there. Although he had a very important and prestigious position in an Iranian based company, he was always preoccupied with going back to Bolivia or South America especially to teach the Faith among the Indians of the Andes.[232]

To some, presumably many, the comfortable lifestyle led by the Khamsi family would have been a lifelong objective and the attainment of one's ultimate purpose in life. For others like Mas'ud, as Dorothy Kamsi-Samandari explains, there was a special capacity to examine oneself, scrutinize one's conduct, and with characteristic resolution avoid the pernicious influence of the forces of materialism:

My father had good contacts with people close to the government, socially very upscale. My father started feeling too afraid of comfort with material and social triumphs. He remembered his love of teaching the Faith and his promise to

---

[231]*Pioneering and Services of Mas'ud Khamsi*, unpublished manuscript.
[232]Personal communication to the author.

the Guardian to devote his life to service and he convinced my Mother and dropped everything to return to South America in 1969.[233]

Similarly, as his friend Dr Shapour Rassekh mentioned, "Even though the path for material success within the companies of Mr Sabet was wide open in front of him, he chose the path of pioneering".[234] Obviously, he did not feel fulfilled spiritually in Iran, missing his experiences of mass teaching in South America.

With this decision, emerged a grave reality that ultimately impacted their pioneering destination in South America. "Very soon my wife recovered from Hepatitis", said Mas'ud, "she was operated for cataract and as we suffered from not being able to teach the Faith in Persia we decided to return to Latin America. Despite all my love and experiences I could not return to Bolivia due to my wife's health and the altitude".[235] Hence, they chose Peru on the western coast of South America because it was close to their beloved Bolivia.

The news of abandoning everything up and relocating with four young children to Peru surprised many people. His daughter Dorothy said:

> This created a shock in his entourage and the whole community far and wide, they didn't expect this from someone in the pinnacle of his successful career and opportunities. It was given for many years as an example of detachment and great sacrifice ... Daddy was doing extremely well in Tehran. He belonged to one of the most financially successful family of Iran, he had a fantastic and successful career and was up for constant growth in an international company.[236]

4.3 Appointed Counselor in Iran

As he was making arrangements to leave Iran to South America, in 21 June 1968, the Universal House of Justice announced to the Bahá'í world the creation of the first eleven Continental Boards of

---

[233] Personal communication to the author.

[234] Personal communication to the author.

[235] *Pioneering and Services of Mas'ud Khamsi,* unpublished manuscript.

[236] Personal communication to the author.

Counselors for the Protection and Propagation of the Faith around the world with Mas'ud appointed to the Western Asian board.[237] This highly important development was first intimated as a World Centre Goal, part of the goals of the Nine Year Plan, by the Supreme Body in its Riḍván 1964 message:

> ...development of the Institution of the Hands of the Cause of God, in consultation with the body of the Hands of the Cause, with a view to the extension into the future of its appointed functions of protection and propagation... [238]

In the months following the announcement of the Nine Year Plan, there was a historic gathering at the World Centre, which spanned a period of fourteen days, focused on consulting both on the progress of the Plan and the implications of the vital goal aimed at perpetuating the functions of the Hands of the Cause, that of protection and propagation. It was during this occasion, following the study of the sacred texts and deliberation with the Hands of the Cause, that the House of Justice arrived at the following decisions:

> There is no way to appoint, or to legislate to make it possible to appoint, Hands of the Cause of God.
>
> Responsibility for decisions on matters of general policy affecting the Institution of the Hands of the Cause, which was formerly exercised by the beloved Guardian, now devolves upon the Universal House of Justice as the supreme and central institution of the Faith to which all must turn.[239]

Therefore the cablegram by the House of Justice joyously announcing the establishment of the Continental Board of Counselors to all National Spiritual Assemblies on 21 June 1968, a

---

[237] The Western Asia area included Afghanistan, Bangladesh, India, Iran, Nepal, Pakistan, Sikkim, Sri Lanka and Turkey.

[238] Bahá'í World Centre. *Messages from the Universal House of Justice 1963–1986*. Compiled by Geoffrey W. Marks. Wilmette. Illinois, Bahá'í Publishing, 1996, p. 32.

[239] Bahá'í World Centre. *Messages from the Universal House of Justice 1963–1986*. Compiled by Geoffrey W. Marks. Wilmette. Illinois, Bahá'í Publishing, 1996, p. 44.

new development of the Administrative Order of Bahá'u'lláh, thrilled Bahá'ís in all countries. This momentous communication was the fulfilment of the World Centre Goal, shared over four years earlier:

> ADOPTION THIS SIGNIFICANT STEP FOLLOWING CONSULTATION WITH HANDS CAUSE GOD ENSURES EXTENSION FUTURE APPOINTED FUNCTIONS THEIR INSTITUTION... FERVENTLY SUPPLICATING HOLY THRESHOLD DIVINE CONFIRMATIONS FURTHER STEP IRRESISTIBLE UNFOLDMENT MIGHTY ADMINISTRATIVE ORDER BAHÁ'U'LLÁH.[240]

Dr Iraj Ayman, Mas'ud's old friend and a member of the National Spiritual Assembly of Iran commented: "As a matter of fact it was a matter of a pleasant surprise when he was appointed as a Counselor because he was not much involved in administrative activities". Dr Ayman added:

> One day he told me that he had received a message from the Universal House of Justice that he is appointed to the Board of Counselors. He told me that "I did not know what does it mean actually". "I have received the cable and I am waiting to receive more information", [Mas'ud said]. I told him that I have not received any information but if you receive let me know. And that is how later on told me the whole thing. But something interestingly happened was that he had already been once in Peru and was familiar with Peru. So he volunteered to go back to Peru as a pioneer although he was a Counselor [in Iran]. And Universal House of Justice approves this. And he left - it was only a few months after he was appointed as a Counselor [in Iran]. And when he left for Peru I received a cable from Universal House of Justice that I was appointed as a Counselor in his stead.[241]

Gradually, the friends around the world started learning to

---

[240] Bahá'í World Centre. *Messages from the Universal House of Justice 1963-1986*. Compiled by Geoffrey W. Marks. Wilmette, US Bahá'í Publishing Trust, p. 130, 1996.

[241] Personal communication to the author.

understand more and work with this new agency of the Universal House of Justice. According to Dr Ayman:

> That particular Board of Counselors, which was in Western Asia at that time, was in a very special condition that no other board of Counselors was like that, because at that time there were four of the Hands of the Cause living in Tehran. And at least three or four other Hands of the Cause were visiting Iran very often. So, always there were a group of Hands of the Cause in Iran and Counselors were actually replacing the auxiliary board members of the Hands of the Cause. And it was a very close association between the Counselors and the Hands of the Cause, everything they were doing together in a way.[242]

The Continental Board of Counselors was a new institution for all. According to the Universal House of Justice the Counselors were assuming some of the functions of the Hands of the Cause. Likewise, the Auxiliary Board members were to be more associated with the Counselors than to the Hands, as it was the practice in the past.

In his new capacity, Mas'ud also travelled to a number of countries including India and Japan.

4.4 Returning to South America

About twelve months later the Khamsi's were leaving Tehran. On the way they visited the Holy Land en-route to Peru as Mas'ud said, "to be close to Bolivia". On 10 July 1969, the same day as the Khamsis arrived in Peru, the Universal House of Justice announced to the Bahá'í world Mas'ud's appointment to the Continental Board of Counselors in South America. He became the first Iranian pioneer to Peru and eventually a Peruvian citizen.

5. Second Pioneering to South America

Settling in a new country is a wonderful experience for anyone. For Mas'ud, Jane and the four Khamsi children leaving friends and family in Iran to come to Peru might have been understandingly sad but exciting enough at the prospects of commencing a new phase of their

---

[242] Personal communication to the author.

life.

The family pilgrimage to the Holy Land gave also all the blessings, confidence and spiritual energies to their mandate to develop nascent Bahá'í communities on that west side of the Pacific Ocean. The three-week trip from Iran to Peru had two parts, one over land and the other by sea.

For Gary Khamsi, his father "chose this means of transport to be able to enjoy the only real vacation he ever took in his life amidst his transition to his new pioneering post".[243] According to Ahmad Khamsi:

> It began with the key leg of Tehran to Haifa, where Dad met with the Universal House of Justice. The rest of the land portion included Haifa to Rome (where we enjoyed not only St. Peter's Cathedral at the Vatican, but the many beautiful Roman ruins), then on to Barcelona, where we boarded the Italian mixed cargo and passenger ship Donizetti, and its long route to Peru. I mean long because it stopped at all the ports along the way! Amongst them were Canarias, Maiquetia (Caracas), Curazao, Cartagena, Panama Canal, Barranquilla, Guayaquil, before finally dropping anchor in Callao. We were warmly met at the dock by Mercedes, Isabel, and Kiko Sanchez and driven to the Bahá'í Centre ...[244]

Kiko Sanchez who was present related:

> They boarded an Italian shipping line that serviced ports between Europe and South America ... it was a long journey. Along the way on board the ship, Mr Khamsi made friends with people whom he later had a relationship with for many years in Peru. My parents picked them up at the port city of Callao, adjacent to Lima, Peru's capital city. It was an impressive sight because they brought an enormous amount of suitcases and trunks. At that time I think their oldest son Ahmad would have been twelve. Dorothy followed close behind in age and then there was Bahia and Gary. Bahia was the youngest daughter and Gary the youngest son. I met them all when my parents arrived from the port. I remember that Mr Khamsi spoke Spanish but

---

[243] Personal communication to the author.
[244] Personal communication to the author.

Jane spoke very little. The children spoke some Spanish. They decided to settle in the National Bahá'í Centre. Mr Khamsi had a project to build a house and they were looking for land. It was spectacular when they settled at the Bahá'í Headquarters. [245]

You walked in through the front door and suddenly came upon the central meeting room where a fireplace was located and where they had placed a huge Persian carpet. The entrance room that faces the street was covered with a large impressive Persian carpet. The room at the back overlooking a small interior garden had yet another carpet. The furniture that Mr Khamsi had brought was beautiful. It was fine and elegant in addition to wooden lamps, etc. The National Centre was really beautiful with all this fine elegant furniture and carpets. They stayed at the National Centre for over a year until Mr Khamsi bought some land and built their house.[246]

5.1 Learning to Travel Teach

No sooner had Mas'ud arrived in Peru in July 1969, than he started travelling in his role as Continental Counselor. For example, we find him in Brazil in December 1969 meeting the Bahá'í community and consulting with the National Assembly and its committees. Mas'ud served as a Continental Counselor for fourteen years from 1969 until 1983 when he was appointed member of the International Teaching Centre.

As a Continental Counselor he travelled extensively. It can be said that he visited every one of the 44 countries in the Americas. Conrado Rodriguez, his personal assistant, said:

> There were always two suitcases in Mr Khamsi's house. One day I asked Jane, "Why the two suitcases?" She replied, "Do you not know the story of the two suitcases? When the World Center calls, and asks him to go to a cold place, he grabs the suitcase with warm clothing and off he goes. Sometime later he gets another call from the House to go to a hot place, and so he grabs the other suitcase with cooler clothing and he's

---

[245]Story told by Kiko Sanchez.
[246]Story told by Kiko Sanchez.

on his way to a hot place. He's gone the next day". Jane, then alludes quietly to the obvious, "Mas'ud sees very little of his children".[247]

It is noteworthy that Mas'ud never forgot his native Iran. On his way back from the 1978 International Convention he visited Iran with his wife. He travelled to various cities including his native Rasht delivering talks in Bahá'í gatherings. His friend Shapour Rassekh said that he "will never forget the trip he made to Iran, during which he attended the National Convention in [the National Centre of] Hadíqih[248]. His presence was a great consolation for a rural Bahá'í family, a member of which had just been martyred".[249]

5.2 Learning to Grow

Although Bolivia and Peru are neighbouring countries, the Bahá'í communities shared similarities as well as having differing strategies for the growth of the Faith. They both shared the Aymara and Quechua nations settled millenniums ago around their political frontier and therefore was home to a large indigenous population. However, Bolivia had been more successful in enrolling indigenous believers in rural and remote areas whereas Peru had made progress with the youth and urban groups.

Not surprisingly Mas'ud appeared to focus in working with the youth and helping to develop human resources among urban believers who later travelled to teach in indigenous areas. In order to create a strong culture of teaching, summer schools in Lima were prioritised and became instrumental in educating believers as a strategy to grow to the provinces.

Mas'ud was very creative in developing communities in such a way that the new believers adopted their newly espoused Bahá'í beliefs and practices naturally without feeling estranged. The teaching stories in this chapter show how wise he was in introducing aspects of Bahá'í identity such as prayer and fasting, particularly to the youth where his main strength was his innate ability to lovingly accompany

---

[247] Story told by Conrado Rodriguez.

[248] A large Bahá'í property in Tehran where summer schools, meetings and conferences were held.

[249] Personal communication to the author.

many souls along their way.

5.2.1 Nurturing the Youth

For Mas'ud, the youth was very important for the development of any Bahá'í community and therefore it became one of the main foci of his endeavours. In a letter to the Peruvian Youth many years ago when he was at an advanced age, Mas'ud remember that "Shoghi Effendi has said: "The youth are the backbone of the community". This means that if there were no youth the community would fall like jelly on the floor. Youth who have already gone through the experience of having served the Cause of God assure us that the joy they felt during their youth was never repeated again in their lives".[250]

Mas'ud later on described how a strong community of youth was formed in Peru:

> In Peru there were great opportunities in the teaching field. The famous pioneer Eve Nicklin[251] had taught the Faith in different departments of the country, but these groups were very small. A very cornerstone of the community of Peru was the family of Enrique and Isabel Sanchez, both members of the NSA, their home a centre for Bahá'í activities. The lack of youth was very noticeable and we started to organize youth activities though they were few - with the help of youth Ahmad Khamsi and Enrique Sanchez we organized picnics at our home to invite more friends. The Bahá'í youth tried to attract more youth at the Bahá'í Centre and we worked with the help of a great potential teacher called Grover Gonzales. Later youth like Fernando Schiantarelli joined and with the help of "grandmother", Angela Pavanel, who opened her house and travelled with them, we organized a youth class at the Bahá'í Centre called "Antorcha" (Torch, in Spanish) and a fireside at Angela's. The number of youth grew fast to 150 in Lima alone.

According to Kiko Sanchez:

The following happened when the Khamsis moved to their

---

[250]Mas'ud Khamsi's letter to the Youth of Peru dated 21 January 1999.
[251]Boris Handal. *Eve Nicklin, She of the Brave Heart*. SC, CreateSpace, 2011.

home. Mr. Khamsi was very enthusiastic about the youth, and took great care of us and was always aware of where the youth were, what we were doing, and whether the youth had their own meetings or not. He began several activities to build-up the community in general but also some interesting activities especially for the youth. For the community, the Khamsi family opened their home and gardens and initiated those famous picnics on Sundays. We would spend the whole day together with the community. We had lunch together, then had our meetings outdoors in the gardens because there were so many people. Topics of deepening and teaching were addressed because the believers brought their non-Bahá'ís friends. Sometimes the meetings gathered together more than a hundred people. We also had other meetings at their home where the youth would bring their own friends. I remember when I was seventeen years old; I had just enrolled in the University. I invited lots of my friends, maybe twenty or thirty, to Mr Khamsi's home. Most of my friends on a political scale were leftists. Mr Khamsi spoke to them and my friends also talked. Some of them became Bahá'ís later on.

During those times the University of Lima [next to Mr Khamsi's house] was also growing. I remember Mr Khamsi driving his yellow car. Many students would hitchhike on the main highway waiting for someone to take them to the university campus. Mr Khamsi would pick up students every day to tell them about the Faith. To start the conversation, he would say, "What are you studying?" They responded: "Economy, administration, etc ... ". "Oh, economy, that's fine", he used to say. Then, he added, "and the economy is developing, all economic reports say that, you know all this of course." The youth would respond with, "yes, of course the economy is improving and there is more research etc." Mr Khamsi would then say, "if this is so, why are we in a crisis every year, possibly a worse crisis every year?" The students then looked puzzled and perplexed. "Of course", they would say. Mr. Khamsi then would continue, "Research shows that there is improvement but the economic crisis increases every year". He used to explain all this to them in the car and told them about the principles of the Faith and its teachings.

Some of these youth started coming to the meetings.[252]

Mas'ud also recalled how the youth began to expand in numbers:

Due to the lack of activities and organization many of the first Bahá'ís were inactive and with the help of Miss Mercedes Sanchez, Auxiliary Board member and outstanding teacher of the faith, we visited each one of the Bahá'ís and started huge picnics so that the new and old Bahá'ís, the youth and children could get to know each other, all these kinds of meetings took place in our house in Monterrico, in the suburbs of Lima, which had a big garden. Between 100 to 200 people used to come and with the visits of Amatu'l-Bahá Rúhíyyih Khánum and Dr Ruhe and his wife Margaret we reached 200 Bahá'ís with their friends, these meetings helped in the teaching work and always a number of visitors accepted the Faith.[253]

A Peruvian youth recalled about this incident about the importance of opening our homes to Bahá'í activities:

I remember a picnic that was in his house, a beautiful circular mansion, with beautiful gardens and fruit trees. We arrived early, about 20 people in all, young and old. Mr Khamsi was very happy receiving us, particularly because he liked believers from the provinces visiting him especially since it required a tremendous effort to travel many hours to the capital. He took us to see his beautiful gardens of which he took great care.

He took us to a side where there were pears and apple trees and showed us a young apple tree that had several fruits and flowers. There was a small red apple tree hanging on its branches but it was still very green. He said: "This is my favourite and I take great care of it".

It was time for the meeting with more than 350 people participating, including children, youth and adults. It was a beautiful meeting of deepening, reflection and joy. There were songs and a lot of dancing - groups from each region presented

---

[252] Story told by Kiko Sanchez.

[253] *Pioneering and Services of Mas'ud Khamsi,* unpublished manuscript.

their songs, dancers and dances.

The meeting was very nice and spiritual. When the friends left, Mr Khamsi and his wife Jane said goodbye to all by the door. We all left with a great desire to continue working on the progress of the Beloved Cause.

I stayed back to help clean the whole house, because of the untidiness that was left after finishing the day's activity. I helped clean the garden which needed a lot of attention. There were broken flowers and pots everywhere, but the saddest thing was to see Mr Khamsi's tree and its favourite little green apple tree all lying on the floor.

Mr. Khamsi smiled, even though he felt sad. We apologized but he said, "It is sad, but we must keep opening our homes to talk about Bahá'u'lláh, there is no time to lose for small material things". For me it was a great example of love and detachment.[254]

In another occasion a kindergarten teacher took 50 children to the Khamsi's residence. According to her, "one of two accompanying teachers, seeing the kindness and hospitality offered to them, gave us, declared herself a Baha'i and told me that she had never seen such kindness. The children played in their garden the whole day and left the place happy, having learned a prayer by heart".[255]

5.2.2 Summer Schools

The importance of the Summer School as an institution was repeatedly stressed by the beloved Guardian, "both as a centre for the preparation and training of prospective teachers and pioneers, and for the commingling and fellowship of various elements in the Bahá'í Community".[256]

For Shoghi Effendi, Summer Schools were the vehicles to consolidate individuals and communities by gathering the friends

---

[254]Story told by Augusto Erquinio.
[255]Story told by Ana Maria Saavedra.
[256]*The Compilation of Compilations: Prepared by The Universal House of Justice (vol. 1)*. Maryborough, Victoria, Bahá'í Publications Australia, 1991, p. 40.

during an extended period of time and offering a program that has the harmonious combination of three elements, that of "devotion, study and recreation".[257] It is through the coming together of these threefold features that the Summer School attempts to ultimately fulfil its "true function of deepening the knowledge, stimulating the zeal, and fostering the spirit of fellowship among the believers in every Bahá'í community".[258] Such a lofty purpose has attached to it a majestic vision, for this mighty institution to be viewed as an embryo of future Bahá'í universities. Shoghi Effendi further elucidated on the purpose in these terms:

> The basic purpose of all Bahá'í Summer Schools, whether in East or West, is to give the believers the opportunity to fully acquaint themselves, not only by mere study but through whole-hearted and active collaboration in various Bahá'í activities, with the essentials of the Administration and in this way enable them to become efficient and able promoters of the Cause....[259]

With summer schools being an increasingly vital institution to foster community development, propagate the Faith, and raise human resources, the Guardian placed great emphasis on the youth having a "peculiar responsibility"[260] in the development and evolution of the summer school into a future university.

Mas'ud not only concentrated in supporting them to make them successful and appealing to the extent that the Peruvian summer schools became internationally known, but also tirelessly encouraged youth to participate:

> In Peru we had very successful summer schools and from my experience I suggested the National Spiritual Assembly to invite outstanding teachers from other countries to give

---

[257] *The Compilation of Compilations: Prepared by The Universal House of Justice (vol. 1)*. Maryborough, Victoria, Bahá'í Publications Australia, 1991, p. 28.

[258] *The Compilation of Compilations: Prepared by The Universal House of Justice (vol. 1)*. Maryborough, Victoria, Bahá'í Publications Australia, 1991, p. 28.

[259] Shoghi Effendi. *Directives from the Guardian.* India/Hawaii, 1973, p. 66.

[260] *The Compilation of Compilations: Prepared by The Universal House of Justice (vol.1)*. Maryborough, Victoria, Bahá'í Publications Australia, 1991, p. 40.

classes, among them we had Dr Ahmadiye from Belize, Habib Taherzadeh from Brazil, Alejandro Reed from Chile, Charles Hornby from Ecuador. The classes were so interesting that we agreed to extend it to two weeks instead of one as it was before. Though each country should have its own summer school, the Universal House of Justice permitted Peru to invite its neighbouring countries such as Ecuador, Bolivia and Paraguay so that they learn to organize their own summer schools. We were told that in Brazil, the youth did not have any interest in participating in their Summer School. I asked that youth from different families to come to Lima to participate in the Summer School, seven youth of both sexes came to Lima to attend this very modest and simple school, and when they returned to their country they enthusiastically asked to have a summer school in Brazil, but in the same way of Peru, and not in first class hotels or luxury places. In great Brazil it was very difficult to find an appropriate place for such a school until the Soltani Institute was built.[261]

For the inherent potential of Summer Schools to be fulfilled they should not be viewed as an isolated event. In a letter written on his behalf, Shoghi Effendi said that Summer Schools rather constitute "a vital and inseparable part of any teaching campaign, and as such ought to be given the full importance it deserves in the teaching plans and activities of the believers."[262] In this manner, following Summer Schools' teaching projects in Peru were facilitated where the youth were encouraged to participate which proved essential in ensuring coherence in the pattern of community life. Kiko Sanchez's remembrances are as follows:

> After one or two weeks of Summer School, almost all the youth with some adults, went on teaching trips. We went to different parts of the country. That was very good for everyone. First, for the opportunity to teach and second, because your parents were not there to do things for you and you learned to manage

---

[261] *Pioneering and Services of Mas'ud Khamsi*, unpublished manuscript.
[262] *The Compilation of Compilations: Prepared by The Universal House of Justice (vol. 1)*. Maryborough, Victoria, Bahá'í Publications Australia, 1991, p. 40.

yourself. Those were very interesting teaching trips. When the summer school ended, we always parted these same groups. It had become a tradition not only during the long breaks but also during mid-year vacations when teaching teams were also formed. It was a tradition to get out and travel teach and Mr Khamsi was always encouraging that.[263]

Mas'ud travelled very often to the mass conversion areas. A friend recalled how he became a Bahá'í in one of those campaigns:

Mr Khamsi arrived in Cusco for the last days of the Forty Days Teaching Plan. I remember that by the Nineteen Day Feast in February 1974, I already had spent about 15 days with the Bahá'í pioneers and other friends. Following the feast, people were dancing and I approached Mr Khamsi to ask and talk to him. He had memorized whole quotations from Bahá'u'lláh's writing. For the third time he asked me if I was ready to become a Bahá'í and to repeat with him "I am a Bahá'í" again and again. Suddenly, the volume of the music was turned down and I was found myself shouting "I am a Bahá'í" and the friends began to sing the welcome song. Looking at them, I remembered everything that each one had taught me.[264]

5.2.3 Caring for others

For his work with the Peruvian youth, they designated Mas'ud as their spiritual father.[265] The well-being of the youth was his main concern trying to get them together, connected and integrated. Such a noble disposition was one of his main legacies to the Bahá'í community. These stories are illustrative as to how little things can make people connected:

When I met Counselor Más'ud Khamsi I was impressed by the clear affection he showed towards everyone particularly towards children. He greeted us smiling, asked how we were and referred to us as his "little friends". I was about ten years old when I was attending an activity with my family at the

---

[263]Story told by Kiko Sanchez.
[264]Story told by Gerson Elias.
[265]Boris Handal. *Eve Nicklin, She of the Brave Heart.* SC: CreateSpace, 2011

Bahá'í National Headquarters. At the end of the meeting, the friends dispersed, some to greet each other and others, especially the young ones, to enjoy some board games. I was watching from a distance the ping-pong game and I had not noticed that Mr. Khamsi had approached me, and with a big smile he said: "Now I'm going to play Ping-Pong with you". I felt that I had to respond to his affectionate invitation even though I knew I was not good at this game. As expected, the ball fell to the floor many times and each time, Mr. Khamsi ran to pick it up cheerfully. After a while, he told me: "Well, we have played, now I'm leaving because I'm tired". This experience clearly illustrated me the importance of being supportive, affectionate and attentive. We should be concerned when we notice that a friend is not fully integrated and is not involved in any activity.[266]

Likewise, a young girl recalled this special home visit:

I was turning 16 years old and Mr Khamsi came to my birthday party. My parents were beginning to know about the Bahá'í Faith. Mr Khamsi participated without many words but his presence won the respect of my mother who at the time did not know the Faith. I remember feeling Mr Khamsi's presence irradiating respect, dignity and a reverence. He had come to my house especially to celebrate my birthday. I was very touched by his love and genuine desire to be part of such a special moment for me, my family and my new Bahá'í friends.[267]

Another youth recounted the following story of kindness and compassion:

In April of 1995, I was involved in a traffic accident and my spine became severely affected. I had to be taken to the capital by plane. I was under guarded prognosis diagnosis for the first ten days and I was told that I might be bedridden for life. Among the first to arrive to the hospital was Mr. Khamsi, who came with a bouquet of flowers... Mr. Khamsi was calmly

---

[266] Story told by Lina Leon.
[267] Story told by Amparo Polanco.

caressing my forehead telling me that I was going to heal and that I should have faith. His words were very premonitory as seven months later I was able to walk again. His presence and his words filled the hospital atmosphere with peace at that moment. [268]

Likewise, this youth many years later remembered another act of kindness:

There was a time, being a young man, when I was going through many difficult personal situations including financial and sentimental problems. It was like all the difficulties had come on my way at once. He agreed to meet me on the same day. I got there around 4 in the afternoon. His house wasn't like most. It had a round shape and was surrounded by garden and trees. Its freshness had a calming effect on my agitated spirit. I was received by an auxiliary board member who told me how lucky I was because whenever he talked to the Counselor it was always about business and then Mr Khamsi would say goodbye. I found him seated in the garden, we greeted each other and he asked me to take a seat. The auxiliary board member soon reappeared with some tea which he placed on the table and left, leaving us alone. Mr Khamsi asked me to say a prayer and after those words he paused and said, "So, Carlos, what's the problem?"

I told him to forgive me for my weakness and began to empty my heart even with tears, telling him of my afflictions in a very emotional heartfelt way. We remained silent for a few seconds until Mr Khamsi with his soft voice asked me "What is life?" He kept thinking and said: "Do you hear the strong song of that little bird?" Actually there was a little bird that sang louder than the other birds. I said, "Yes" to Mr Khamsi. And he asked me "Can you see it?" to which I answered that "... no, because the bird is hidden in those trees". Mr Khamsi addressed me with calm and affection: "You cannot see him but because of his singing you know that he exists - if he did not sing for sure nobody would know it exists".

---

[268]Story told by Jesus Asencio.

When we said goodbye, he accompanied me to the door and gave me a chocolate saying: "Sweeten your mouth with this chocolate since life is sometimes very bitter. We have problems but this should not stop us from continuing to sing by teaching while we stay alive. If we allow ourselves to be absorbed by difficulties then we are dead".[269]

To conclude the section let's read this story told by Gary Khamsi about understanding and supporting teaching work:

> When I was 18 years, two months after getting my first driver's license I caused an accident with two other vehicles. There were no personal injuries but my Dad's car was unusable for two weeks. Three hours later, I told my father that I was sorry I could not go to a youth committee meeting because of the accident. Without even hesitating, he offered me the other car to the meeting. With good reason after what has happened, he could have told me to take a public bus. With this he gave me two messages, we must support people who may feel insecure due to some mistakes made, and, above all, that the work for the Faith cannot stop.[270]

5.3 Learning to Teach

Mas'ud also took the responsibility of accompanying friends in teaching experiences to remote indigenous communities. Taking the Faith from urban to remote places was indispensable to bring about 'Abdu'l-Bahá's "promise" to the native people of America. As well as in Summer Schools, youth were chosen first for that training and became the prime strategy to form a constant flow of travel teachers. The following story told by Kiko Sanchez is illustrative as to how Mas'ud got the youth involved in the process of mass teaching:

> I remember one of my first trips with Mr Khamsi. Ahmad [his son] and myself were fifteen and thirteen years old respectfully and we accompanied Mr. Khamsi into the interior of Peru to Chavin de Huantar, which is in a valley called the Conchucos Alley. We had to cross a tunnel to get to this

---

[269]Story told by Carlos Nunez.
[270]Personal communication to the author.

place. The narrow tunnel had a low roof and the bus had the entire luggage at the top covered with a canvas. On the bus there were also all kinds of animals inside. We were there for several days visiting the communities and it was very nice to see Mr Khamsi relating to the villagers, talking about the Faith, deepening on the teachings, and take care of some mundane tasks. Our hotel was a simple hotel with no shower. We had to wash ourselves with water from a sink in the inner garden of the hotel. It was a half-wash and then every day we went out to visit communities three or four kilometers away from the town. When we were walking along the road we felt a strong smell of sulfur. The smell was like rotten eggs and we found out that some hot springs there were close and next to the river. One day Mr Khamsi took us to this place to take a bath. So, with our shorts and towels we went down to the river. The place had an archeological excavation on the left wall, like a big cave, from where hot water gushed out to the river. You had to go over some large stones that marked the border between the river and the place where the water was coming out. On one side the water poured out and formed a small pool where bubbles abounded. The river was on the other side. We bathed there with soap in very nice warm water. The three of us had a lot of fun bathing. Mr Khamsi was always tremendously enthusiastic. We left very clean, and well bathed but smelling of sulphur – a distinct smell of rotten eggs! Nevertheless we were spotless. With our hair finely combed, we returned to town and found that people were not bothered by our offensive smell because they were so used to it. We spent several days in the area visiting communities.

Mr Khamsi took notes of everything such as the Bahá'ís who were being visited and their places of residence. I remember that before we went out to visit people around town and in the countryside, we would always pray together and review quotes from the Writings. When he spoke about the Faith to the villagers, these quotes would come up.

The day we returned home we were waiting for the bus. It came from inside Conchucos Alley and it travelled overnight through Chavin de Huantar, from where we needed to go. We were waiting at the bus agency. The bus was supposed to arrive at seven o'clock in the evening and it was nine o'clock, then ten o'clock, and the bus did not arrive. It was very cold and Ahmad and I were complaining. Then Mr Khamsi with a blanket or a poncho made a tent. So we were sitting on the floor and somehow he was holding the tent with his head. Inside, he put a lighted candle. The candle began to warm the atmosphere and from time to time he raised it to let in air. Inside we were warming up until the bus finally arrived. And when the bus arrived there was only one free seat and no seats for Ahmad and me. Not only were the seats full but the aisle between the seats was full as well. Ahmad and I decided to take out our sleeping bags and we climbed up the bus to the cargo rack above, accommodated ourselves inside our sleeping bags and underneath the tarp. This is where we traveled as two additional bags of cargo. I remember when we passed through the tunnel we felt the roof above at very close range from our faces.[271]

5.4 Learning to Fast

How did Mas'ud teach the virtues of fasting and obedience to the Bahá'í laws to the youth? Many of the youth came from Christian families for whom fasting was not only unknown but also a strange ascetic practice. In an environment where not being Christian was an antithesis to social standards, learning to fast was a challenge for the newly enrolled, particularly the youth.

Consequently, collective observations of fasting took place which lead to the youth developing steadfastness and enriching their spiritual life as Baha'u'llah had instructed: "Fast ye for the sake of your Lord, the Mighty, the Most High. Restrain yourselves from sunrise to sunset".[272]

Those meetings were held either in Mas'ud's home, at the Bahá'í centre or in a country club to which he belonged. Maria Eugenia

---

[271]Story told by Kiko Sanchez.
[272]The Universal House of Justice. The importance of Obligatory Prayer and Fasting. *The American Baha'i,* 31:7, 2009.

described in the following story how Mas'ud created a space where the youth began gaining their Bahá'í identity through following the Fast:

> The activities organized by Mr Khamsi and his family around the time of the fast, were very rewarding for me and for all the youth who were invited. His family and the Sanchez family during the weekends used to go to El Bosque Country Club. He used to bring all the food needed to prepare the breakfasts and the dinners at the Club. Those were times of recreation and leisure as well as serious study and meditation on the Writings and stories of the Faith. I sense that he took great care of all the details. This was something I believe is very important for the youth. That we not only go to a spiritual retreat with nothing to do except pray and meditate but that there are also spaces available for us to play. The most important thing of those fasting retreats was that he fostered a feeling of coexistence among the Bahá'ís. It helped us develop the habit of obedience to the law of God, such as the vital law of fasting. Many of the youth belonged to a new generation of believers and experienced difficulties at home in order to practice the law of fasting; this was so because our non-Bahá'ís parents did not really understand, and we did not have the facilities to organize our time nor prepare our meals. Therefore, these special retreats that Mr. Khamsi organized during the fast were very important; several weekends dedicated to creating a unique space to focus on acquiring greater knowledge of the Faith and the mystical significance of fasting and prayer. Through collective study, reflection and physical exercise these precious days of fasting did indeed, wholly prepare us for the rest of the year. They were a spiritual foundation for me.

I remember we had to get up very early, it was still dark, and we had to help prepare breakfast together with the older women. After that we went outside and sat on the grass where Mr Khamsi told us stories, translating them from a book he had in Farsi. He took time to translate these stories because in those there was not as much Bahá'í literature as there is now. Nowadays, you can find books and stories translated from distinguished believers of heroic age. We filled our spirits with such deeply motivating stories because we listened carefully to all those inspiring past events. The narratives were a very important complement for me. In other words, it was not only the fact that we had to read a book and know about the law but also about its component, the fire of the spirit. I believe that they were the best times of my life.[273]

It is also worth mentioning Mas'ud's special sense of humour. These are little vignettes told by local believers reveal his sparkling personality and wittiness:

> When I began attending Bahá'í firesides Mr Khamsi once told me that Christ has already returned. I told him that he must be mad. After some months noticing that I had become a Baha'i he told me: "Abraham, who is mad now?" [274]

One day a Bahá'í arrived to the Bahá'í Centre at lunchtime and said to Mr Khamsi that now he has become a *Hare Krishna* follower. Mr Khamsi turned to him and smiling he said: "Congratulations but you have gone back 6,000 years!".[275] Another believer recalled:

> Mr. Khamsi would always tell us how important it is to obey the Bahá'í Institutions. Once he told us about a pioneer serving in a South American country who said Mr. Khamsi wished her to pioneer to China. When the Assembly learned of this, they asked her why she wanted to leave for China? She responded saying that Mr. Khamsi had appeared to her in a dream and he told her to go to China. As it was not deemed wise for this Bahá'í lady to leave her pioneering post, Mr. Khamsi was informed and he visited the lady and found her actively preparing her suitcase for the trip. He asked her, "Why do you want to go to China?" She answered: "You told me to go in a dream." To this Mr. Khamsi responded, "But we need you here!" She replied that her dream was very real and therefore she must go. He then lovingly asked her, "How is it that you believe me in your dream but not here in real life?" This question caused much

---

[273] Story told by Maria Eugenia Gonzales.
[274] Story told by Abraham Reyes.
[275] Story told by Vicente Lopez.

laughter and she decided to remain at her pioneering post. Mr. Khamsi always reminded us that our dreams, as profound as they may be, should be consulted upon before taking action with our institutions and obey them in order to receive divine confirmations.[276]

I took Mr. Khamsi to the barbershop near the Bahá'í Center where he always cut his hair. Whenever he arrives they embrace him, he then takes off his coat and he seats himself in a swivel chair. There are mirrors in front and in back of these chairs. All of sudden Mr. Khamsi realized that his hair was uncustomarily long and so he moved it from side to side and says to me, "Mister Conrad, do I look like a rock and roller?" I was with my back to Mr. Khamsi and so I turned around and looked to the right and to the left and said, "No Mr. Khamsi, you do not look like a rock and roller." "Why not" he replied, and I said, "because rock and rollers have painted fingernails and wear earrings ..."[277]

5.5 Learning to Give

From all the multiple conferences that Mas'ud participated perhaps the most relevant was the one held in Bahia. This city is cited by 'Abdu'l-Bahá in the Tablets of the Divine Plan: "Likewise the city of Bahia, situated on the eastern shore of Brazil. Because it is some time that it has become known by this name, its efficacy will be most potent".[278]

The Bahia International Teaching Conference was called by the Universal House in Justice in 1977 to fulfil all the goals of the Five Year Plan. *Bahá'í News* reported about this very successful conference:

> Over 1300 believers from 37 countries gathered at the Castro Alves Theatre from January 27 to 30. Seventeen indigenous tribes of the Americas were represented. The Conference was illumined by the presence of three Hands of the Cause of God:

---

[276] Story told by Farid Tebyani.
[277] Story told by Conrado Rodriguez.
[278] 'Abdu'l-Bahá. *Tablets of the Divine Plan*. Wilmette, US Bahá'í Publishing Trust, 1993, p.31.

Mr Enoch Olinga the official representative of The Universal House of Justice, Mr Paul Haney and Dr. Rahmatu'llah Muhájir. Also in attendance were six members of the Continental Board of Counselors in South America. Twenty Auxiliary Board Members and 47 National Spiritual Assembly representatives were also present. A panel coordinated by Counselor Masu'd Khamsi, with the participation of eleven National Spiritual Assemblies and many indigenous believers, presented an account of the accomplishment of the goals of the Five Year Plan.[279]

A Peruvian youth recalled a particular presentation of Mas'ud during the conference about giving to the Funds where he again mentioned his famous "tuman":

We were at the Bahia Conference in Brazil in 1977. The venue was divided into three sections. The ground floor was for Spanish-speaking believers, the second level for those of English-speaking background and the upper level for the friends who came from Iran and Europe. This was before the Khomeini revolution and Iranians had a lot of economic power. Mr Khamsi began talking about donating to the Fund for teaching the Faith in South America, speaking simultaneously in Spanish and English. After a while he changed to Farsi and I noticed the tone of his voice had changed as well. Luckily, I had a Persian-Brazilian friend to whom I asked to translate for me what he was saying to the Persian community. My friend said that Mr Khamsi was reprimanding them. There was too much tension in the hall. At one time, some Iranian friends made a gesture to leave the hall but firmly he asked to close the doors that nobody can leave until he finishes. He lowered the tone of his voice but resolutely talked about what Shoghi Effendi said. He talked about a letter that Shoghi Effendi sent him for a contribution he made many years ago for the construction of the Wilmette Temple. He said, "for him and everybody it is a treasure. I am now satisfied for having helped with the construction of that Temple. No matter how

---

[279] *Bahá'í News*, March 1977.

much you contribute now you cannot add one more stone to the building". Mr Khamsi said there are boxes on the stage to place your contribution. Now it is the time to donate! Just then a humble Bolivian Indigenous lady arose to make the first contribution. That was a lesson of detachment to all. Then everything became magic and a huge contribution was raised. The Persian friends donated to the purchase of 4WD vehicles to be used for teaching the Faith in the rural areas of Bolivia...[280]

Mas'ud's services to the Institution of the Ḥuqúqu'lláh were also admirable either as a member or educating communities about this sacred law. In June 1973 Mas'ud was appointed Trustee of the Continental Funds for South America a service that was later extended to the whole Americas. From August 1992 to October 1997, he further served as a Deputy Trustee of Ḥuqúqu'lláh, reporting to the Chief Trustee of Ḥuqúqu'lláh, Hand of the Cause of God Dr. 'Alí-Muḥammad Varqá and afterward became Deputy Trustee on the Regional Board of Trustees of Ḥuqúqu'lláh for South America until November 2001.

5.6 Learning to Nurture Scholarly Ability

Mas'ud was constantly seeking to foster scholarly capabilities within different individuals. The following two stories are cited below as an example of encouraging others in the field of Bahá'í literature:

> During my trips to Ecuador as a Counselor I always stayed at Charles and Helen Hornby's house. On different occasions I noticed Helen lying down on the floor with a pile of books and small pieces of paper looking into the books and making notes on the papers. One day I asked her what she was doing so enthusiastically, she said she was doing a personal reference file so when looking for the exact reference she would not waste time looking into so many books. To me that was wonderful since the Beloved Guardian Shoghi Effendi made a reference book, but about very important subjects of the Faith. I encouraged her to go on with such a valuable work, but told her she should not think of the work only being useful for

---

[280] Luis Wong's personal communication to the author.

herself, I told her that as a Bahá'í, if she was doing something useful, she should share it with others, it would no be hers. That book is called "Lights of Guidance"[281] (a Bahá'í Reference File). Later on, in order to correct and complement this book she asked authorization from the World Centre to go to Haifa, and here she devoted herself to investigate all the books and to record the information for her last edition that was printed in India.[282]

According to Helen Hornby, Mas'ud had told her: "Bahá'ís cannot be selfish, that when one does something like this it must be shared, now this is no longer yours".[283]

"El Concurso en Lo Alto" (The Concourse on High)[284], a collection of ten biographies of martyrs and saints of the Heroic Age of the Faith, was another book that got published only because of his encouragement and directions. He even managed to get the publication financed by Amatu'l-Bahá Rúhíyyih Khánum and Mr Salim Nounou.[285]

There were no Bahá'í books written or edited in Spanish by native Spanish speakers. All the books we had at that time and most of the books even today are translations and do not have the Spanish flavour I was always looking for someone that could start such a necessary and valuable work. Finally I found a very talented youth, although he was a relatively new Bahá'í he deepened quickly. As he knew the Bahá'ís should know the Islamic religion very well, he also deepened into the history and principles of this religion. His name is Boris Handal Morales, who at that time lived close to the Bahá'í Centre in Lima, Peru, and by contact with my son Ahmad who was the same age and lived at the Bahá'í Centre he accepted the Faith.

---

[281]Helen Hornby. *Lights of Guidance: A Bahá'í Reference file*. Bahá'í Publishing Trust, 1983.

[202]*Pioneering and Services of Mas'ud Khamsi,* unpublished manuscript.

[283]Helen Hornby. *Lights of Guidance: A Bahá'í Reference file*. Bahá'í Publishing Trust, 1983.

[284]Boris Handal. *El Concurso en Lo Alto*. Lima, PROPACEB, 1985.

[285]Salim Nounou (1905-1990).

He wrote the book in 1985. [286]

6. Amatu'l-Bahá Rúhíyyih Khánum

The Hand of the Cause of God and the Guardian's widow Amatu'l-Bahá Rúhíyyih Khánum always praised and admired Mas'ud's services and devotion. His mass teaching work was appreciated by the Hands of the Cause during their six year interreign between the passing of Shoghi Effendi in 1957 and the election of the Universal House of Justice in 1963.

Mas'ud Khamsi was invited to participate by Rúhíyyih Khánum in the famous Green Light Expedition and accompanied her to various Bahá'í events. In addition both served as members of the International Teaching Centre in Haifa. This chapter explores how the Hand of the Cause worked together with her Counselor through various projects and the deep reverence the latter showed for the former.

6.1 Introduction

Mas'ud had known Khánum during his first pilgrimage to the Holy Land in 1953:

> In the afternoon when I was coming to the gardens I saw Shoghi Effendi. And I saw Rúhíyyih Khánum from the car. In those days, the Persians cannot meet Rúhíyyih Khánum according to the Persian costume, the man could not see unchadored[287] women. So Shoghi Effendi respected Islam and the Persians could not see Rúhíyyih Khánum. But I saw Rúhíyyih Khánum. I went to Dr Hakim's room which is in the gardens and saw Rúhíyyih Khánum for the first time but not face to face. The first time I saw Rúhíyyih Khánum in America was at the opening of a conference. So Rúhíyyih Khánum invited for lunch [both] Jane and me to have lunch with her. So that was the first time.[288]

Later, through Mas'ud's tireless efforts, he was known to her as a hard working member of the Continental Board of Counselors for

---

[286] *Pioneering and Services of Mas'ud Khamsi,* unpublished manuscript.

[287] A chador is a head covering cloth for women in Middle Eastern countries.

[288] *Interview with Mas'ud Khamsi.* Lima, Peru. Tape provided by Masud Samandari.

South America. Counselors individually and as a board reported directly to the International Teaching Centre.

6.2 The Green Light Expedition

The Green Light Expedition led by Amatu'l-Bahá Rúhíyyih Khánum into the Amazons, the Orinoco and the Andes basins took place between February 1975 and August 1976. Mas'ud said of this expedition that "it was unique in the Bahá'í history of South America; there has never been anything like it: 100% results have been produced by putting in 100% effort". Thirty-six tribal groups were visited during a six-month period. As a result, a film was produced totally narrated by Khánum – a complete transcription containing the details of the expedition are enclosed in appendix 2 of this book for the reader's perusal. The story in appendix 1 relates to the Green Light Expedition in the Peruvian and Bolivian Andes.[289]

The expedition was Khánum's response to 'Abdu'l-Bahá's call in the Tablets of the Divine Plan:

> O that I could travel, even though on foot and in the utmost poverty, to these regions, and, raising the call of "Yá Bahá'u'l-Abhá" in cities, villages, mountains, deserts and oceans, promote the divine teachings! This, alas, I cannot do. How intensely I deplore it! Please God, ye may achieve it.[290]

It was of course a great privilege for Mas'ud to accompany Khánum on these trips. In a short recount of his pioneering experiences written at the instructions of the Universal House of Justice, Mas'ud annotated:

> A great honour and opportunity conferred in my life was to be invited to participate in the Green Light Expedition, organized by our dear Hand of the Cause of God Amatu'l-Bahá Rúhíyyih Khánum, which lasted approximately a year from the beginning in New York, going through the Amazonian basins

---

[289] Amatu'l-Bahá Rúhíyyih Khánum Mary Sutherland Maxwell. *The Green Light Expedition*. 1975. Video available on YouTube: https://www.youtube.com/watch?v=pW4qAmfpjG8

[290] 'Abdu'l-Bahá. *Tablets of the Divine Plan*. US Bahá'í Publishing Trust, 1993, pp. 41-42.

of Venezuela, Surinam, Brazil, Colombia, Peru and Bolivia until the return of the group to the United States, and the editing of 42 hours filming. Since there are slides[291] and a video of this important and historic trip I do not need to explain it in detail. I can only say that in all the Bahá'í world, including Persia, there was an enormous enthusiasm about pioneering at that time. In Lima, Peru a TV station showed the 2 hours long movie and it was also shown in some provinces.[292]

David Walker, one of the four-crew members documenting the expedition through film and photography, recalled that Mas'ud was also involved in the logistics and being the project manager:

> Rúhíyyih Khánum invited Mr Khamsi on the expedition primarily as her business manager, but also as her translator. Rúhíyyih Khánum used her own money to pay for the expedition and the film (She sold her father's collection of Japanese art to raise money for the project). So naturally she wanted to conserve funds as much as possible, and Mr Khamsi was an astute businessman and consummate bargainer. He was responsible for all of the logistics of the expedition, arranging flights, boats, hotels, etc. Moreover, whenever Rúhíyyih Khánum spotted an Indian artefact that she wanted for her "ethnographic museum", she would whisper to Mr Khamsi, "Mas'ud, get me that rattle," and a few moments later he would join us with a big smile saying, "Here it is, Khánum!"[293]

David Walker also praised Mas'ud's business acumen:

> I first met Mr Khamsi on February 4, 1975, at the Pan American Terminal at Kennedy Airport in New York City, as we piled up our equipment for the flight to Caracas. We were several hundred pounds overweight, which put Mr Khamsi right to work, negotiating with the ticket agent. It wound up costing about $500, considerably less than it might have had every

---

[291] Video available on YouTube: https://www.youtube.com/watch?v=pW4qAmfpjG8

[292] *Pioneering and Services of Mas'ud Khamsi,* unpublished manuscript.

[293] Personal communication to the author.

overweight piece been weighed.

Later, in April 1976, as we were finishing up the editing of the film and getting ready to make prints (each print was four reels), Rúḥíyyih Khánum again called Mas'ud to New York to come and negotiate the cost of prints with the DuArt Film Lab. DuArt was one of the major labs in New York, and we had done work with them for many years. They charged us depending on the length of the film and we naturally paid the going rate. We had never heard of bargaining over the cost, but sure enough, Mas'ud was able to talk them into significantly reducing the cost of each print. We were astonished! [294]

It seems that Mas'ud's additional unscripted job was to teach the young crew a greater sense of reverence for the Hand of the Cause and the Guardian's widow! According to David Walker:

> We film makers (three for the movie, one for still photographs) were all young guys in our 30's. Mr Khamsi was charged with keeping us in line and smoothing feathers when we clashed with Rúḥíyyih Khánum about things she wanted filmed and things we felt needed to be in the film. We had our share of explosive moments, but they were quickly overcome, and Mr Khamsi was invariably on hand to play the role of referee.

> Throughout the trip Mr Khamsi demonstrated a wonderful sense of gentle humour which lifted our spirits. His Persian deference to Rúḥíyyih Khánum was an education for us American youth, although she did not expect the same from us. She felt free to scold us when we got too rambunctious, but her annoyance passed quickly and she remained to the end of her life a true and steadfast friend.[295]

6.3 A Sense of Reverence

Mas'ud's sense of deference for Khánum, who was not only a great person but also a Hand of the Cause of God and the widow of the Guardian of the Bahá'í Faith, was evident to all.

---

[294] Personal communication to the author.
[295] Personal communication to the author.

Jim Jensen, a pioneer to Ecuador in his twenties, described how at a conference he observed Mas'ud's feeling of reverence towards Khánum:

> Rúhíyyih Khánum wanted to meet with all the pioneers that were present and Mr Khamsi was there. I got to see him in the presence of Rúhíyyih Khánum and he was completely transformed, he was like a humble servant. He was always a humble person without ego and when he dealt with us in Ecuador he was loving and kind, but he was also proper and he looked elegant all the time and he looked serious and prominent. Now, he was in the presence of Rúhíyyih Khánum and he is like a servant and he was so humble, bowing his head, sitting straight and kind of bowing towards her and translating her words into Spanish for some of the people there. That was very interesting, a total transformation in the presence of Rúhíyyih Khánum.[296]

A letter dated Naw-Ruz 1976 written by Amatu'l-Bahá's portrays her appreciation for such a friendship:

> My Dear Mas'ud,
>
> Words are useless to try and convey to you my deep appreciation for your friendship. I have very few people in this world who are really close to me and to whom I can turn in time of need – knowing they are there and will come to my aid. You are one of them.
>
> I can only say may the Báb, Bahá'u'lláh, the Master and the Guardian reward you for, alas, I could never do so for all your help.
>
> Rúhíyyih[297]

This sense of reverence was perceived by many people. Observing that heartfelt attitude of respect a youth commented:

---

[296] Story told by Jimmy Jensen.
[297] Original letter in the collection of the Khamsi family.

[Mas'ud] was always respectful, very kind, with a deep love. It was the kindness and respect coming from a deep love. It was the formal kindness and respect that Persians might have but the kindness and respect emanating from a profound love.[298]

Likewise, a young Bahá'í[299] who was taking a summer break from his studies in the United States and was able to participate in one of the Green Light Expedition events commented:

> I still remember Amatu'l-Bahá's cry of delight when Mas'ud arrived to the conference; he had been delayed briefly on some important matter in the capital and joined us on the second day of the conference. That spontaneous expression of joy on her part upon his re-joining the team, the unfailingly gracious way in which he related to her, an absolutely wonderful combination of respect, consideration, solicitousness, and boundless affection, tempered with straightforwardness and good humour made a deep impression on me.
>
> For someone who had just emerged out of six months in the jungle, you would not have been surprised to see Mas'ud dressed in worn-out fatigues and look the part of a haggard explorer. Not a bit. Mas'ud always looked like he had just emerged from a tailor's shop in Bond Street in London: clean-shaven, the very embodiment of pulchritude and refinement, as I have always thought the Blessed Beauty would like us all to be elegant... I always sensed that Mas'ud's outer demeanour, his princely manners, were a perfect reflection for the richness of his inner self. They were the exterior expression of the chief animating force of his life which was love for the Blessed Beauty, manifested in a life-long, tireless, enthusiastic, commitment to the promotion of the interests of His Cause. [300]

His aristocratic appearance was much the reflection of his spiritual nobility. Similarly, another young believer commented about Mas'ud's personal disposition and deportment:

---

[298]Story told by Jimmy Jensen.
[299]Story provided by Augusto Lopez-Claro.
[300]Augusto Lopez Claros, Messages of Condolence.

I first met this handsome, distinguished gentleman, in the expansive, stylish lobby of Dan Carmel, Haifa's first exclusive hotel, perfectly placed on the mountain allowing for a panoramic view over the Mediterranean Sea and beyond. It was in the late 1960s and Mr Khamsi was visiting the Holy Land on pilgrimage with his entire family. I was struck by them all – their affability, charm – natural, splendorous individuals without flaunting it. The backdrop to this group of royalty was perfect. The name of the street (Hanassi) where Dan Carmel is located means president in Hebrew and the hotel's elegant interior is only outmatched by the magnificence of the view outside, overlooking Haifa Bay and the Galilee and Golan landscape. I felt grand as a lad that afternoon of stateliness but was drawn immediately by the warmth of Mr Khamsi and his unassuming demeanour. How can simplicity reside in such nobility so effortlessly, I thought? As though the personage was oblivious to the material qualities, incarnate or otherwise, wishing to subjugate him. This is forever, how I remember dear Mas'ud Khamsi - the star we gazed upon in admiration never turned upon himself but always looked to the sun which made his brilliance even brighter.[301]

6.4 The Green Light Expedition in Lima

During the Green Light Expedition, when Khánum arrived in Peru she stayed at Mas'ud's place where many meetings with the local community took place. Unfortunately, Khánum arrived very sick as a Bahá'í friend recalled:

> It was a difficult situation for the Green Light Expedition because the boat in the Amazon, the Peruvian part of the Amazon, was a small boat and they were a bit cramped. That's why I believe, because of age, and so much time on the water sailing, that when they arrived to Lima, Rúhíyyih Khánum came down with pneumonia. Mr Khamsi took her to the hospital. They wanted to treat her pneumonia with antibiotics and insisted she rest. Then Rúhíyyih Khánum said to Mr Khamsi: "Mas'ud, I'm not going to touch any of those chemicals, I'm

---
[301] Story provided by Shahbaz Fatheazam

not going to take that". Mr Khamsi called my house and talked to my father and said: "Dr Sanchez [a Bahá'í doctor] please come here and convince Rúhíyyih Khánum that she has to take her medicine". My dad went and I translated. Mr Khamsi stood aside and introduced my dad. They already knew each other and she looked quite emaciated. My dad spoke to her: "The Bahá'í Writings say that in the future diseases will be cured with the principle of restoring balance and we will use medicine that natural and pleasant to taste". "However", my dad said very confidently, "that is in the future. For the time being, what we know now is this medicine and you have a serious illness and the only thing we can do now is to use this medicine". Mr Khamsi was listening and Rúhíyyih Khánum looked at Mr Khamsi, looked at my dad, nodded and then took her medicine".[302]

To make things worse, soon after Khánum was involved in a car accident in Lima:

Amatu'l-Bahá Rúhíyyih Khánum spent about a month in Lima recovering. Mr Khamsi used to take her to El Bosque Country Club to have some sunshine because of Lima's strong haze most of the year. When they were coming back they had a car accident. An ambulance driving in the opposite direction climbed over the central division of the highway and fell sideways on the lane where Mr Khamsi was driving his Volkswagen beetle. Mr Khamsi managed to apply the breaks but his car hit the ambulance. Rúhíyyih Khánum was on Mr Khamsi's side and suffered some blows. However, behind Mr Khamsi was Mark Sadan who was the director of the Green Light Expedition film. He was a big and tall fellow and by falling on him, Mr Khamsi broke his forearm that had to be plastered. The steering wheel also broke.[303]

Once recovered, Khánum made a trip to the north of Peru with the purpose of visiting the Aguaruna tribe. The Aguarunas is the only

---

[302] Story provided by Kiko Sanchez.
[303] Story told by Kiko Sanchez.

indigenous group from Peru mentioned in Shoghi Effendi's map on the Ten Year World Crusade in 1952. Luis Guerrero, a homefront pioneer in that area, recalled:

> Mrs Mary Maxwell [Amatu'l- Bahá Rúhíyyih Khánum] visited my home in Chiclayo. I went to pick her up from the Tourist Hotel in my car and brought her to my home. She bought a fish and prepared it together with my wife Rosario. At lunch she let me know with her interpreter that she wished for me to go to the Aguaruna tribe. Since she could not get there herself, she wanted me to go on her behalf. She was coming from her Green Light trip through the Amazon. However, they could not reach the tribe following the pathway they had chartered through the Amazon. They discovered that Aguaruna tribe was settled on the Marañon river and not the Amazon.[304]

Next year, Luis Wong with Mas'ud went to visit the Aguarunas fulfilling Khánum's request and many Aguarunas became Bahá'ís:

> We departed by bus with Mr Khamsi and other Bahá'í friends. An Aguaruna man served as our guide. After twelve hours of travel we arrived to a park with concrete benches that served as our bed until the truck that was going to transfer us arrived. Mr Khamsi was lying down on the concrete bench for twenty minutes when the truck arrived. We continued the trip until dawn and we went down to walk through the jungle to the Marañon riverbanks. There we crossed the river by raft until we reached the Temashnun Community. At Temashnun there was a meeting of the Apus who are the Chiefs of the tribes from Ecuador and Peru. Mr Khamsi spoke to them about the Bahá'í Faith ... [305]

Rúhíyyih Khánum also took time to gather with the Bahá'ís of Lima. "Khanum went to visit communities in Lima", Gary Khamsi recalls, "being well received by several homes where she spoke to host families and friends". A local believer invited her and a group of Counselors to her place. Marta Lopez narrated what transpired that

---

[304]Personal communication to the author.
[305]Story provided by Luis Wong.

day:

> I had the privilege of inviting Rúhíyyih Khánum to my home. She came with all the Counselors of South America because at that time they were having a summit meeting in Lima. I remember asking Counselor Donald Witzel, "Donald", I said, "Khánum will come to lunch at my house and I do not know what to cook ... Mr Khamsi has forced me to invite her... Who am I to ask Amatu'l-Bahá to come for lunch to my house? I am an ordinary Bahá'í". Finally, I invited her and she was happy that I invited her. I thought of some very nice recipes for lunch. I made typical Peruvian food but since I did not know what Amatu'l-Bahá Rúhíyyih Khánum was used to eating, I made a plate of baked chicken instead. I also made potato salad because I thought these were international that she would surely be able to eat. She served herself and served white rice that I made with tadikht[306], like a rice cake. She was somehow impressed how I had been able to make such a big rice cake.
>
> Amatu'l-Bahá took a piece of chicken, some potato salad and a little bit of white rice. She was very discreet in serving herself. Then I remember that two Counselors said: "Khánum, you have to try this Peruvian food". She was not willing to and said, "I'm afraid of my stomach, it can be spoiled". "No", a Counselor said, "here in the house of Marta we always eat Peruvian... she is very careful preparing her food". Therefore she tried a little bit of Peruvian food because a Counselor put it on her plate and she said, "this is delicious". Afterwards she got up and she helped herself to a little of everything, very moderately. When we finished having lunch she told me that the food had been very delicious and that she really admired my cooking hands.[307]

In Lima Rúhíyyih Khánum stayed at the Khamsi family home although she spent about one month in a hostel to recuperate from her ailing. Gary Khamsi, the youngest of the four children, recalled these interesting facets of Rúhíyyih Khánum's personality as she stayed

---

[306] The browned crispy rice formed at the bottom of the cooking pot.
[307] Story told by Marta Lopez.

at the family home: "Since the Green Light team were exhausted, we respected their rest. At night she would call my sisters because she liked to comb their hair. At that time Bahiah had it very nice and very long. She was very sweet with me in Lima".[308] He remembers "the nice tone of her voice and readiness to laugh, I loved the sound of her laughter ... I was surprised when she gave me a rock music cassette!!"[309]

6.5. At the World Centre

The friendship between Khánum and Mas'ud was a lasting one. In 1983 Mas'ud was appointed as a Counsellor member of the International Teaching Centre, necessitating his family's move to Haifa. According to Azam Matin, a pioneer in Lima who looked after Mas'ud when he was at an advanced age:

> He had many memories with Shoghi Effendi and Rúhíyyih Khánum. He developed a friendship with Rúhíyyih Khánum when he and Jane lived for ten years at the Bahá'í World Center and frequently associated with Rúhíyyih Khánum there. She used to invite some members of the Univeral House of Justice and Hands of the Cause to get together. One of Mr Khamsi's striking virtues was his courtesy. That was his striking virtue - he always showed respect to anyone.[310]

When the Khamsis were leaving the Holy Land to go back to their pioneering post in Peru, Khánum wrote to him:

Haifa 13 March 1993

My very dear Mas'ud,

It is going to be extremely difficult for me not to have you here in Haifa. Our deep friendship is of long standing and memories of the epic South American trip we made together ever fresh in my mind. But, I am well aware that wherever you and dear Jane are it will be a beacon of light for Bahá'ís and non-Bahá'ís alike; what we lose here others will gain there! The sea of life seems

---

[308] Story told by Gary Khamsi.
[309] Story told by Gary Khamsi.
[310] Story told by Azam Matin.

to have tides and sometimes we find ourselves abandoned on the shore and then comes a new tide and we are afloat again! We have to put up with so much in life and hope at the end we are acceptable to God.

God bless you and Jane and yours!

Until we meet again, much loving affection and many treasured memories!

Rúhíyyih

Communication between Khánum and Mas'ud continued even after leaving the World Centre. Conrado Rodriguez, Mas'ud's personal assistant, recounted:

> When Mr Khamsi spoke of the Guardian he always started with tears. Mr Khamsi was much loved by the Guardian and by Amatu'l-Bahá Rúhíyyih Khánum. Once I noticed that Mr Khamsi was crying. I asked him, "Why are you crying Mr Khamsi?". He said, "I am communicating with Amatu'l-Bahá Rúhíyyih Khánum. She is not well because of the pollution in Israel ... I want her to come here to Lima, to my house that is already built but she cannot because she has many tasks and duties..." Mr Khamsi was very concerned with Rúhíyyih Khánum's physical health.
>
> The years that I worked with Mr Khamsi were the happiest years I have ever lived. At that time there were no computers but teleprinters (telex). I noticed on one occasion that Mr Khamsi was communicating with someone through the teleprinter. He was kissing every sheet coming out from the machine and he was very happy. I asked Mr Khamsi the reason for all those kisses.
>
> He said: "My dear Conrado, I am talking with Rúhíyyih Khánum".[311]

7. Pioneering

Having himself been a homefront pioneer as a youth and later an international pioneer with his family, Mas'ud always encouraged others to pioneer and remain in their posts. He was aware of such an

---

[311] Story told by Conrado Rodriguez.

exalted station to which Bahá'u'lláh had referred to in laudable terms:

> They that have forsaken their country in the path of God and subsequently ascended unto His presence, such souls shall be blessed by the Concourse on High and their names recorded by the Pen of Glory among such as have laid down their lives as martyrs in the path of God, the Help in Peril, the Self-Subsisting.[312]

During one of his visits from Haifa to Peru a friend told Mas'ud that "Many people are worried that now that you are in Haifa you will never come back to Peru". He smiled and calmly replied, "God willing, I am a Pioneer and I will lay my bones in Peru".[313] He even managed to raise a young alpaca[314] at his garden where in a wheelchair he used to entertain multiple visitors.

7.1 Encouraging New Pioneers

The Islamic Revolution in 1979 was a big blow to the Iranian Bahá'í community. Many believers including a Continental Counselor and all the National Spiritual Assembly members were summarily executed or simply disappeared. Bahá'í properties were confiscated, individuals sacked from their employment as well as students expelled from schools and universities. It was a period of horror where the Islamic fanaticism was displayed at its worst.

During these tumultuous events, the Universal House of Justice, in messages addressed to the dear Iranian believers resident in other countries throughout the world, brought much comfort and solace, reassuring the friends that they are nothing but expressions of the "mysterious forces of this supreme Revelation"[315].

> In such an afflicted time, when mankind is bewildered and the wisest of men are perplexed as to the remedy, the people of Bahá, who have confidence in His unfailing grace and divine

---

[312] The Universal House of Justice. *Wellspring of Guidance: Messages 1968-1973.* Wilmette, US Bahá'í Publishing Trust, 1976, p. 102.

[313] Story told by Dr Omar Brdarevic.

[314] A native Peruvian animal.

[315] Letter from the Universal House of Justice "To the dear Iranian believers resident in other countries throughout the world" dated 10 February 1980.

guidance, are assured that each of these tormenting trials has a cause, a purpose, and a definite result, and all are essential instruments for the establishment of the immutable Will of God on earth. In other words, on the one hand humanity is struck by the scourge of His chastisement which will inevitably bring together the scattered and vanquished tribes of the earth; and on the other, the weak few whom He has nurtured under the protection of His loving guidance are, in this Formative Age and period of transition, continuing to build amidst these tumultuous waves an impregnable stronghold which will be the sole remaining refuge for those lost multitudes. Therefore, the dear friends of God who have such a broad and clear vision before them are not perturbed by such events, nor are they panic-stricken by such thundering sounds, nor will they face such convulsions with fear and trepidation, nor will they be deterred, even for a moment, from fulfilling their sacred responsibilities. [316]

Throughout this period, a massive number of believers had to leave the country through the mountains of Azerbaijan and Kurdistan to flee to Turkey and Pakistan. Eventually these friends re-settled in Western countries through humanitarian visas arranged by the United Nations Organization. A large number of those friends settled in major American urban centres in the State of California.

According to Dr Iraj Ayman, former Continental Counselor in Iran,

During the first year of the revolution in Iran, I came to the United States in the spring of 1979 for a short visit to attend an international conference on educational research and visiting our children. While I was in the States I received word from the NSA in Iran advising me not to return because my name was on the blacklist of Bahá'í leaders to be executed. Very soon our home and all our belongings in Iran were confiscated. I had to remain indefinitely in the United States.

---

[316] Letter from the Universal House of Justice "To the dear Iranian believers resident in other countries throughout the world" dated 10 February 1980. Available at: https://www.bahai.org/library/authoritative-texts/the-universal-house-of-justice/messages/19800210_001/1#658643603

The Universal House of Justice was advising Persian friends who were in Europe and North America to pioneer to other countries around the world. I recommended to the Persian Desk at the Bahá'í National Office to organize a series of regional gatherings of Persian Bahá'ís for encouraging them to consider pioneering to other parts of the world. We managed to organize a few of them. It so happened that at that time Mas'ud came to the US to participate in the regional gathering of the Counselors in the Americas. So, we invited him to attend those gatherings of the Persian friends and persuade Persian friends to consider pioneering in South America. The main guest speaker in those gatherings was Hand of the Cause Dr. Varqa or Hand of the Cause Mr Khadem. Mas'ud participated in the conferences in San Diego, in Santa Monica, and in Wilmette. He was persuading, advising and assisting those interested to go to South America especially to Peru. He was successful in recruiting a few pioneers to proceed to Peru ... and delivered very effective talks in those conferences and arranged private counseling for interested friends helping them to make up their mind and proceed to the goal-countries in South America.[317]

Several cables reached the Universal House of Justice about the conferences in Wilmette, San Diego and Santa Monica where Mas'ud participated:

THREE HUNDRED PERSIAN BELIEVERS GATHERED TOGETHER IN THE SHADOW MOTHER TEMPLE WEST IN PRESENCE OF HAND CAUSE DHIKRULLAH KHADEM COUNSELORS EDNA TRUE IRAJ AYMAN AND MANUCHIHR SALMANPUR THREE NATIONAL SPIRITUAL ASSEMBLY MEMBERS TWO AUXILIARY BOARD MEMBERS OFFER DEEPEST LOVE SERVITUDE SUPREME BODY. DETERMINED DISPERSE FULFILL GOALS CONSOLIDATE WEAK CENTERS. OVER FIFTY SOULS OFFER PIONEER. REQUEST PRAYERS HOLY SHRINES BESEECHING CELESTIAL CONFIRMATIONS ... (From a cablegram received 19 February 1980)

TWO HUNDRED AND FIFTY PERSIAN FRIENDS GATHERED

---

[317] Personal communication to the author.

SAN DIEGO CENTER 24 FEBRUARY PRESENCE HAND CAUSE VARQA DEEPLY GRIEVED PASSING DEAR HAND CAUSE BALYUZI. OFFER HEARTFELT SUBMISSION SUPREME INSTITUTION. FIFTY BELIEVERS DETERMINED RESPOND FILL PIONEERING TRAVEL TEACHING GOALS. OTHERS HOPEFUL MOVE LATER. BESEECH PRAYERS HOLY SHRINES BESTOWAL CONFIRMATION SUCCESS. (From a cablegram received 26 February 1980)

FOURTEEN HUNDRED PERSIAN BELIEVERS GATHERED SANTA MONICA CALIFORNIA 24 FEBRUARY PRESENCE HAND CAUSE VARQA COUNSELORS KHAMSI SALMANPUR AND AYMAN TWO NATIONAL SPIRITUAL ASSEMBLY MEMBERS AND AUXILIARY BOARD MEMBER JALIL MAHMOUDI. SPIRIT DEDICATION INTENSE. COUNSELORS REMAINED LOS ANGELES FOLLOWING TWO DAYS TO CONSULT WITH PROSPECTIVE PIONEERS ... (From a cablegram received 2 March 1980)

Mas'ud advised them that "the Guardian had told [the Persian believers] that they had to leave, that they had to go and live outside Iran. That they must live to teach the Faith. He told them about the Guardian's wishes and that they had to comply with the Guardian... They were not in the United States to get rich and live a mundane life. They had to put their lives at the service of the Faith".[318]

Ms Violette Haake, former member of the International Teaching Centre, attended one of the gatherings where Mas'ud spoke. She and her husband volunteered to go to Peru: "We went to Peru at that time but then found out that since we were not familiar with Spanish we would not be of any service to the community but nevertheless because he [Mas'ud] gave such a wonderful talk in San Francisco we started considering going pioneering to other places, we ended up in another area. So we owe him this wonderful opportunity that we came across because if we could have come to Australia, we could not have had any of the bounties that Bahá'u'lláh has showered over us. So we owe him a lot".[319]

---

[318] Personal communication to the author.
[319] Story told by Violette Haake.

What follows are stories from two other people who attended Mas'ud's talks:

It was the first week of August 1981, my wife Molok told me that Counselor Mr Khamsi is here in Dallas to give two evening talks in the Bahá'í Centre. Tonight the talk is in English and tomorrow night for the Persian-speaking friends. This was the first time I met Mr Khamsi. In his talk he asked if there was anyone ready to go pioneering in South America should come to the stage. After talking to Molok and getting her permission I went up with other friends to the stage and stood in front of the audience and every one began cheering us. The meeting finished and the majority of these people showed up next night.

Again, the following night Mr Khamsi asked for pioneers to South America. He said again, "Anyone who wants to go please come to the stage". Molok told me, "Go to the front ... you must go to a pioneer post". I accepted and went to the stage.

After the meeting Mr Khamsi gave me the name of Nasser Haddadan [a Persian pioneer in Peru] and the Lima Bahá'í Centre telephone number. The next day I contacted Nasser and he told me to phone the Lima University Computer Department to talk to his boss for a job. He also mentioned the salary. I accepted the amount and tried to talk next day to the Computer Department but the lines were busy. At night I called Nasser to tell him the situation and he told me his boss has doubled his offer for the job. The next day I went to Houston to the Peruvian embassy to get the visa and after a few days we arrived in Peru.[320]

Moojan Matin recalled his own story:

I met Mr Khamsi in 1979. I heard that a Persian Bahá'í, a Counselor, was coming to the San Francisco Bahá'í Center in California and he wanted to speak to the Persian Bahá'ís in the area. About 400 Persian Bahá'ís gathered for that purpose in the Bahá'í Center of San Francisco. It was a full hall. I went to

---

[320] Story told by Zia Ghofrany.

accompany my grandfather whose name is Abbas. He, along with another Counselor, was inviting the Persian friends to leave the United States and pioneer particularly to Latin America. It was the beginning of the Iranian revolution where scores of Bahá'ís were leaving for the United States, Canada and Australia. The Universal House of Justice was worried now that Iran was convulsed that the friends instead of going to the above countries would not take advantage of the moment and go directly to pioneering posts where the Faith needs their services more. That was basically Mr Khamsi's topic. He said that the Universal House of Justice does not need you here in the United States. Now that Iran is convulsed and with problems and everyone is leaving, go to Latin American countries, to Africa, where the Faith needs you. This was his main topic. At the end of the program he said that those who are interested in leaving to Latin America in three months raise their hands. So immediately I volunteered. My grandfather accompanying me told me, "Moojan, if the Universal House of Justice sends a personage such as Mas'ud Khamsi you have to obey the House. The House says leave the United States, you have to leave". Later when the meeting was over, I talked to him about my subject and he asked me: "Are you going in three months?" "Yes", I said to Mr Khamsi, "in three months I'm in Lima". When we arrived in Peru, the only person I knew was Mr Khamsi. [321]

Mas'ud did all what he could to protect the Iranian friends that came with temporary UN refugee status to Peru. At that time all Iranian embassies in Latin America had instructions of rejecting any passport renewal requests from Iranian Bahá'í citizens. This is the amazing story told by Yolanda Torres Urteaga, a Peruvian believer:

> One day [Mas'ud] told two Persian families [with UN refugee status] to travel to Chiclayo, in northern Peru, that there their migration problems would be resolved and that they would be able to stay in Peru. They should just contact my uncle Alberto Guerrero and everything would be solved. It was the decade of the 80s and Mr Khamsi was worried because the Bahá'ís of Iran

---

[321] Story told by Moojan Matin.

who lived outside of their country had been called or rather forced to return by order of the Iranian government and the only way they had to save themselves from that request was to initiate their procedures to opt for Peruvian citizenship. My uncle in obedience to the Counselor and using the position he had at that time as a special attorney in an important Bank wrote a letter stating that he knew them as honourable people and that he endorsed these families for being Bahá'ís. This document was presented to the police where my uncle was also known for working in the bank and because he knew the head of that institution as they had studied together in primary and secondary school.

Perhaps, doing everything he did would have costed my uncle his job but once again we can appreciate that the hand of God is present and protects his loved ones. Obedience to the institutions is vital for all Bahá'ís and this is an example for future generations because when you serve with a pure heart the doors open and everything is solved.[322]

Mas'ud also had a Persian secretary. According to Shahnaz Talebzadeh assisting him with his work, "At that time many Persian pioneers were arriving to Peru, and they needed a lot of attention and he asked me to solve their translation problems, residence procedures and other needs until they settled in various cities".[323]

7.2 Nurturing Current Pioneers

An important facet of Mas'ud's job as a Cousellor was to encourage current pioneers to be steadfast in their post as an Iranian pioneer remembers: "He was our Counselor coming to Paraguay every 2 or 3 months, he always advised the pioneers to be firm in their pioneering position and not to be afraid of the difficulties and to go ahead and feel like soldiers of the Blessed Beauty and help to strengthen the National Spiritual Assembly".[324]

These two stories reflect the way Mas'ud never neglected the

---

[322]Personal communication to the author.
[323]Story told by Shahnaz Talebzadeh.
[324]Story told by Houshang Balazadeh.

welfare of pioneers whether they were homefront or from overseas:

> I remember that every year I met the Persian friends for Naw Ruz and we were happy with Chelo Kabab[325] and sweets and other Persian delicacies. They were meetings where the Counselor Mr Khamsi talked to us and deepened us and made us feel heavenly! It was there where the pioneers could take spiritual strength to continue working for the Faith all year long! He told us of the tremendous successes of humble people who had raised to be pioneers like Mr Musa Banani in Africa, who after many hardships and difficulties met Hand of the Cause Mr Olinga, who conquered the continent of Africa. Or another Bahá'í who had to sell his land to return to his country, but at the insistence of Shoghi Effendi stayed, and then found oil on his land. Another Bahá'í who in Japan suffered a lot but one day wrote to the National Company of Japan and told them that their electric rice cookers should let the rice burn and brown a little at the bottom, and this would greatly increase sales in Iran. That pioneer received a huge monthly check from the National Company every month! [326]

> [Mas'ud] had a special concern for traveling teachers and pioneers. He was attentive to the situation of each one, visiting them at their posts, encouraging them and looking after their welfare. His farewell phrase that I cannot forget is "you have to persevere". I remember that I was at my homefront pioneering post in a small town in Peru about two hours away from the provincial capital. The telephone communication system was incipient and I did not hear that Mr Khamsi had stopped in town on his return from Bolivia and wanted to meet with the pioneers. When he did not find me, he sent a special vehicle to pick me up despite the distance and the time. [327]

> After the summer school ended, Ahmad Khamsi who was 16 years old, said to me [a very young American pioneer] "You have not come back to Ecuador yet. Come and stay at my

---

[325] A traditional Persian dish consisting of meat and rice.
[326] Story told by Farid Tebyani.
[327] Story told by Mirna Leon de Donaires.

house" and so I was very embarrassed at that invitation from the Counselor. He said: 'Just come to my house for a couple of days before you go back' and so I was able to sleep at their house, eat at their table and see Mr Khamsi in a completely different setting, with the family and the children. I was very happy to be in that family environment because I had been out of California for six months now and that was the first time to be able with a family, the whole family speaking English. But Mr Khamsi was always so proper and respected that I was very much in.[328]

With his business acuity Mas'ud was a source of practical advice to pioneers including general business guidance. "He encouraged many pioneers to go back to the US or other universities and get a diploma so that they could serve at higher levels in their communities," said Dorothy Khamsi-Samandari, "to buy land and build houses on them or buy their own apartments, not pay rent so that they contribute to their own future not make someone else rich … to write their will and testament, to keep family unity".[329]

The story about Eve Nicklin (1895-1985) is probably the best corollary to this section about caring for our pioneers. Eve was an American pioneer who became known as the Spiritual Mother of Peru. She settled in twelve cities within six South American countries for nearly five decades. On arriving in Peru in 1941 she was a woman in her late forties, without money or knowledge o the language, no Baha'i literature in Spanish and surviving on a bare income as an English teacher in schools and hospitals. A fall at the Lima summer school in 1978 forced Eve's return to Lima from her pioneering post at a small town in Peru. Having no family connections and being already an octogenarian, she remained under the loving care of the Khamsi family who took responsibility for her wellbeing and hiring a nurse to look after her. Eve went to live in a geriatric clinic and finally stayed on the second floor of the National Hazíratu'l-Quds for her four last years of her life — visited and always surrounded by her many spiritual children. Less mobile, Eve always maintained her always

---

[328]Story told by Jimmy Jensen.

[329]Personal communication to the author.

encouraging nature, deepening the friends, sharing stories about the early history of the Bahá'í Faith in Peru as well as showing them and explaining her many teaching pictorial albums.[330]

Mas'ud used to say that in the future, schools, hospitals, universities and all types of humanitarian institutions would be named after her. A believer recalled that Mas'ud had great love for Eve Nicklin and talked to her with great affection, "he looked and talked to her with much tenderness".

8. Bahá'í World Centre Services

In 1983 Mas'ud was appointed a member of the International Teaching Centre in Haifa for a five-year period. The National Convention of Peru joyfully cabled the Bahá'í World Centre: "... the friends applaud the appointment of Mr Khamsi". An emotive farewell took place at the airport to wish Mas'ud and Jane well in the next stage of their life now at the Holy Land.

8.1 A Member of the International Teaching Centre

"To my surprise and high honour", Mas'ud recalled, "the Universal House of Justice named me as a member of the International Teaching Centre. I am not going to explain those 10 years of service in detail, but I want to make clear that it increased my knowledge of the Faith greatly, the experience and learning I got from the Hands of the Cause, members of the Universal House of Justice and other deep and important Bahá'í friends will be an unforgettable treasure in my life".

Mas'ud remained in Haifa for nearly a decade since he was reappointed for another term in 1985 serving directly the Universal House of Justice in that position, and visiting national Bahá'í communities the around the world.

This institution of the International Teaching Centre was created by the Universal House of Justice in 1973 with all the seventeen living Hands of the Cause as *ex officio* members along with three Counselors. By 1988 the number of Counselor members were raised to nine although only a few Hands had survived, namely, Amatu'l-Bahá Rúḥíyyih Khánum, 'Alí-Muhammad Varqá, `Alí-Akbar Furútan,

---

[330]Boris Handal. *Eve Nicklin, She of the Brave Heart.* SC, CreateSpace, 2011.

Collis Featherstone, John Robarts, Ugo Giachery, Jalál Kházeh and William Sears. Out of these eight Hands, only the first three resided in the Holy Land assisting directly in the development and functioning of this institution. As we are aware the last Hand to pass away was Dr Varqa in 2007.

Counselor Donald Rogers from Canada had joined the International Teaching Centre in 1988. Mr Donald Rogers wrote:

> One of the unique features at this time was to function as nine Counsellor members in the work without the day-to-day participation of the Hands of the Cause. This was an important transitional moment. Mas'ud's loving service at this time was an important factor in achieving unity in our resolve. His generous hospitality extended to all of us and to the body as a whole had a galvanizing affect. Further, his reverence for the Institution of the Hands was demonstrated most lovingly by his respect for and tenderness with Hand of the Cause Amatu'l-Bahá Rúḥíyyih Khánum, in itself, a spiritual education for us. His wise counsel and insightful comments on the teachings of the Faith during our consultations served to strengthen both the institution and its members. For example, we were enlightened by his comments on the Kitáb-i-Aqdas as we studied an advanced copy of the approved English translation.[331]

Mas'ud's activities extended to other fields such as youth programs, Spanish-speaking gatherings, and the formation of the "El Viento Canta" (The Wind Sings, in Spanish) musical group as well as engaging with the foreign diplomatic board.

8.2 Youth Programs in Haifa

Many years after the Khamsis left the Holy Land the friends still remembered the morning meetings that they used to have with the youth at their home in Haifa:

> When we arrived at the Holy Land the youth rendering services told me about their isolation and the lack of programs for them,

---

[331] Personal communication to the author.

to such an extent that some of them went out to clubs or other amusement centres. With the experience acquired with youth in Bolivia and Peru, my wife and I invited youth to our home to stay and sleep for the weekend starting Friday evenings, on Saturday very early they prepared their breakfast and we started the study of spiritual texts such as the Hidden Words or the Book of Certitude. The number of participants reached 26 and it was a well-known permanent program particularly during the fast. Very soon the youth started deepening classes with some well-read friends of the community, they gathered by languages and subjects.[332]

8.2 Latin Nights

At the same time a small group of Spanish speaking staff began to strengthen their Bahá'í identity at the World Centre:

> There were also special activities through the Golda Meyer Development Community Institute. Amatu'l-Bahá Rúhíyyih Khánum and other ladies made friends with the director of this institute. My wife Jane and I made use of that relationship and every time that groups from other countries came for the institute courses, through the director, we invited the Latin American participants and students to an evening called "Noche Latina" (Latin Night) at our home.[333]

These Latin Nights continued for a long time and were a space where the friends could deepen about the Faith in their native language drawing from Mas'ud's experience and knowledge.

8.3 El Viento Canta

Perhaps one of the most successful Latino activities was the creation of the folk music group "El Viento Canta" (The Wind Sings) which was inspired and supported by Mas'ud and Amatu'l-Bahá Rúhíyih Khánum. Many of that youth group grew up in Peru under Mas'ud's tutelage and were serving at the World Centre. Their first presentation was at the seat of the Universal House of Justice. Rúhíyih Khánum and

---

[332] *Pioneering and Services of Mas'ud Khamsi*, unpublished manuscript.

[333] *Pioneering and Services of Mas'ud Khamsi*, unpublished manuscript.

Mas'ud sat on the first row. At the conclusion of the performance, Rúhíyih Khánum came to the stage to see their costumes and realized that these were not completely genuine. She said, "These are not authentic. I know the costumes, come to my house and I will give you authentic clothes to use in other performances". When the friends when to the House of 'Abdu'l-Bahá, Rúhíyih Khánum gave them original costumes which included a native skirt and a chullo (an Andean hat with earflaps). After that evening "El Viento Canta" found themselves performing in various events including weddings and special celebrations as they were preparing for an European tour with the support and encouragement of Rúhíyih Khánum and Mas'ud.

"El Viento Canta" also performed at the Peruvian Embassy in Tel Aviv and at the International Bahá'í Convention followed by tours to many countries in Europe, Africa and Asia teaching the Faith through their music as they themselves later reported:

> It was destiny that led these young people to meet at the Bahá'í World Center in Haifa at the same time in the late 1980s when Mr Khamsi was serving at the International Teaching Center. Our first presentation was for the World Center staff including the presence of the Hand of the Cause Rúhiyyih Khánum, some Counselors and Members of the House. After these presentations the group thought that it would be good to leave the World Center together making a proclamation and teaching trip in Western Europe. However, Mr Khamsi had more challenging goals. Under his guidance, the group sent letters to 10 National Assemblies in Europe, offering their services for any activity in areas they thought were most needed in their countries. It was a challenging goal but Mr Khamsi was determined that El Viento Canta contribute in the way that 'Abdu'l-Bahá promised. One night he read us this passage from the *Tablets of the Divine Plan* regarding the indigenous people of the Americas: *"... should the Indians be properly educated and guided, there can be no doubt that they will become so illumined as to enlighten the whole world....* "[334]

---

[334] 'Abdu'l-Bahá. *Tablets of the Divine Plan.* Wilmette, US Bahá'í Publishing Trust, 1933, p. 33.

Mr Khamsi took over the job of contacting the friends in the European countries to be visited and later when the 1988 International Convention was held in Haifa, Mr Khamsi arranged several presentations of the Viento Canta for members of National Assemblies of Europe so that they could see the group and how the group provided an opportunity for cultural education, entertaining and with a message of spiritual hope. To motivate the delegates Mr and Mrs Khamsi offered a special presentation for the Hand of the Cause William Sears in the room of one of the hotels with the intention of gaining interest and promoting the group among the busy delegates. Also with the support of the Hand of the Cause of God Amatu'l Bahá Rúhíyyih Khánum, the Viento Canta was invited to sing at a special dinner at the House of 'Abdu'l-Bahá where all the living Hands of the Cause were present including the Counselors of the International Teaching Center and Continental Counselors from around the world. As a result the Viento Canta's travels were expanded not only to Western Europe but also later to Africa. Also the recent opening of the Iron Curtain gave them the opportunity to visit countries in Eastern Europe and Asia. Among those countries were Siberia, Mongolia, and China to mention a few. Mr Khamsi's vision was always years ahead of ours and he planned goals that we would never have imagined before.

More than 40 countries, thousands of souls were touched and transformed by the melodies of Bahá'u'lláh's message through radio and television presentations, many newspaper articles, public parks and local and national theaters. There were generations of children who grew up listening to the music of this group around the world.[335]

8.4 External Affairs

Mas'ud became very skilled in conducting external affairs activities a skill that, without doubt, he learned from his father Siyyid Ahmad and

---

[335]Report supplied by Cesar Cortes Peralta (Perú), Roxana Hadden (Perú), David Hadden (USA), Conrad Lambert (United Kingdom), Bernadette Cortes-Wohlwend (Lichtenstein), Claudia Delgado Hernandez and Miguel Cortes Peralta (Peru).

great-uncle Siyyid Naṣru'lláh following 'Abdu'l-Bahá's advice: "Some of the loved ones should establish ties of friendship with the notables of the region and manifest towards them the most affectionate regard. In this manner these men may become acquainted with the Bahá'í way of life, learn of the teachings of the Merciful One, and be informed of the pervasive influence of the Word of God in every quarter of the globe".[336]

In Mas'ud words:

We were very good friends of the Ambassadors of Peru and their wives, they were always our guests and we took them to the Holy places and to the building of the Universal House of Justice, we invited outstanding Bahá'ís like Amatu'l-Bahá Rúhíyyih Khánum, David and Meg Ruhe, among others, even Amatu'l-Bahá invited them to her house (House of the Master). As I said before I took the group "El Viento Canta" to a reception for the Ambassador of Peru. It seemed that the Peruvian diplomat during meetings with his colleagues had enthusiastically explained them about his visit to the "Bahá'í Organization", as a result many of them wanted to visit the Bahá'í Holy places in Haifa.

On one occasion with the authorization of the Universal House of Justice I invited the Ambassadors of Peru, Bolivia, Colombia, Venezuela, Panama and The Dominican Republic, and the wife of the Brazilian Ambassador to a Chinese restaurant where Amatu'l-Bahá Rúhíyyih Khánum talked about the Faith, her talk was translated into Spanish and the Ambassador of Peru thanked us for the Bahá'í hospitality. [337]

According to a staff member, "Besides his work as a Counselor, Mr Khamsi would help as an unofficial ambassador to international dignitaries who were visiting the Bahá'í World Centre; often the office of the mayor of Haifa would contact the Universal House of Justice for permission to visit the Seat with diplomats, Ambassadors and other V.I.P. I think it was 1986 when the mayor of Lima and his wife visited

---

[336] *The Compilation of Compilations: Prepared by The Universal House of Justice (vol. 2).* Maryborough, Victoria, Bahá'í Publications Australia, 1991, p. 265.

[337] *Pioneering and Services of Mas'ud Khamsi,* unpublished manuscript.

Haifa and met with Mr Khamsi to tour the Seat of the Universal House of Justice, thus developing good will and relations between Peruvian representatives and the Bahá'í Faith".[338] Mas'ud had previously acquired the Peruvian citizenship.

8.5 International Trips

During his time at the International Teaching Centre Mas'ud participated in several overseas events. To mention a few: the dedication of Guaymi Cultural Centre (Panama, February, 1985) accompanied by Hand of the Cause of God Amatu'l-Bahá Rúḥíyyih Khánum, first Bahá'í International Peace conference in San Francisco (August, 1986); a Bahá'í National Teaching Conference in Bangladesh (October 1987). On a trip to India Mas'ud was asked to place the corner stone of the Panchgani Academy.

Similarly, he participated in a large-scale teaching campaign in southern Brazil (September, 1987), and in a mass teaching campaign around Lake Titikaka which sits between Peru and Bolivia. According to Bahá'í News:

> The unified efforts of Counselor Mas'ud Khamsi of the International Teaching Centre, Counselor for the Americas Isabel de Calderon, four Auxiliary Board members, and members of the National Spiritual Assemblies of Peru and Bolivia have combined to rekindle Peru's Lake Titicaca region. A two-day mass teaching workshop attended by 60 Bahá'ís was followed by a five-day teaching campaign in which 1,764 new believers were enrolled in the Faith. 738 youth and 1,026 adults. These successes were achieved in spite of a strike last September 28 during which roads in the area were closed. A highlight was the teaching work at a high school in Villa Quebrada where the principal and all the teachers and students embraced the Faith. The campaign was capped by a two-day conference to evaluate the results and determine future directions. Ten volunteers offered to continue with the consolidation work.[339]

---

[338] Story supplied by Marko Sebastiani
[339] *Bahá'í News*, February 1989.

The highlight of those travels was possible going back to his roots in Baku, the land of Siyyid Nasrulláh and Siyyid Ahmad, his great-uncle and father, respectively.

One special privilege was being named as a representative of the Universal House of Justice for the First Convention of the National Spiritual Assembly of Azerbaijan in [in 1992] Baku where my father and my grandparents lived for a long time. Due to Communism, the Faith there was suspended until 1992, specifically the Assembly of Baku was banned. Fortunately, as I had some relatives in this country during the week I stayed in Baku with my wife, 11 people became Bahá'í, some of them were my relatives.[340]

When Mas'ud passed away in 2013, the National Spiritual Assembly of Spain wrote: "During his service as an International Counselor at the Bahá'í World Center he made numerous visits to Spain that left a great impression and inspired the hearts of the friends who had the good fortune to listen to him and to partake of his presence".[341]

Faithful to his promise, after he retired from the International Teaching Centre, Mas'ud returned to Peru and served for several years on the National Spiritual Assembly despite his advanced age.

9. Socio-Economic Development

Socio-economic development was one of the chief landmarks of Mas'ud's life. Drawing from his understanding of the Writings, he was of the belief that spiritual and material well-being goes hand-to-hand particularly for disadvantaged populations which usually were the focus of mass teaching. "Be anxiously concerned with the needs of the age ye live in, and center your deliberations on its exigencies and requirements"[342], is Bahá'u'lláh's exhortation.

Based also on his family background on socio-economic development and his business perspicacity, Mas'ud always looked

---

[340] *Pioneering and Services of Mas'ud Khamsi*, unpublished manuscript.
[341] National Spiritual Assembly of the Bahá'í of Spain, Messages of Condolence.
[342] Bahá'u'lláh. Gleanings From the Writings of Bahá'u'lláh. Wilmette, US Bahá'í Publishing Trust, p. 213, 1990.

at linking the propagation of the Faith to raising people's and communities' material progress in the field of education, health, agriculture, culture or any other dimension bringing human and societal improvement.

9.1 An Entrepreneurial Mindset

Coming from a family with members such as Siyyid Naṣru'lláh and Siyyid Ahmad who had a strong entrepreneurial acumen, it was natural that Mas'ud thought that raising standards of living with planned socio-economic activities was the Bahá'í approach, particularly in collaborating shoulder to shoulder with rural and indigenous communities.

Mas'ud wrote:

At the beginning of the Century, in a letter 'Abdu'l-Bahá, recommended my father to cultivate tea in Persia. In one Tablet after receiving the first tea from my father's plantation, he recommended my father to spread this plant until Persia was self-sufficient in tea and did not need to import it. This was directly an economic development recommended by 'Abdu'l-Bahá, On another occasion and other Tablets, he recommended my father to make friends with the Russian Consul in the city of Rasht, where my father lived. I consider this to be a social development. These two things were in my mind since I was a kid and later I helped Indians from Bolivia for their economic development such as improving their animal breed and poultry, researching better grains for their crops, and I also worked to establish schools for their social development. In 1979 with the authorization of the Counselors for the Americas, I wrote a letter to the International Teaching Centre suggesting to ask the Universal House of Justice to create an office devoted to projects and recommendations to all Latin American Spiritual Assemblies to start Social and Economic Development projects. This suggestion was accepted by the Supreme Body and after communication and clarification of some items between them and the International Teaching Centre and more explanations from my part, in October 1983, the Universal House of Justice announced to the Bahá'í world through a circular about the establishment of the Social and Economic Development Office and that each country should try to create a committee or an organization for such a purpose.[343]

His sense of practicality led to an earlier stage of entry by troops in South America and to initiate projects and conversations with Bahá'í institutions and individuals. Dorothy Khamsi-Samandari wrote:

> Daddy used to say it is very difficult to teach starving people, we must care for their health and physical development as well as their spirit, therefore educational institutions, Bahá'ís schools to educate children, Bahá'í radios to teach populations to develop in health, nutrition, family values, hygiene, agriculture, animal husbandry, history, culture, music and dances, organizing local languages and folklore festivals, etc. and finding good jobs... As a result of these mails and the same necessities in the United States and the times the socio-economic conferences in December for many years took place in Orlando and carved the way for many communities to establish Bahá'í schools and Bahá'í institutes and Bahá'í radio stations and projects for medical centres ...[344]

9.2 Bahá'í Radio Stations

One of Mas'ud milestones was the creation of Bahá'í radio stations. At that time using dedicated radio broadcasting channels for teaching the Faith was an idea still embryonic. Already the beloved Guardian had advised as early as in 1943:

> In connection with the radio work ... he would suggest that the main consideration is to bring to the attention of the public the fact that the Faith exists, and its teachings. Every kind of broadcast, whether of passages from the Writings, or on typical subjects, or lectures, should be used. The people need to hear the word 'Bahá'í' so that they can, if receptive, respond and seek the Cause out. The primary duty of the friends everywhere in the world is to let the people know such

---

[343] *Pioneering and Services of Mas'ud Khamsi*, unpublished manuscript.
[344] Personal communication to the author.

a Revelation is in existence; their next duty is to teach it.[345]

As with his interest in establishing radio stations operated by national assemblies, Mas'ud recounted:

> My radio and TV knowledge in Persia particularly at listening to friends who had programs of the Faith in Ceylon and New Delhi in India, encouraged me to have short programs in Bolivia about the Bahá'í Faith on different occasions. On my visits to countries such as Peru, Ecuador and Colombia I encouraged the friends to make use of this excellent tool. The first Bahá'ís of Puno listened to the radio of La Paz and they had interest in knowing the Faith deeper, as Bolivia sent a teacher there were many declarations in Puno. In Ecuador, Mr Raul Pavon was using this media. During a trip Rúhíyyih Khánum gave a fur coat to be sold for funds and these funds were used to establish radio programs. With this and the technical support of Mr Kamran Mansuri, Mr Raul Pavon's dream came true. With the authorization of the Universal House of Justice and the technical assistance of Engineer Dean Stevens, he managed to establish the first Bahá'í radio station in Otavalo, Ecuador.[346] Gradually, other countries got excited about having their own radio station. The Universal House of Justice agreed that in places where there were concentrations of Bahá'í communities and funds could be obtained they could establish radio stations. Then Peru[347], Chile [348], Bolivia [349] and Panama[350], thanks to contributions of my personal friends they supported the establishment of these radios. It is interesting to mention that during a visit in company of Amatu'l-Bahá Rúhíyyih Khánum, the President of Panama, knowing that we had a project to establish a radio station in Guaymi, got very

---

[345] The Universal House of Justice. *Wellspring of Guidance: Messages of the Universal House of Justice 1963-68.* Wilmette, US Baha'i Publishing Trust, 1969, p. 312.

[346] Established in 1977.

[347] Established in 1981.

[348] Established in 1986.

[349] Established in 1984.

[350] Established in 1985.

excited and ordered to immediately give all help needed to obtain the licence for this radio, and seriously expressed that he would like to be invited for the inauguration of the radio. All these 5 stations have next to them a Teaching Institute.[351]

In particular, Radio Bahá'í of Lake Titikaka was established at a time when the persecutions in Iran were at its peak. The station was located at an altitude of 3,875 meters above sea level, higher than Mount Fuji, on the shores of the world's highest navigable lake in between Peru and Bolivia, the land of the Aymara and Quechua nations, where about 130 Local Spiritual Assemblies had been formed.[352] Its dedication sounded like a Divine response to the oppressors of the Faith reverberating Bahá'u'lláh's words 150 years ago:

> And if they cast Him into a darksome pit, they will find Him seated on earth's loftiest heights calling aloud to all mankind: "Lo, the Desire of the World is come in His majesty, His sovereignty, His transcendent dominion!"[353]

Dean Stevens recalled the exciting first day of the Peruvian Bahá'í radio on the commemoration of the Martyrdom of the Báb, a project in which Mas'ud had a leading role and invested considerable energy and time:

> Let me start with one vivid memory, of the day of the Martyrdom of the Báb when we dedicated Radio Bahá'í of Lake Titikaka. We were all together when we pushed the button to commence that historic transmission, but when I turned around to embrace dear Mas'ud, he had disappeared. I found him alone, with tears streaming down his face. Both of us had strongly felt the presence of the Báb Himself at that moment! I never again saw Counselor Khamsi so affected.[354]

Dr Omar Brdarevic, a former member of the National Spiritual

---

[351] *Pioneering and Services of Mas'ud Khamsi*, unpublished manuscript.
[352] *Bahá'í News*, September 1981.
[353] Bahá'u'lláh. *The Summons of the Lord of Hosts.* Wilmette, Bahá'í Publishing, 2002, p. 51.
[354] Personal communication to the author.

Assembly of Peru has observed about how much Mas'ud assisted the taskforce composed of young Bahá'ís:

> He always supported us for the work we had to do. It was more than 500 hours of radio work required by the Universal House of Justice to obtain from that body the approval for having a Radio Bahá'í in Peru. So we were working hard to design and organize events and programs. In the background Counselor Khamsi was encouraging us at all times. Especially, when it came time to get the license for the radio station, he was working very closely with the National Assembly at all times. He was involved at all levels. When experts from outside came like Dean Stephens, he was always part of the consultative process.[355]

9.3 Nur University

Nur University was the first Bahá'í-inspired tertiary institution in the world. It was established by Eloy Anello, an American pioneer in Bolivia who was later appointed as an Auxiliary Board member and then a Continental Counselor.

Eloy had previously approached Mas'ud to obtain guidance for beginning a school in his locality. Dorothy Khamsi-Samandari explains how Eloy's mind was routed into a different dimension:

> Daddy on one occasion told him [Eloy Anello] not to start a normal school he intended to open in Bolivia, but a University, that the Blessed Beauty would be behind him, Eloy said "how can I do that it's way beyond me?" and Daddy took out a check of US1,500 to begin the paper work, this was the beginning of Nur University. He told him to aim high and go back to the United Stated and get a valid degree in Education, which he did, and employ professionals not amateurs, which he did. Eloy credited my father with this on repeated occasions and said that after that, Dr Mohajer also pushed and supported this initiative and along with the Universal House of Justice prayed and supported furthermore this endeavour. Eloy told me to come visit soon as he was suggesting naming a Conference

---

[355]Story told by Omar Brdarevic.

Room or Hall after him.[356]

Mas'ud became a founder member of the University and an ardent supporter. He was of the idea that through Nur University we could enhance education in remote and rural schools. Its principles are explicitly based on the spiritual teachings of the Bahá'í Faith. The University started functioning in 1985 after arduous bureaucratic and political challenges to get the government licence since Nur was to become the first private university in Bolivia. According to Manoucher Shoaie, the University Principal, "After the foundation of Nur University, he always supported the University intellectually and morally, either when he was in Peru or when he resided as a Counselor in the Holy Land. He sometimes facilitated contacting those Bahá'ís who wished to be friends of Nur and contribute in different ways to the implementation of their educational projects".[357]

9.4 Institutes

The creation of teaching institutes was another landmark of Mas'ud's services. At that time most of the Bahá'ís endowments consisted of centres mostly located in urban settings for administrative purposes and community meetings. As mass teaching was blooming there was a need to have facilities where travel teachers can stay for various days for their training with dormitories and other amenities. These are Mas'ud's memories on how teaching institutes began to develop:

9.4.1 In Bolivia

Bolivia was certainly one of the first places to experience the process of having an institute. Mas'ud recounts:

> As the number of Bahá'ís and areas of teaching kept growing, we found out that we needed more travel teachers and human resources to take care of so many communities. As I was acquainted with the history of the first Teaching Institute in Persia (Daro tabligh) in charge of the wise and famous Bahá'í Sadr us Sudur I thought about having an Institute in Bolivia. The Beloved Hand of the Cause of God, Mr Abu'l-Qásim Faizí

---

[356]Personal communication to the author
[357]Personal communication to the author.

knowing my idea, asked a friend in Pakistan to provide me with funds. With that money I arranged a simple Institute in Cochabamba with different rooms, a kitchen, a dining-living room and a private construction for the custodians and teachers of the courses. Mr Athos Costas and his wife Angelica were the chosen ones, and we started courses for Indians, for the literate and illiterate, for Bahá'í and non-Bahá'í teachers, courses for children, teachers, etc. I am sure that the unprecedented development of the Faith in Bolivia and the current number of Bahá'ís around 300,000 or 400,000 is based on the institutes such as Soltani Institute in Chuquisaca, Sucre, Sacaca Institute in Oruro, etc. [358]

9.4.2 in Peru

The Peruvian Bahá'í community followed suit to their Bolivia counterpart and soon began to have its own teaching institutes in Indigenous areas as Mas'ud explains:

> With my experience in Bolivia regarding institutes, I visualized the need to have institutes in Peru for both teaching and deepening. With the authorization of the National Spiritual Assembly I purchased a site in Cusco with funds of a Persian friend, Mr Tashakor and we built the first teaching institute in Peru. Years later in Puno we built an institute next to the Radio Bahá'í building [in 1980]. It was built with a contribution from a relative of Dr. Muhájir suggesting we called it the Muhájir Institute. I obtained vehicles from friends outside Peru for places such as Puno and Cuzco where communication and contact with other indigenous communities was very difficult.[359]

It is noteworthy that the previous year, in 1979, his childhood and youth companion and later Hand of the Cause Dr Muhájir, both of the same age, had passed away in his arms in the Ecuatorian Andes while on a teaching trip coming from Peru where he was encouraging the establishment of Radio Bahá'í of Puno and its institute. The later was

---

[358] *Pioneering and Services of Mas'ud Khamsi*, unpublished manuscript.

[359] *Pioneering and Services of Mas'ud Khamsi*, unpublished manuscript.

named Muhájir after him. In recalling that tragic day in Quito Mas'ud wrote:

> We then all went to the Bahá'í Centre to take part in the meeting of the pioneers. After a short talk Dr Muhájir left the room. The meeting continued. Suddenly Helen Hornby entered the room and asked for prayers for the Hand of the Cause. I rushed out and found him lying down on the caretaker's bed on his side with his head supported by his hand. He told me he had sharp pains in his heart and neck, and asked me to rub his neck while he rubbed his heart. I insisted on calling a doctor but he refused, so as not to alarm the friends, and as it was a Saturday we thought it better to take him to a nearby clinic. We walked quietly past the friends who were now gathered in the yard, got into the car, and Charles drove us to the Clinic Americana Adventista.
>
> The doctor asked Rahmat [Dr Muhájir] about his condition and his speciality; he laughed, but did not answer. The doctor was preparing an injection and was rather anxious as he knew he was dealing with an important personage. Rahmat patted him on the back and said, 'Don't be afraid. Death is nothing to be afraid of.' He himself adjusted the oxygen machine and inhaled some oxygen, which did not seem to help. His pain was becoming more excruciating and we sent for a heart specialist. After a few minutes he turned to me and said, 'Mas'úd ján, I am fainting.' He repeated, 'Ya Bahá'u'l-Abhá' several times. Those were his last words. In his hand, Dr Muhájir was holding kept pieces of Bahá'u'lláh's hair in a small silk bag.[360]

9.4.3 In Brazil

The Soltanieh Institute has become a major educational establishment in Brazil with magnificent accommodation and conference facilities spread around fourteen hectares. According to Mas'ud:

> The Soltani brothers Husayn and Ghodrat, deep Bahá'ís and pioneers in Brazil for a long time, wished to immortalize their parent's memory, who as pioneers passed away in Brazil and

---

[360] Írán Furútan Muhájir. *Dr Muhájir: Hand of the Cause of God, Knight of Bahá'u'lláh.* London, Bahá'í Publishing Trust, 1992, pp. 580-581.

according to Bahá'u'lláh's words are considered as martyrs. When they consulted with me, I suggested that they build a Summer School in the name of their parents since Brazil did not have one and they always had to search with difficulty a place for this purpose.

The NSA thought that the fund to build a summer school could be invested to build or purchase 10 local centres that were considered within the Six Year Plan for Brazil. Finally, I convinced the National Spiritual Assembly that in Brazil there were other economic resources to build those 10 local centres but a Summer School needed the capital that only Soltani brothers could provide.

In a meeting of Counselors, near Mogi Mírin, a property of Soltani brothers and their summer house, we decided to place the first comer stone. "Two sovereigns" which is the translation for the word "Soltan" and "King" have placed the first stone in Soltani's property. At the beginning they thought about building a school with 100 beds, but later as the work progressed they decided to do it for 300 beds and finally it was for 500 beds with private and public bathrooms, conference room, libraries, dining room and kitchen besides beautiful gardens. Now most of the celebrations, conferences and meetings including the Brazilian Annual Convention are held there, and recently they can provide food for 1,000 people and therefore they plan to build another conference room for 1,000 people. This school has often been blessed by the visit of Amatu'l-Bahá Rúhíyih Khánum and other Hands of the Cause of God. The Universal House of Justice wishes this will become in the future a university of the Faith and presently it is called Superior Education Institute.[361]

9.5 Rural Schools

Another significant achievement of Mas'ud in Bolivia was the establishment of rural schools for the education of children. In Mas'ud's words:

---

[361] *Pioneering and Services of Mas'ud Khamsi,* unpublished manuscript.

The Beloved Guardian informed the world that Dr Rahmatu'lláh Muhajir started to open children schools after the success obtained in mass conversion in Mentawai Islands, Indonesia during 1954 and 1956. This is why I started schools with children from the indigenous communities of Bolivia. Once on a visit I discovered that the Minister of Indigenous Affairs knew very well about the Faith through Colonel Gallardo and his wife Fabiana Gallardo who was French, they were the first teachers in Bolivia. With the authorization of that Ministry and the enthusiasm of the Bahá'ís we got to establish 42 schools in different departments of Bolivia, they were very simple constructions built by the Indians themselves. Later on we established a very strong relationship with the Ministry of Education. Before I left Bolivia in 1962, the Minister asked the Bahá'ís to participate and assist the first literacy campaign in Bolivia.[362]

With Mas'ud the social and economic dimensions of the teachings of Bahá'u'lláh were brought forward at a time where individuals and societies were learning about progressing mass teaching throughout South America. At the beginning, the inspiration seemed to come from early interventions in Iran, the Cradle of the Faith. When those experiences were translated to the Latin context the *adopting* became *adapting* and therefore a new model emerged at a more sophisticated level such as radio stations, hospitals and universities.

This process of learning continues and nowadays, national communities and friends through personal initiatives are understanding that personal and social transformation are two faces of the same token when it comes to carrying "forward an ever-advancing civilization" under the guidance of the Universal House of Justice.[363]

10. Protecting the Bahá'í Community

No effort was spared by Mas'ud to protect the Faith, both internally

---

[362] *Pioneering and Services of Mas'ud Khamsi,* unpublished manuscript.
[363] Bahá'u'lláh. *Gleanings from the Writings of Bahá'u'lláh.* Wilmette, US Bahá'í Publishing Trust, 1990, p. 215.

and externally. Likewise, with great courage and assertiveness he asserted the validity and strength of the teachings of Bahá'u'lláh to the public. In that, Mas'ud was a lion like his predecessors Siyyid Naṣru'lláh and Siyyid Ahmad, becoming the embodiment of the Tablet of Ahmad verse: "Be thou a flame of fire to My enemies and a river of life eternal to My loved ones".[364]

10.1 Looking after the Youth

The Covenant was a major theme that Mas'ud emphasised in his engagements with the community. There were several occasions when individuals raised themes which were not entirely compatible with the teachings of the Faith. Some of them insisted on their ideas and wanted these to penetrate the community influencing thoughts at the level of culture. Mas'ud was adamant in protecting the community in his role as a Counselor.

The following are some stories narrated by believers revealing Mas'ud's vigilance as a stalwart defender of the Cause.

> Mr Khamsi did not go to the youth meetings on Fridays but he was one of those who was vigilant that these meetings go well. When he named his auxiliary members there was always a young auxiliary member who was there to protect the youth from some Bahá'ís who sometimes wanted to capture the enthusiasm of the youth but with their own ideas. He was always very vigilant. I remember when I was not so young, I was in my twenties, a pioneer arrived with some strange ideas and some very rare quotes from Shoghi Effendi which he said he had found somewhere, and then organized a meeting. Mr Khamsi sent me there so that if he came with rare statements I would challenge his claims and ask for the sources and references. Mr Khamsi was like this, always taking care of the youth.[365]

When the defence of the Cause was at stake, Mr Khamsi's reaction was adamant and acted without any hesitation. On

---

[364] US Bahá'í Publishing Trust. *Bahá'í Prayers: A Selection of Prayers Revealed by Bahá'u'lláh, the Báb, and 'Abdu'l-Bahá*. Wilmette, US Bahá'í Publishing Trust, pp. 208-209, 1991.

[365] Story told by Kiko Sanchez

one occasion, a pioneer organized a deepening seminar about the Teachings. Mr Khamsi, as a Counselor, considered that the study materials for the participants, as well as the display of the images on large posters, were the personal interpretation of the pioneer and not according to the authorized Scriptures of the Faith. After advising the pioneer and given his resistance, Mr Khamsi immediately contacted the Bahá'í institutions at different levels, and based on the instructions received, the seminar was suspended.[366]

Many of the people who entered the Faith in those years did so because they saw it as a group with advanced ideas or as a club where they can travel and get to know different people and places. At a seminar in the Bahá'í Centre where a broad range of contemporary topics were going to be addressed, a certain medical doctor began talking about contraceptive methods and techniques to avoid having more babies and so forth. Mr Khamsi was listening very carefully without interrupting and when he did, very firmly, stood up and turned the address around. He clearly said that "this does not work and let's see what the Bahá'í Faith says in regards to that". He then began talking about the spiritual dimensions of marriage and what the Baha'i Writings and Bahá'u'lláh and 'Abdul-Bahá said. It was the first time that I saw him talking with such firmness that I had not seen before. In other words, he was like a shepherd taking his flock to good pastures.[367]

10.2 Covenant-breaking

Several missions were given to Mas'ud as an Auxiliary Board member for Protection for the Hands in the Western Hemisphere to deal with Covenant-breakers. One of the saddest occasions was when two close friends, with whom he had started mass teaching in Bolivia, had broken the Covenant after the passing of Shoghi Effendi.

Similarly Mas'ud had to deal along with the Hand of the Cause Abu'l-Qásim Faizí with a case of members of a National Spiritual Assembly in South America that had broken the Covenant. "We are following the

---

[366]Story told by Manoucher Shoaie.
[367]Story told by Luis Wong.

agreed steps of meeting" it says in the reports of the Hands in the Holy Land, "and trying to save these people before expelling them from the Faith, in case all, or some, of them because of their inexperience, lack of sufficient knowledge of Covenant-breaking or Covenant-breakers, may have been unduly influenced and will renounce such baseless claims once the situation is clear to them".[368]

When Covenant-Breakers passed through Peru and contacted the media, Mas'ud immediately gathered the youth and the community to advise them:

> One of the many experiences with Mr Khamsi that reinforced my knowledge about the Covenant was when a newspaper published Covenant-breakers' material. Some Bahá'ís received letters from the Covenant-breakers and their letters began to spread. He spoke about the Covenant-breakers directly, openly, and talked about the faithfulness that we should have to the Universal House of Justice. He was very emphatic, talking without hesitations, about the love to 'Abdu'l-Bahá, the love to Shoghi Effendi and the love to the Blessed Beauty. One of the things that Mr Khamsi said very clearly was that the Covenant-breaker "might be a lamb in front of you, telling you by heart Bahá'u'lláh's words but he is a wolf. You have to pay attention to your ears, to any key word that he might say and right there you point". His words were a blessing. He was always protecting the youth from what might come.[369]

10.3 Proclaiming the Faith

Another record documenting how Mas'ud defended the Faith took place at the 1980 Radio Bahá'í Conference that took place at the University of Puno in Peru. Those were the times where Marxist ideas were strong among the students and the country was in political turbulence. It shows how valiant Mas'ud was and how he did not fear defending the Faith, even when there was verbal and physical provocations around him.

---

[368] Bahá'í World Centre. *Ministry of the Custodians: An Account of the Stewardship of the Hands of the Cause 1957-1963.* Haifa, Israel, Bahá'í World Centre, 1992, pp. 375-376.

[369] Story told by Hector Núñez.

A Bahá'í described the incident:

I was in charge of recording the Conference procedures and for the moment I left the post. As I went out I saw a mob outside the university where leftist students like wolves had aggressively surrounded a Baha'i. I asked to talk and I said that I worked for a mining company and knew very well how workers should address each other. I pointed out to them the correct way unions are supposed lead the working class and I even said, "there is no greater abuse today than a worker abused by another worker". Then, I told them, that dignified behaviour is derived from the spirit of man. When I was addressing them, the mob kept shouting and protesting loudly. I said to them: "I can offer you something. I can offer you a meeting with a person who can talk to you about what you are interested in". "Yes, there's no problem", they said. "Well", I said, "just allow me five minutes" and they agreed.

Next, I rushed to the conference hall and I saw Mr Khamsi was sitting at the front with all the counselors. I leaned towards him and said: "Mr Khamsi, there is a group of university students outside, they are like fifty, sixty. Could you talk to them about the Faith?" to which he responded: "Very good, young man, find a room". Therefore I returned to the group of more than sixty students who upon seeing me again began to applaud confrontationally. I told them, "The meeting is going to happen and please let me know which room would you choose right now. Is that okay?" "Yes", they replied very agitated. After choosing the room I went to Mr Khamsi and said: "Everything is ready, the meeting will be here in the main hall of the auditorium".

Mr Khamsi remained on stage with his Auxiliary Board members like a general with his officers. He then established some ground rules because there was still a lot of loud shouting going on. He told the youth leaders who wanted to talk without permission or limits that they were welcome to express their ideas but only for 15 minutes at a time. After that the Bahá'í view would also be presented for 15 minutes and so forth until the subjects had been discussed thoroughly. Several times during the youth leaders' presentations they attempted to dominate and take over the conversation and Mr Khamsi firmly reminded them that their 15-minute period was up and they needed to yield the microphone to the Bahá'ís. The way Mr Khamsi talked to this group of students about communism was excellent. When they started to confront him, Mr Khamsi said, "Do you know communism? Do you know the parents of communism? I do know their land and I know their parents ... "

Mr Khamsi was virtually besieged by all those youth who were shouting their communist slogans at him but with unshakable calm he conversed with solid arguments refuting the questions and challenges put forward to him. He did not shy away from the noise or anything. With a smile and logical proofs he made them aware of the truths of the Faith and the power and capacity of the Bahá'í teachings. He invited them to investigate the Faith. People suddenly became quiet and the noise disappeared. When he finished talking about how the Bahá'í teachings relate to the world, they applauded.

For me, as a youth and a young married man, it was an amazing experience that gave me a lot of confidence of what being a Bahá'í means. It was out of the ordinary seeing Mr Khamsi not only talking about what is a Bahá'í but also about political change and what are its fundamentals. He began talking about change, about the needs of the world and then he talked about the message of Bahá'u'lláh. It was for me a master class of how to teach the Bahá'í Faith.[370]

Dean Stephens, the Radio Bahá'í engineer, commented further about the same occasion:

Then there was Mas'ud the Lion, on the occasion of the radio conference in Puno when the Marxists arrived: "You don't know anything about the Bahá'í Faith, but we know all about your beliefs - and we reject them! Come study the Faith of Bahá'u'lláh with us!" As you no doubt remember, a number of

---

[370] Story told by Hector Núñez.

them did just that.[371]

10.4 The Street Quarrel: A Teaching Story

One day Mr Khamsi went to visit Fernando Schiantarelli, a home front pioneer living in the city of Huancayo in the heart of Andes. Fernando later related an episode that happened during that visit showing Mr Khamsi's capacity in the field of teaching:

> It was Sunday morning and we went for a walk in the city. The weather was perfect. When we got to the main square, we saw a respectable group of people surrounding someone we could not recognise. As there was no rush, the inertia of distracted walking, led us into the crowd. There were about 80 people listening attentively to a man with dark skin and cropped hair who spoke to them with the passion of those who have found the truth and want, not only to share it, but to convince whoever wants to listen to them that their path is the only one path to eternal salvation.
>
> I told Mr Khamsi to keep walking, but he said he wanted to listen. I did not have anything else to listen to either. Who could say no or contradict Mr Khamsi? Not me at least. Mr Khamsi was my spiritual father and he inspired my deepest respect. And respect entails obedience.
>
> From what I could understand after a few minutes of passionate speech, the man was a criminal, converted to Christianity during his stay in prison and that now, he was giving his testimony of how the Bible had rescued him from the wrong path and given himself to salvation. But the path he had travelled was bitter and stormy. Thanks to his powerful tone of voice and well-articulated language, the audience, composed mostly of peasants, listened attentively. It was the version of a police chronicle, but live and with a supposedly happy ending. The man boasted how evil he had been. Of his alcoholism, other addictions and a most exhaustive list of sins that one can imagine. Evidently, he tried to dramatize the advanced degree of his wickedness as an argument to demonstrate the powerful

---

[371] Story provided by K. Dean Stephens. Personal communication to the author.

force of transformation of the message that had saved him and that he now shared with the group.

I turned to my right to see Mr Khamsi, and to my surprise he was no longer with me. I thought he was tired and was gone. But I could not find him either near the group or far in the square. I turned again to the speaker and saw a head of white hair that was a couple of meters away from that impassioned man who tried to convince us that his path was the only one that led to heaven. Suddenly, Mr Khamsi raised his hand as if to ask a question. My survival instinct warned me that we were in trouble.

Mr Khamsi had as usual a distinguished bearing and commanded immediate respect. The speaker, surprising everyone, stopped his passionate speech to attend to that gentleman with neat white hair and well-groomed clothes. "Sir", Mr Khamsi said kindly betraying his foreign accent only on the first syllable. "I have news for you. Christ has already returned, and his name is Bahá'u'lláh".

The speaker did not expect to be interrupted and less so with a message of that nature. A restless murmur was heard among the audience that until then had remained silent out of curiosity or confusion.

While all this was happening I managed to make my way and came to the side of Mr Khamsi. Only then did I realize that the speaker was smaller than he appeared and was on a wooden box that helped him to be more easily seen by the listeners. Mr Khamsi's face exuded tranquillity with a hint of a smile that emphasized the certainty of his words. But the speaker's face lit up immediately and I could see his eyelashes were as daggers.

"According to what the Bible says clearly the return of Christ has already happened. Didn't you know? His name is Bahá'u'lláh". People began to gather stretching their necks not to miss details of what was happening.

"The Antichrist arrived !!!", the speaker proclaimed as if he were a Roman emperor dictating his sentence. Now the man was evidently beside himself and shouted his opposition and rejection of what Mr Khamsi had said. It was blasphemy according to him. Not only that, he came down from the box and advanced directly towards Mr Khamsi until their faces were only a few inches apart. Mr Khamsi did not back down one millimetre.

"What do you say Sir?", the man asked. A group of about 10 individuals, dressed in suits and ties just like the speaker, came out unexpectedly from all sides and surrounded us immediately. The speaker had come with his entourage of apostles. Mr Khamsi was only with me. Now Mr Khamsi's voice and that of the speaker were mixed in a quick exchange of arguments. It was a tremendous altercation of religions showcasing wisdom against fanaticism, from inclusive and harmonic principles against exclusionary and separatist concepts. While they argued with the fervour that fuelled their respective truths, I looked at those surrounding us in case the discussion escalated into violence. It was then when I felt that the presence of Mr Khamsi not only irradiated a transcendent security but an insurmountable shield of protection.

"Let's go" said the speaker after 10 minutes of discussions that had put him on the defensive. One of his entourage lifted the wooden box, breaking the circle of curious entertainers and walking away until they disappeared from the square. The crowd dissolved immediately in whispers.

"Let's go, Fernandini". That's how Mr Khamsi referred to me. His face showed a mischievous smile that only sprouts when someone has the satisfaction of his triumph with the cloak of humility and compassion for the defeated. "Why did you do that, Mr Khamsi? Why did you get into this fight?" I asked. "Fernandini, in the Korán there is a verse that says: "Never believe in those who preach their sins". And so, quietly, we continued our journey, enjoying the good weather and the beautiful city of Huancayo.[372]

---

[372] Story written by Fernando Schiantarelli.

11. Returning to Peru

At the approximate age of 71 years, Mas'ud returned to Peru after serving for ten distinguished years at the International Teaching Centre in Haifa. Despite health problems, he was elected as a member of the National Spiritual Assembly of Peru from Riḍván 1996 to Riḍván 1998. Afterwards he requested not to be elected due to health reasons.

The meetings were held every Saturday and Sunday of each month and used to take ten hours. At the meeting, a member Martin Mansilla recalled, he was "slow and soft and at other times with firmness and great wisdom, due to his age he was fatigued".[373]

11.1 Serving at the National Spiritual Assembly

"Years later, in the mid-nineties", Martin Mansilla recounted his experiences as a young man recently elected as National Secretary, "Mr Khamsi and his wife Jane returned to reside in Peru and I had the honor of sharing with him our administrative service as members of the National Spiritual Assembly. In this important institution of our beloved Faith, I received his support, advice and guidance at various moments of my service as National Secretary".[374]

Mas'ud's personal assistant recalls of those years his spirit of sacrifice:

> Many of the friends do not know that Mr Khamsi came from the Holy Land very exhausted. When I entered his room it was as if you were pouring a bucket of water on him. He was very wet and Jane was constantly cleaning and drying him. This happened many times.

> When Mr Khamsi was elected a member of the National Assembly I said to myself, "the Peruvians have made a big mistake" because of his fragile health. When he was elected a member, he told me, "In any circumstance where I am, on Monday, Wednesday and Friday we have to go to the Secretariat". In this way, Mr Khamsi taught to me about Bahá'í obedience.

---

[373] Story told by Martin Mansilla.
[374] Personal communication to the author.

Mr Khamsi was almost dead in bed but I had to obey. I would cry until I had no tears left to the thought of reminding him to go to the National Centre. When Jane was not in the bedroom I would whisper in his ears, "Mr Khamsi, Mr Khamsi", and he would say to me "Yes, Mr Conrado, I hear you". I would say, "Mr Khamsi, we have to go to the Secretariat" but when I saw Jane coming I would run away because I felt guilty that I was generating him more pain. Next Mr Khamsi would ask his wife, "Jane, please bring my suit". And Jane, being a responsible wife, would reprimand him. I would hide somewhere and Jane would call me, "Mr Conrado, please persuade Mas'ud not to go to the Bahá'í National Center given his conditions". Giving up, Jane would finally say quite upset at him, "if you want to go to the National Centre, then go..." Mr Khamsi would call me to help him dress. I had to take him on my shoulders, carry him and I would sit him in his car. I also had to put his feet on the clutch and on the accelerator. It was like he was driving but he was not driving, giving me the impression that a higher force was driving instead.[375]

As National Assembly member Mas'ud had the opportunity of participating in the eighth 1998 International Bahá'í Convention at the advanced age of 76 years. Azam Matin, another National Assembly member said:

> I always looked at Mr Khamsi as someone who has been here for a long time. When I looked at him, I was thinking of ourselves staying here for a long time and growing old like him, in this place where sometimes one is experiencing a different culture and is far away. Mr Khamsi was in all Bahá'í activities but actually as a person he was alone, because you usually have your classmates, from your neighborhood, when you grow up, you have your circle that you meet from time to time. In that way, I saw Mr Khamsi alone. Then we went to the Holy Land together in 1998 for the International Convention. One day I found him talking with a group of people like him, they were people of his time, from his environment. It gave me such

---

[375] Story told by Conrado Rodriguez.

a joy that tears came out. I really thought that here is where Mr Khamsi belongs, and what patience he had to live in Peru for so many years. Of course, one has a general love for humanity but there is another love by affinity that you have with your own people. And that's what I think he lacked. When I saw him in that state I became very happy.[376]

Mas'ud, at the age of almost 80 years, attended the inauguration of the terraces around the Shrine of the Báb in which another participant witnessed:

I recall during the opening of the Terraces in Haifa Mr Khamsi (June 2001) came in a wheelchair and carried a cane. At the end of the ceremony the friends began to walk up the steps to the Shrine of the Báb. Mrs Khadem was also sitting nearby in a wheel chair. She said, "Too bad I am too old to climb the steps, but it is just a joy to be here and be part of the occasion". But Mr Khamsi jumped out of his wheel chair and began climbing, with the aid of his cane and a friend [his son Gary]. When Mrs Khadem saw that she jumped out of her chair and said, "If Mas'ud is going to climb up, so will I!"[377]

"I was surprised that he got up and asked me to help him", said Gary Khamsi, "and although we did not speak when we were climbing up so he did not lose energy, I imagined that each step forward was like every mountain in the Andes that he went up to reach the indigenous people who he loved so much. And he reached the top, just as he reached the people's hearts in areas so remote and difficult to reach".[378]

11.2 Generosity

Generosity was one of the virtues that Mas'ud learned from his ancestors Siyyid Naṣru'lláh and Siyyid Ahmad, as Bahá'u'lláh extolled His followers: "To give and to be generous are attributes of Mine;

---

[376]Story told by Azam Matin.
[377]Story provided by David Walker.
[378]Personal communication to the author.

well is it with him that adorneth himself with My virtues".³⁷⁹ Mas'ud's personal assistant stated:

> Many people came to his house looking for help especially material assistance. Mr Khamsi always said that if he cannot receive them personally then his advisor would. He was obviously referring to me, that I was going to talk to them. Many people came with some requests almost demanding to talk to Mr Khamsi. However, Mr Khamsi told me that "I cannot show up because I'm not feeling well" and therefore they have talk to me. Mr Khamsi had a safe where he entrusted me with money and envelopes. He said to me, "Mr Conrado, some people are coming, Bahá'ís and non- Bahá'ís, here is the money and the envelopes. You see how much you can support them". I let them know that such monies were the result of Mr Khamsi's hard work during his life and now he is retired. However, I told them that he is not a charity. A Jewish friend came on one occasion and Mr Khamsi said to me, "you see how you help him" … that money was sacred, because he had earned it in his lifetime with so much effort.³⁸⁰

Although Mas'ud worked all his life, "His admiration for the Guardian was limitless and he always made of his life what he thought the Guardian wanted him to do. All his life was dedicated to the service of the Faith. If Mr. Khamsi put some business, it was to survive but he was not interested in it. His main interest was always in serving the Faith, there was nothing else in his life but to serve the Faith",³⁸¹ a believer said. His daughter added, "He really wanted to be free to only teach, especially among the Indians and the youth".³⁸² Mas'ud certainly lived for the Faith.

11.3 External Affairs

From his great-uncle Siyyid Naṣru'lláh and his father Siyyid Ahmad,

---

³⁷⁹Bahá'u'lláh. The Hidden Words of Bahá'u'lláh. Wilmette, US Bahá'í Publishing Trust, p. 39, 1985.

³⁸⁰Story provided by Conrado Rodriguez. Personal communication to the author?

³⁸¹Kiko Sanchez, personal communication to the author.

³⁸²Dorothy Khamsi-Samandari, personal communication to the author.

Mas'ud must had learned the importance of approaching prominent people. During his services throughout Latin America we can see him meeting high government officials and diplomats. He was aware of the need to make the Faith known to prominent people. For instance, a Bahá'í traveller teacher recalled the following encounter with a leading politician who had recently been elected president of Peru's Assembly of the Constituent in charge of writing a new constitution.

> After a teaching trip to the Amazon in October 1978, we brought a Bahá'í indigenous couple to Lima to be present at the meeting that took place with the president of the congress Victor Raul Haya de la Torre. At the interview, dear Counselor Mas'ud Khamsi told the President of the Parliament that he was aware that he was a follower of Zoroaster, which the president confirmed. He said "you Bahá'ís come to support and not to ask like most religious groups do. You are like white doves and please continue going to those places that we can not reach". Our Counselor was aware of all information on a world level of which the President was himself surprised.[383]

President de la Torre also said "I receive with much sympathy this visit," be said, "because it represents ideals that we also profess, even though imperfectly ...". According to *Bahá'í News*, "President de la Torre was impressed with the diversity of the Bahá'í delegation that included young and old, men and women, Indians and whites, villagers and city people."[384]

"His services in Lima when he returned from the Holy Land", says Azam Matin, "were in the field of external affairs". Mr Khamsi was always concerned about external affairs in order to create bonds of fellowship to demonstrate the greatness of the Bahá'í Faith. He invited ambassadors and personalities to his home. The ambassador of Israel was one of his friends along with the Peruvian diplomat Juan Alvarez Vita who once was the United Nations representative to oversee the situation of the Bahá'ís in Iran.[385]

---

[383] Story provided by Carlos Nunez.
[384] Bahá'í News, issue 576, March 1979.
[385] Story provided by Azam Matin.

Moojan Matin added:

Mr Alvarez Vita was very close to Mr Khamsi. He was sent by the United Nations to observe the situation in Iranian prisons. He told us once that he was not very successful because they would not let him in, they would take him to better prisons, or cover-up the situation. Following this, Azam and I managed to have a friendship with this man until now.[386]

Mas'ud was also a friend of the officials for the Ministries of Foreign Affairs and Justice and Human Rights and many others whom he invited to his home together with representatives of the National Assembly, such as the former Counselor Isabel de Sanchez. "We learned from him", said Moojan Matin, "because of Mr Khamsi's experience we keep having many similar initiatives".[387]

11.4 Last Years

He continued to have an extensive flow of correspondence till the end of his life. One day, as his personal assistant recalled, over 150 letters arrived to his home to which Mas'ud remarked: "Let's respond to the friends". Even with a line but he felt he had to respond to all. The same person remembers Mas'ud emotional intelligence and affection: "He could read my soul as soon as I arrived to his home. He used to observe me carefully and sense if something was bothering me. We used to go to his room to have tea. Sometimes, before serving tea, he pointed at his legs and making a sound with his hands. I knew it that I had to put my head on his lap and he began to caress my head and hair saying: "Do not worry, who does not have problems in life?".[388]

As he was aging Mas'ud's mobility slowed down. Very often he had to stay in bed and later lived in a nursing home, fragile and with failing memory, where he used to receive the Bahá'ís. His spark had not diminished though. A visitor leaving his room recalled Mas'ud telling him jockingly, "Please close the door from outside".

"In the last years when Mr Khamsi could not read anymore", Azam

---

[386] Story told by Moojan Matin.
[387] Story told by Azam Matin.
[388] Story told by Conrado Rodriguez.

Matin remembers, "he asked us to go to his house to read for him Payyam-i-Bahá'í the Persian magazine from France. Whenever we went to his home we used to read magazines, books, all in Persian, for him".[389]

Mas'ud had a profound and ineffable affection for the land of the Incas. According to a friend:

> His love for Peru and the Peruvian community were genuine. On more than one occasion he said, "Peru is my pioneer post and here is where I want to be buried. I'm never going to leave Peru". When he went to the Holy Land, he said he was there for a specified period only, but his purpose was to return to Peru and finish here the rest of his life. He could have gone to live overseas with one of his children. But he did not want to. He wanted to die here in Peru which was his pioneering post.[390]

Mas'ud Khamsi passed away on 5 March 2013 in Lima at the age of 91 years of age. As a binding testimonial of love and gratitude, he was buried with a prayer book in his hands containing innumerous names of believers and communities with whom Mas'ud associated in life and served together. The International Centre wrote of this legacy: "He will long be remembered for his steadfast devotion, humility, and warm sense of humour, as well as his love for the youth and indigenous peoples, whom he cherished and constantly encouraged". [391]

After a vigil at the National Haziratu'l-Quds he was laid to rest during the Fast, at sunset, with prayers in Spanish and Persian at the Huachipa cemetery.[392] What better resting place than at the heart of the Andes mountains which he loved so much, where his long-life friend Hand of the Cause Rahmatu'lláh Muhajir is also interred, the scene of the magnificent services he promised silently once to the Guardian of the Faith exactly 60 years before at the Holy Land. Five years later, Jane "joyously reunited her beloved husband, Mas'ud

---

[389] Story told by Azam Matin.

[390] Story told by Kiko Sanchez.

[391] Letter from the International Teaching Centre to the Continental Board of Counsellors in the Americas dated 8 March 2013.

[392] In Quechua, *a household divinity*

Khamsi, in the Abhá Kingdom".[393],[394]

To pay tribute to such a brilliant soul that never put an end to his services the Universal House of Justice emailed all National Spiritual Assemblies on 7 March 2013:

> Our hearts were grieved to learn of the passing of dearly loved, stalwart promoter of the Faith of Bahá'u'lláh, Mas'úd Khamsí, whose long record of distinguished service we recall with such admiration. In 1957, in response to the goals of the Guardian's Ten Year Crusade, he left Iran as a pioneer to South America, participating in some of the earliest efforts to reach its highly receptive indigenous populations. Following his return to Iran, he was appointed to the first contingent of Continental Counselors in 1968 as a member of the Board for Western Asia. He departed once again for South America within months and, for the next fourteen years, served as a Counselor in that continent. In 1983 he was appointed as a member of the International Teaching Centre, in which capacity he laboured for a decade. His endeavours thereafter continued unabated, even at an advanced age. In every service he rendered—in the treks he undertook on foot from village to village across vast mountain ranges; in his efforts to encourage young people; in the travels he pursued, bringing his zeal for teaching to some of the remotest parts of the globe—he displayed a generosity of spirit, a warmth of heart, and a determination and courage that were borne of utter consecration and complete loyalty to the Cause of Bahá'u'lláh. We extend our deepest sympathy to his dear wife, Jane, his children, and other members of his family and assure them of our fervent supplications at the Sacred Threshold for the progress of his devoted soul in the realms of God. We advise the holding of befitting memorial gatherings in his honour in all Houses of Worship and in Bahá'í communities throughout the world.

---

[393] Letter from the Universal House of Justice to the National Spiritual Assembly of the Baha'is of the United States dated 28 December 2018.

[394] Jane passed away in Miami surrounded by her family at the age of 96 on 22 December 2018.

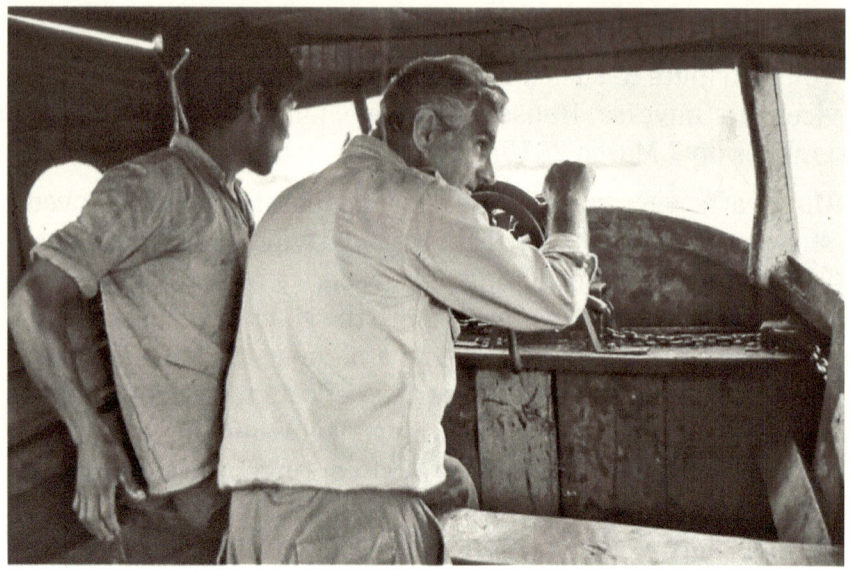

Figure 31: At the Green Light Expedition.
Source: The American Bahá'í Archives.

Figure 32: Leonora Armstrong, Spiritual Mother of
South America, Amatu'l-Bahá Rúhíyih Khánum and
Counselors at the Lopez residence.
Courtesy: Vicente Lopez.

Figure 33: In a Bolivian village with Amatu'l-Bahá Rúhíyih Khánum.
Source: The American Bahá'í Archives.

Figure 34: El Viento Canta.
Source: Bahá'í World Centre.

Figure 35: Hand of the Cause Amatu'l-Bahá Rúhíyih Khánum, members of the Universal House of Justice Mr Ali Nakhjavani, Mr Borrah Kavelin and Dr David Ruhe with El Viento Canta team and the Peruvian Ambassador and wife at Mr and Mrs Khamsi's home in Haifa in 1988.
Source: Rolando Cortes

Figure 36: Consulting with the National Spiritual Assembly of Peru.
Source: Bahá'í Peruvian National Archives.

Figure 37: In a summer school in Lima next to
Eve Nicklin (centre), Spiritual Mother of Peru.
Source: Bahá'í Peruvian National Archives.

Figure 38: At the inauguration of Radio Bahá'í of Lake Titicaca in Peru in 1981. Mas'ud Khamsi is standing on the left hand side. Andres Jachakollo is sitting on the front row second from the left.
Courtesy: Mehran Manie

Figure 39: Members of the International Teaching Centre featuring the Hands of the Cause of God Amatu'l-Bahá Rúhíyih Khánum and Ali Akbar Furutan (front row, third and fourth from right).
Mr Khamsi is standing second on the back row.

Figure 40: Mr Khamsi with Hand of the Cause of God 'Alí-Akbar Furútan. Courtesy: Iran Furutan

APPENDIX 1:
The Robbery, a Green Light Expedition Story[395]

Here is a small story woven into a much larger and exquisite tapestry: Rúhíyyih Khánum and the Green Light Expedition in the last phase of their journey into the Southern Andes of Peru and Bolivia.

Rúhíyyih Khánum's historic visit to our pioneering post woven into a gracious anecdote of Mr Khamsi on the last leg of the Green Light Expedition in Peru and Bolivia.

So, we lived in Puno, Peru. Patricia and myself with our two daughters Sandra and Ridvan. We were pioneering there during the 5-Year Plan from 1975 to 1980. This was also the time when the historic Green Light Expedition led by Amatu'l-Bahá Rúhíyyih Khánum and a group of a dozen or less special companions who were in charge of filming, sound tracking, writing, logistical, financial arrangements, interpreting, public relations, and many other technical and practical support functions. During this leg of a long expedition which began at the base of the Orinoco river in Venezuela winding its way south-west to the Amazon Basin in Peru, into the Amazon river and up other important tributaries leading west; over land and into the Eastern slopes of the Andes rising 5-6 thousand meters above sea level, and then over the top and down the western slopes to the fertile valleys and breadbaskets of Peru's major population centres, namely, the Pacific coastal region and Atacama desert where the Capital City of Lima with around 4-5 million inhabitants (circa 1975) is situated and half-a-dozen cities of a quarter-million or more at that time, north and south of Lima along a littoral more than 2 thousand kilometres long. Once the Expedition reached Arequipa, Peru's second largest city in the highlands of the Southern Andes, the Expedition climbed aboard

---

[395]Story told by John and Pati Kepner.

the old British built train up and over the Andes on the western slopes and arrived at the desolate Altiplano (high plains) city of Juliaca in the State of Puno. This dusty and windy city is about 250 kilometres north of Peru's furthermost southern-highland border with Bolivia.

Here is where my story begins and how it weaves its way through a much larger story involving the Hand of the Cause of God Amatu'l-Bahá Rúhíyyih Khánum, Counselor Ruth Pringle (nutritionist and companion of the Hand of the Cause during the expedition) and Counselor Masu'd Khamsi, personal friend of the Hand and in charge of all financial and logistical arrangements for the Hand of the Cause and the entire expedition's camera crew, who were filming and documenting this incredible journey from the jungles of South America and now well into the high desert plains of the Andes surrounding the highest navigable lake in the world, the majestic deep blue Lake Titicaca at 3,835 meters above sea level.

The provincial capital of Puno, nestled on the shores of this huge lake (8,300 square kilometres) about the size of Puerto Rico. It shares with Bolivia its uncontaminated water (in 1975), whose reported depths in its centre are fathomless; fed by myriad streams from the towering Andes mountain range completely surrounding the lake and sustained by glacial melt. This lake up until a few decades ago was navigable by two British built steam ships that were shipped to the coastal port of Iquique in Northern Chile, disassembled there and transported on the back of mules over the Andes to Lake Titicaca's shores at Puno. A Peruvian government naval base was established there around the same time. The two ships (El Ollanta and El Inca) were assembled on dry dock and introduced into the frigid waters of its new home in the Andes. When Rúhíyyih Khánum learned of this story she became extremely interested in crossing the lake from Puno to the Bolivian port of Huaqui, where a bilateral agreement between the two countries enabled a British built short-train to pick up passengers and take them on their final ride across the flat Altiplano to the deep seated Capital City of La Paz situated on the slopes of an enormous "bowl" drastically cut out of the Andes by millennia of erosion; a drop which takes you from 4 200 meters above sea level in El Alto, a town of a quarter of a million Indigenous inhabitants at the time circling atop the bowl, to altitudes of 3 400 meters after cris-crossing down roads and zig-zag train tracks to the city's depot near the centre. Then beyond the train and railways, along other city roads leading straight down to 2 800 meters at the southern depths of the bowl, where most foreign embassies are located along with golf courses, the famous Valley of the Moon, and a more elite residential environment.

So, as the only pioneers living in Puno at the time of the Green Light's arrival, we were notified by the NSA of Peru to accommodate them the best we could. We were informed that they would be arriving on Monday morning. It was 1975 (can't remember month or numerical day). They would be arriving to Juliaca by train from Arequipa. We knew this was a train that travelled all night (12 hours) and arrived at dawn to Juliaca. It then unloaded passengers there, refuelled and an hour later departed for the city of Puno only 50 kms away which took the same train another hour to reach. Up to this date, I do not know how or why we decided to pick them up in Juliaca or if it was their idea or that of the NSA. My guess is that there was a feeling that they had better get to their hotels quickly after having spent the whole night on a slow train climbing the Andes and getting higher and higher every hour. The altitude, as anyone who has travelled to these levels knows fully well, can be harsh on one's body within the first 24 hours by causing what they locally refer to as "sorochi" or altitude sickness. We did not have to worry about the Hand of the Cause and her companion Counselor Ruth Pringle. They were to fly up to Juliaca later that morning. I would pick them up after leaving the crew at their hotels. We were mostly concerned about getting the Hand of the Cause to her hotel in Puno for rest and medicinal herbs and teas that would comfort her stomach, together with some light and controlled meals which Pati prepared for her. All of this allowed her to relax for a few days before crossing the lake on her dreamed of voyage on steam ship Ollanta. The latter left Puno only once a week on Wednesdays at 9 pm and arrived at 7 am to Huaqui on the Bolivian side.

I remember arriving in my Toyota Land Cruiser to Juliaca shortly after the train's arrival from Arequipa. It was around dawn. When I arrived at the platform, I found the Green Light Expedition members scattered everywhere walking up and down or sitting close by their equipment and suitcases. Mr Khamsi who was in charge of the group in the absence of Rúhíyyih Khánum was nowhere in sight. A few minutes later he arrived. He had hurried off minutes before in search of his briefcase which had been stolen from him just before he got down from the train when he realized it was gone. He arrived empty handed. The thief had a gotten away. Inside the briefcase was his passport, important documents and a considerable amount of money. He was the administrator and financial officer of the Expedition, appointed by Rúhíyyih Khánum. Needless to say he was upset and asked me if I could take him to the airport soon so he could fly back to Lima, get a new passport and replenish the funds he needed for the rest of the Expedition's journey. This would take a few days and he told me to take charge of the travel logistics and funding and that he would catch up with us in Bolivia. I remember feeling pretty bad thinking that maybe my late arrival to the train station as they waited for me to pick them up at the side of the train, might have been the reason his briefcase was stolen. I remember mentioning this to him with a heavy heart. He assured me however that it had been stolen from inside the train as the train was arriving as everyone began standing and crowding the aisles removing their suitcases and belongings from the overhead racks.

There were so many suitcases and camera equipment that it literally filled up the entire Land Cruiser. I did have space however for Mr Khamsi up front. The rest of the crew members took taxis and we all proceeded to Puno. I dropped Mr Khamsi off at a hotel where he could get cleaned up and make a reservation for his urgent trip that same morning to Lima. The plane from Arequipa with Rúhíyyih Khánum and Ruth Pringle on board would be arriving to Juliaca around 10 am. I would be there with Mr Khamsi to receive them and for them to bid farewell to him as he boarded the same plane back to Arequipa and then on to Lima.

Fast forward a week to the high mountainous village of Sacaca in the State of Potosi, Bolivia. This is where Rúhíyyih Khánum was invited by the NSA of Bolivia to meet with the Community and hundreds of Indigenous believers from all over the Andes of Bolivia. It was my unbelievable honour to drive (12 hrs.) and escort Rúhíyyih Khánum from Puno to El Alto (gateway to La Paz at 4,200 Mts. above sea level) where there was an official escort by the NSA to take her to her hotel in the centre of La Paz city. We accompanied her all the way to her hotel and got to carry her bags and accommodate her and Ruth in their room. After she got settled in her room, I received a call on the lobby phone. It was Rúhíyyih Khánum asking me to come to her room with a bunch of different alpaca wall hangings of the Greatest Name which she had seen in Puno as we passed by the Artisan's home and workshop to pick them up and take them to Bolivia for the big conference in Sacaca. I was hopeful I could sell them to friends whom I knew would appreciate the skilled artisan's work (as did Rúhíyyih Khánum), native materials designed and crafted into beautiful wall hangings of the Greatest Name of God.

So, once in her room with a fellow Bahá'í pioneer and friend of mine James Selph who she specifically asked for me to bring along, she greeted us and told Jim, "I understand you are a black-belt in Aikido? This impresses me a lot. I also know you are an Auxiliary Board member. To be honest, I am most impressed with your achievements as a black belt". This raised some smiling faces in the room. Apparently, she was interested in having Jim teach her some Aikido moves. I remember hearing her say she was currently taking some Yoga classes. I believe they talked about this subject awhile as I began to unpack my wall hangings at her request. She then asked me to place the hangings on the wall and to hold them there while she observed them and consulted with Ruth about their looks, sizes and the particulars of each one. She then chose one that she liked best and she told me she was planning on placing it in the room of the Guardian at Bahji. She mentioned that she wanted to do this because of the great love the Guardian had for the Indigenous peoples of the Andes. As we know, these same people who she was going to meet with the following day in Sacaca were the Indigenous people who began to enter the Faith in troops while the Guardian was still living in 1957 during the 10 Year Crusade. She mentioned how this entry by troops of the Quechua and Aymara peoples of Bolivia gladdened his heart so very much.

Fast forward to Sacaca the following day and an incredibly magnificent occasion of unity, song, dance and prayer high in the Andes. Rúhíyyih Khánum was escorted to the village where the event took place. She spoke to the heart and inspired the friends deeply. At the end of the day, Pati and I were asked to escort her back to where the 4 wheel drive vehicles were waiting, about an hour or so from where they left her in the morning to reach the village on horseback. As we were approaching the vehicles with Rúhíyyih Khánum atop her horse and riding majestically like a Queen through the Altiplano with magnificent snow covered mountains behind her, with Pati carrying our daughter Sandra in her arms walking along side our Queen and I on the other side also walking alongside her, Mr Khamsi appears out of nowhere and walks toward us with a huge smile on his face. As soon as Rúhíyyih Khánum sees him she shouts out a joyful "Oh Masu'd! Oh Mas'ud!" Mr Khamsi approaches her and greets her joyfully and raises his hands. It is here that we all realized that he had a brand new briefcase chained with a lock to his wrist. This caused Rúhíyyih Khánum to heartily laugh out loud and we all joined in the laughter.

APPENDIX 2:
The Green Light Expedition Film Narrative (extracts)

As narrated orally by Amatu'l-Bahá Rúhíyyih Khánum.[396,397]

Our journey began in Caracas [Venezuela]. This was a fulfilment of a long cherished dream of mine to visit the Indians of South America. I asked the Counselor from South America, Mas'ud Khamsi, to be our business manager and Dr Nosrat Rabbani my lady companion and the medical advisor of the expedition. My expedition also included four young Bahá'ís, experts in filmmaking, Mark Sedan and David Walker, from the United States, Rodney Charters from New Zealand, and Anthony Worley from Brazil. From Caracas, we flew to Puerto Ayacucho, the capital of the Federal Territory of Amazonas.

Venezuela - the Amazonas

The small Bahá'í community of Puerto Ayacucho met us at the airport and helped us load our provisions onto the truck. It took us over an hour to reach Venado a huge flat hunk of rock into the Orinoco river. This is the place where all traffic above Puerto Ayacucho leaves for the interior. Some weeks previous to our arrival, Mr Khamsi had rented a large river barge which was waiting for us and for our 60 pieces of equipment, baggage and provisions.

This was the ship that was going to take us 1700 km to visit 8 different Indian tribes in the interior. This is to be our home for 32 nights and we named her the Queen Mary. The little white room at the

---

[396] Amatu'l-Bahá Rúhíyyih Khánum Mary Sutherland Maxwell. *The Green Light Expedition*. 1975. Video available on YouTube: https://www.youtube.com/watch?v=pW4qAmfpjG8

[397] Narrative transcribed with the assistance of Jim Jensen and Jamshid Ardjomandi.

back was our bathroom.

On the Venezuelan part of our journey we were accompanied throughout by Leco Zamora, a Mataco Indian pioneer from Argentina. Every evening our boat was moored on a sand bank for the night. Our first job in the morning was to roll up our hammocks and get them out of the way. Life aboard the Queen Mary was in no way difficult. In fact, the only real inconvenience were the black flies which in this particular moment were so vicious that I wore my mosquito net hat.

Wonderful as the water was for drinking it was usually very dangerous to swimming. The Indians always seemed to know where is safe to go in and our captain strongly advised the men that they should only bathe from the rocks. We soon found out why. I caught three man-eating piranha fish in less than two minutes.

Every morning we held prayers for the success of our expedition and that we would be guided to do the right thing and meet the right people during the day. Along the Orinoco River and also in the neighbourhood of Puerto Ayacucho itself there are great many Bahá'í communities. Some of them are over ten years standing. This is the Bahá'í community of Buenos Aires Island. These people have been Bahá'ís for around twelve years.

Over and over again after we had had prayers we found that the door would open in the most remarkable ways for us to meet the people that we wanted to see.

These Piuroa Indians invited us to their village, as it was an hour's walk from the river they agreed to come back and take us there the following morning. The Indians invited us to hold a meeting in the local schoolhouse and to tell them about our teachings. I am very happy that I could come and see them.

In the whole Amazonian Territory of Venezuela the most important town after Puerto Ayacucho is San Fernando which was founded over 200 years ago by missionaries and was very much like an old fashioned colonial town. Although I do not attend church services I like very much when I am travelling to go into churches to pray that the people of the area in which I am travelling and teaching, may be guided to the message of Bahá'u'lláh.

Three days later we reached Laventa Rosa which to our own joy we discovered it as an entirely Bahá'í village. These people have migrated up to the river and taken enough land and established themselves. They took us and showed us where they planned to build their local Bahá'í Centre. They had already set aside this piece of land with this object in view.

Now we entered the Bentuari which is much narrower and shallower than the Orinoco. Because of this, we found that we very often got grounded on sandbars and it was necessary for all of us to get out and push. The captain took no more chances and picked the channel himself very carefully.

Yuca, which is known in other countries as cassava or manioc. It is the universal staple of the Indians throughout South America in the jungles. It is prepared by roasting the flour over a pan. We found the Indians extraordinarily friendly people. If you met them with an open heart and a friendly spirit you immediately received the same response. We were able in many of the villages to purchase papayas, bananas and even fresh eggs.

As our boat could not navigate in the shallow waters of the tributaries, we hired a dugout canoe and installed our own outboard motor, and used it for side trips.

We made a special trip up the Manapiare river to visit the growing town of San Juan of Manapiare. Our first view of the town was this huge garbage heap on the shores. San Juan is the government outpost and an active centre for missionaries. It is now linked to civilization by a new road. We met two Americans who belonged to an Evangelical group called The New Tribes Mission. One of them had just flown in for a visit to see how the work was progressing. The other had lived in Venezuela with his wife and children for over 20 years.

We also met the Catholic father, a Jesuit priest from Spain. Although we admire in many ways the work of the missionaries we were greatly troubled by the evidences of what our civilization does. To me the great tragedy is that if we Bahá'ís don't hurry up and go out and teach these people while there is still time they will go down into that same valley of shadow, so to speak, that we went down into. I look it at this way, here are the primitive people, the tribal people, the villagers, the simple people, the illiterate people, that are so much nicer and friendly for the human standpoint so much better, more spiritual in many cases that we are. And this is the culture and civilization of Bahá'u'lláh that will come in with the new world order as it develops and it has to come in the future. Now, the youth of today, our youth, are beginning to come out of this valley of materialism and climb up towards this new world order. They are beginning to reject so much of what we have in the world today, this materialism. But these people want to have everything that there is in the 20thcentury, which is perfectly natural. So they have to come forward; they have nowhere to go else except forward into the progress of our century and our way of living but if they could come forward as Bahá'ís, if they can become Bahá'ís in their own culture now, in their own villages, in their own civilization so to speak, then to me, they will be lifted from this mountain over to that mountain. They won't have to go down to the valley of the shadow the way we have. That is the whole urgency. In my mind that is the reason why if we don't get up go out and teach this people every hour that passes we are losing all our opportunities, and these will never come again. They, instead of having all of this suffering and disillusionment and corruption and bitterness they can come with all their wonderful qualities to this height, they can fly over in other words instead of crawling down into that valley and coming up to the top.

And I think that's what Bahá'ís have to realize that there isn't time. Every day we are losing ground we see it here on this river, you see how people are changing all the time. Wherever the touch of civilization comes, it withers. They lose their identity are no longer interested in spiritual values to the degree that they were before they began to become, so to speak, semi-civilized and go down into the bog of the very civilization that is destroying us and we want to get rid of it.

The people themselves of the tribes talk to their own people, more clearly, better, more concisely than we do, but the pioneers have prestige. When we go with Leco, Leco can teach better. We help Leco to teach because they say he's come with all these people, from this very civilization we want to save them from wasting their time, so to speak. The two, the two together, that's the key to the whole situation.

We met a Piaroa Chief. We invited him aboard our boat to have coffee. He said that fifteen years before he would have been afraid to go on a boat that was owned by white men. ... this shows how much people are changing. It also shows how the spirit of the Bahá'ís gives people confidence. He was a widower whose wife had died when their last child was born and he was bringing up a group of small children himself. The attachment of the children to the father and the extraordinary tenderness that he showered upon his children was very, very touching and very indicative of the nature of the Indians. We discovered that eight years ago the Piaroa Chief was already in contact with some of the Bahá'ís ... If a man such as this accepts Bahá'u'lláh's teachings he will not only be a very fine believer but instrumental in bringing in many, many of his people into the Cause of God.

The Makos as a tribe have never been converted to Christianity. We were fortunate to meet their more important chief, who called a meeting to hear about the Faith.

We are not missionaries but we have a very wonderful message, and this lady said we should tell this to our head chief. And this is a very good thing she said. We believe also that great respect should be shown to the *capitanes* whoever they are and wherever there are ... To the degree to which they are interested and want to ask any questions to that degree we tell them of our beliefs and the purpose of our trip. It was not our purpose to force it on them.

Finally we reached the waterfalls at Tangua. This was the furthest the Queen Mary could go. We were told that beyond the falls, there was an island called Monotiti where we could contact one of the most interesting and primitive tribes in Venezuela and Brazil called the Yanomamos. We walked about thirty kilometres on this one trip. It was the longest walk of my entire life. The Yanomamo Indians have the custom of sucking a plug of tobacco stuck in their lower lip.

Fundamentally, unity in diversity which is such a strong principle in the Bahá'í Teachings means that we are all alike and are all different. One feels one's human kinship with people. At least one should feel it and if one doesn't feel it, then there is something wrong with you, that you don't feel it, because it is there. But, it presupposes not having the concept that those people are different from you, far from you, alien from you, you have to think that those people are human beings just like me. One has to have the sense that these people, that the other person is loved by Bahá'u'lláh and I hope that Bahá'u'lláh loves me. That we all belong to God, that His love is a portion to all men irrespective of race, irrespective of education, irrespective of advantages or disadvantages.

You don't necessarily have to speak a person's language to have a bond of understanding. That can be something that you feel between each other and I have felt it many times with people with whom I couldn't be speaking one single word.

If we don't let the Bahá'ís know the needs of these people, if they don't see the faces of these wonderful people, their simplicity, that they are between two worlds and no longer in the old world of their tribe which is a good existence and they had the dignity and the nobility of their customs and are not in our world, because nobody loves them, and nobody really cares for them and nobody respects them. These are the kinds of people all over the world that we have to teach the Cause of God to. These wonderful people that are out in the jungles, in the savannahs, in the deserts of the world, we have to go and teach them. And it is very, very difficult for people to understand them if they don't see them that the beauty of their faith, their politeness to us, their patience, their kindness, was a very wonderful experience to me to be with these people. Of all the tribes' people that we have met on this trip, these are the ones that I like the best. Because so far these are the least touched by western civilization.

Shoghi Effendi said we have a cancerous materialism. It eats away at the very flesh of the bones of the spirits of men and we have been devoured by it in our civilization. These people when they are touched by it, it destroys them. Then how can the Bahá'ís ignore the fact that these are the ones that we have to teach. This is the next, to me, the next great step in the progress of the religion of God is to teach these people, it's of supreme importance.

Suriname – The Bush Negroes

The second part of our trip took place in Suriname where we went to visit the Bush Negroes. This lake was created by flooding the whole valley. We arrived at the village of Redi Doti. It was almost like returning to Africa to come to a Bush Negro village. The Bush Negroes are a very independent people who have preserved their African heritage in the New World. Their ancestors were brought as slaves. They ran away into the jungle and established their African way of life and were never recaptured. No Bahá'ís have been into the interior before to visit the Bush Negroes. This young man is a student in Paramaribo who invited us to come to his village. These are his grandparents. The Bush Negroes are the cleanest people that I have ever met in any part of the world including my own part.

A great many of the Bush Negroes still follow the old pagan religion of Africa. Many of the homes have a small shrine in front of them to protect the people from evil spirits. Voodoo as it is called in our part of the world, JuJu as it is called in West Africa, means magic. Sometimes the people held religious services of their own which we did not intrude upon. The headman, or captain of the village, very kindly placed their meeting hall at our disposal – and we were able to live in it during the period of our visit to Reddi Dotie.

The thing that is interesting to me is what percentage of the Bush Negroes are still pagan because this is mostly a pagan village. Obviously it is full of pagan shrines and they are very attached to the spirit world and to a spiritual world. What they need is to connect this with a living religion without superstition. This is the way one has to teach in Africa, the people have to slowly give up their fears because a great deal of the religion is based on fear and superstition.

To me the best example we are ever going to get out is that it is like a building that is wired electrically. Now the current is in the wall. If I want to plug in a huge electric saw in a factory I can do so and it uses thousands of watts. If I want to plug in only a ten-watt bulb and I make the organic connection because the power is in the walls. Now, this is what the Bahá'ís don't realize. When a villager, who is ignorant and illiterate and everything else, when he accepts the Faith of Bahá'u'lláh, he is making a tiny perhaps organic connection with reality. Now supposing an atom bomb comes they are killed and we are killed and everybody is killed in one second. Do we as Bahá'ís believe that those people that accepted Bahá'u'lláh are in exactly the same condition as those people who didn't? This is not in accordance with any religious teaching in the whole world.

Well, the point is to bring your receptacle to the ocean of truth and whatever the size of it is, fill it. So, this is the point, if a man has a huge receptacle and he fills it with one teaspoon for what use is it? But if he only has a tiny little cup and he fills it brimming over, this in the sight of God is much more important and it's right in Bahá'u'lláh's own Words in the Gleanings. But they think because they are educated, and big and wealthy and important, and they have condescended to accept the Revelation of Bahá'u'lláh that they have filled themselves and are that big worthy, so to speak; when maybe they've only got a teaspoon full of service and of devotion and a poor little man that only has the capacity of a teaspoon, he's filled his teaspoon brimming over. And personally I believe that the teaspoon in the sight of God is more important than a half empty container of somebody who has much more capacity.

On the second part of our visit to the Bush Negros we flew over the Suriname river on our way to Boto Passi. We loaded all our things on a canoe and went upriver to the Kamaloea where we were to meet our Bahá'í friends. We were received with great warmth and hospitality by Bahá'ís and non-Bahá'ís alike.

Our visit to Kamaloea was one of the warmest experiences on the whole Green Light Expedition. We had a special meeting the night of our arrival and the captain of the village, or chief, was very anxious to hear more about the Bahá'í teachings.

The next morning we discussed with our Bahá'í friends how we could best help their teaching work. They are speaking Taki Taki which is the language most commonly used in Suriname and is similar to pigeon English.

Like all Africans the people have a very strong sense of protocol. This man is the Captain, or chief, of the village. Yesterday we arrived by plane and we had so many pieces of luggage and everybody was so kind to us. He gave permission for them to help us and everybody helped; a little boy like this was carrying this thing on his head. And when I got up this morning I said to our Bahá'í friends: these people, the Boto Passi, are so kind I want to go back and see them.

We decided to visit the nearby village of Lafanti and hold a meeting there. A number of people accepted the Faith. The Bush Negroes make their own canoes by the same method used in Africa, curing them with both fire and water. This village was the most beautiful I have ever been in my entire life.

We decided to hold the election of the first Spiritual Assembly of Kamaloea which would be the first Spiritual Assembly of the Bush Negroes anywhere in Suriname. As this Bahá'í could not be present at the evening meeting, he cast his vote and Jamshid wrote it down for him. All too easily we city people forget that half the world's population is illiterate. Plans were made for the election of the Spiritual Assembly that night. The captain who in meantime had become a Bahá'í is casting his vote for the first Spiritual Assembly.

Some of our Bahá'í friends took us down the river. On our way down river we stopped at this village to see if we could see the only Bahá'í who lived there. Although everybody else was out working their plantations, he happened to be at home.

We were nine hours on our way down the river from Kamaloea to Mamadam. Mamadam is the place where the government ferryboat picks up passengers twice a week and takes them over to Afobaka on the other side of the lake. This is to be our home for three nights where we slept with about 40 other passengers waiting for the arrival of the ferryboat. That night our Bahá'í friends cooked dinner for us - a delicious soup of piranha and plantain.

Some of the people living in the hut were very anxious to know more about the Bahá'í Faith. Our friends from Kamaloea were very enthusiastic teachers. After discussing the Faith practically the entire night with our friends, this man expressed the wish to become a Bahá'í and Jamshid enrolled him the morning of our departure. These Bush Negro Bahá'í's were amongst the finest that I have ever met anywhere in the world and we parted from each other with great regret.

Our Bahá'í brothers embarked in their canoe and went back up the river to Kamaloea. Everything was loaded onto the crowded government ferry and we set out for the five-hour journey across the lake. We found marked interest from our fellow passengers in who we were and in what we believed.

Brazil – Manaus

We flew over the Amazon river which at this point was over 20 kilometers wide. The whole area was flooded because the rainy season had begun. It was a great revelation to all of us to discover that Manaus, in the heart of the Amazon Basin was such a modern city with shipping in its ports from all parts of the world. It has every convenience of civilization including one of the most beautiful opera houses in Latin America. We arrived to attend the first historic Bahá'í conference of the Amazonian region and were greeted very warmly at the airport by members of the new Bahá'í community. During our week's visit there were many lectures given to students at both universities and high schools.

[Talking to students:] I would rather talk to an audience, like yourselves, of young people than any other kind of audience in the whole world. Nobody knows better than the youth how many problems face us in the world today. As I see it, one of the greatest problems facing the human race, and that means you, is how to bring the two thirds of the world's population who live in villages into the advantages of the 20th century, the advancement of the 20th century without ruining their human characteristics that are so wonderful.

Colombia – Leticia

From Manaus we flew to Leticia in Colombia on the frontier between Brazil and Peru. Leticia is a small, very pleasant town ideally situated for pioneering as many Indian tribes can be reached from here.

Boats on the Amazon are enclosed because of the very heavy rains. For eighteen days ten of us lived and slept on this one. She was noisy, smelly and slow. We called her, appropriately, the Mutt. This was the beginning of our journey up the Amazon in Peru. Gradually a daily pattern of living on the boat was established ... The rainy season floods the riverbanks but the villagers are used to it and build their homes on stilts reaching their homes by canoe. Various Christian missions are rapidly spreading throughout this entire area.

The only quiet place [in the boat] was the roof where we held prayers every morning. It was also the only place where we could have a conversation because of the noise of the diesel engine inside was absolutely deafening. The trouble was that it was very difficult to get up and down because there was no deck on our boat.

This Ticuna village had been recently converted to Christianity. There were many crosses along the river such as this dated 1970-1972. We wondered why we Bahá'ís had come so late. Indian fathers are as devoted to their children as their mothers and we saw so many

THE GREEN LIGHT EXPEDITION FILM NARRATIVE (EXTRACTS)

evidences of their care and tenderness.

We had expected the Amazon River to be a wild and unpopulated area and we were very surprised to find that all along the riverbank there were villages and settlements ... The Amazon is the land of mirror images - one glides through a dream of exquisite beauty.

In search of Indians left touched by our civilization we went up the smaller rivers. We'd at last come to this Yagua family living according to their own customs. The Indians are a very quiet people, a very restful people, who think before they speak. They have a dignity and a nobility which constantly impressed us. No people tame wild animals like the Indians. Their homes are full of much loved and cared for pets.

When the time comes for me to have to leave this planet, the only thing that is going to be the hardest to depart is from the jungles. I have this mad, mad love for the jungles. I never feel that I can see enough of the jungle, be in the jungle enough, and whenever in my life I travel away from the jungle area, it is infinite heartache that I'm leaving this marvellous, marvellous land of trees and of nature, and the beauty.

Going deeper into the jungle we came to another more isolated Yagua village. This man probably continued to wear the costume of his ancestors. He very kindly demonstrated for us how they shoot poison darts through these long blowpipes.

We went back to the Amazons and visited another Yagua village.

Going up another river we visited the Bora tribe. This huge hut, called a Cocomera, is the meeting house for the villagers. We decided to go upstream, a day's journey, to see a Cocomera in another village which was still being used as a communal dwelling. In the Bahá'í teachings there is a tremendous emphasis on the family, on respect for parents, mutual kindness and understanding. This is something that exists in villages.

Peru – Iquitos and Pucallpa

Our journey to the Amazons was at an end. We are approaching Iquitos, an inland port, 4 000 km from the sea. Recently, oil has been discovered in this part of the world. To cities such as this the indigenous people flock in great numbers, only to live in squalor and poverty. The filth produced by modern towns flows into the riverbanks. Here in Pucallpa many poor people have built their houses floating on the river itself.

We decided to visit the Shipibo people who are both very gifted artistically and also very shrewed. The women wear very beautiful embroidered skirts. To me it is very impressive the way in village life even very small children work, and they love working.

Peru – Lima

This was our last contact with the Amazonian Indians. We were leaving the wonderful world of the jungles to fly to Lima, the capital of Peru. In the home of Mr Khamsi we discussed our recent experiences.

I've always been very romantic about this part of the world and I thought the primitive peoples are going to go and teach the untouched primitive people living in their original culture. And now I don't feel that way about it. If the Bahá'í's ever get to the primitive people, God bless them, it will be a wonderful service. But in the meantime, get to the people that are no longer primitive. Get to these areas before it is too late, don't you feel so?

You know there is something that I want to say because I think it ought to be said and I know that we all know it, but perhaps the Bahá'ís don't realize it. The missionaries are a highly praiseworthy and admirable group of people. Just because we talk about the missionaries doesn't mean they that are not wonderful people; they have a dedication that we Bahá'ís could learn from. They have a systematized, intelligent way of going to their teachings that we should learn. The only trouble with the missionaries is that they're teaching something that is outdated. Instead of teaching them the religion of God for today, they are teaching teach something that is two Dispensations back. But, they are wonderful.

... I know that the sky is the limit and the Bahá'ís have to realize it and that they have to have more imagination. There is no lack of good will on the part of the Bahá'ís but what they need is the imagination to see that it could apply to me not to you, but I can go. When they understand it then I think we will have a tremendous influx in these areas.

... If I had the opportunity, if I were younger, believe me I would not hesitate to pioneer to places like this. People have to behave as if there was a crisis and this is a crisis in world history. And this is why the Guardian and now the House of Justice is constantly appealing to the Bahá'ís to fulfil 'Abdu'l-Bahá's Divine Plan, because there isn't any more time to lose. And I think that this is what I hope this film will do, really. This is the whole purpose of the film. Is that if the Bahá'ís look at this film can feel that they came with us, that they saw these people, that they saw the difficulties, that they saw the possibilities, and they saw the beauty of it all. And in their hearts will arise the desire to go out and teach in such an environment, such people the Cause of God, well then the film would have fulfilled its objective, because that's the whole purpose of it.

Remember Bahá'u'lláh says seize your opportunity for it comes but once. And the Báb says: mount your steeds, Oh Heroes of God. Now let the Bahá'ís get up and go.

Bolivia – Oruro

The last stage of the Green Light Expedition took place on the Altiplano in the Andes. We went to Bolivia to attend an Indian Bahá'í conference. The friends gathered from many towns and villages all over the Altiplano. From Sacaca we set out for the top of the mountains accompanied by about 150 Bahá'ís. Each group of Bahá'ís villagers had brought their own instruments. Almost all of them played their flutes all the way up to the top of the mountain.

[Talking to the conference participants:] Beloved friends, I have come a very, very long way to see your faces again. And I cannot tell you how happy I am to be here. When I was coming over these mountains to reach this place I had a very strong feeling that, although we are a small group of people, that we were not alone. In the Bahá'í Teachings we have a thing called the Supreme Concourse, the souls of those wonderful, wonderful people who have served humanity, who have great qualities and who have died and have gone to another world. And I had a very strong feeling that above our heads, we couldn't see them, but the members of the Supreme Concourse were with us. And I believe that those who you love, your ancestors, your parents, your grandparents, are watching this meeting and sharing in it. Now, whatever we receive here, when we leave here we will take it with us and share it with others – our joy, our love, our spirit of brotherhood – not only we, but there is another very beautiful thing, it is Bahá'u'lláh's promise: He said when you mention God, when you pray, the scattering angels take these words and they scatter it all over. And we must be sure that already the spirit of this meeting will go out in the air and affect Bolivia. You are the beginning of the great flood of the Message of Bahá'u'lláh amongst your people. So we are all very, very blessed and that is why I say this is a feast of love and is a feast of thanksgiving.

Peru - Cusco

This is Cusco. Capital city of the old Indian civilization, the golden city whose temple of the sun was covered by sheets of pure gold - gold which led the Spanish Conquistadors to totally destroy the great empire of the Incas. We arrived in Cusco to attend the first all Quechua-speaking conference ever to be held which had been arranged by the Counselors of South America. Many of the Bolivian Bahá'ís had come to attend. It took this bus load of Bahá'ís from Ecuador over a week to drive the 2 000 kms from their country to Cusco. The Andean believers flocked to register for the conference. The Bahá'ís from Peru, Ecuador and Bolivia spent one whole day discussing how much they could understand each other's dialects so that Bahá'í literature could be made standard for all these countries. It was a colourful group of people who gathered at Sacsayhuaman for the opening day of our conference. This great fortress built by the Incas took 30,000 people 80 years to construct. We went up to the highest point to hold our meeting, the place where the Incas believed the sun was tied. I told my Indian brothers and sisters about themselves, that their ancestors had built an empire second only to the Romans. That the achievements of the Incas in government, road building, architecture, arts and crafts were as great as any the world has ever seen.

The government of Peru had recently made Quechua the second official language. This gentleman had come from Cusco to attend our conference as representative of the Quechua speaking Academy of Peru. Macchu Pichu was a fortress hanging in the clouds. Built by the Incas over 500 metres above the valley below. We all came by train from Cusco to visit this famous place, one of the last strongholds of the Inca empire.

We held our meetings and prayers again on the spot where the sun is tied. The first mass conversion in the Western hemisphere began in Bolivia, how much joy it brought to the heart of the Guardian. I remember how he announced it to the Bahá'í world and how thrilled we were. And now here was a Bolivian Bahá'í addressing other Andean Bahá'ís at the top of the historic Macchu Picchu. The Indians are a deeply spiritual people - a noble race of man with a unique destiny if they accept Bahá'u'lláh. What would happen to all these wonderful people we have met. So many of them, so many tribes, scattered over such a vast area. Who will go to teach them, to keep the small fires that we have lit burning, to turn it all into a great conflagration.

'Abdu'l-Bahá said, "O that I could travel, even though on foot and in the utmost poverty, to these regions, and, raising the call of "Yá Bahá'u'l-Abhá" in cities, villages, mountains, deserts and oceans, promote the divine teachings! This, alas, I cannot do. How intensely I deplore it! Please God, ye may achieve it".[398]

---

[398]'Abdu'l-Bahá. *Tablets of the Divine Plan.* Wilmette: US Bahá'í Publishing Trust, pp. 41-42, 1993.

Bibliography

Abadian, Hossein. Armenians Socio-Political Activists & Iranian Constitutional Revolution (1905-1911). In *Proceedings of International Academic Conferences* (No. 2503649). International Institute of Social and Economic Sciences, June 2015.

'Abdu'l-Bahá. *Selections from the Writings of 'Abdu'l-Bahá*. Bahá'í World Centre, lightweight edition, 1982.

'Abdu'l-Bahá, *Some Answered Questions*. Wilmette, US Bahá'í Publishing Trust, 1990.

'Abdu'l-Bahá. *Tablets of the Divine Plan*. Wilmette, US Bahá'í Publishing Trust, 1993.

'Abdu'l-Bahá. *The Secret of Divine Civilization*. Wilmette, US, Bahá'í Publishing Trust. 1983.

'Abdu'l-Bahá, *The Will and Testament*, Wilmette, US Bahá'í Publishing Trust, 1990 reprint.

Amatu'l-Bahá Rúhíyyih Khánum Mary Sutherland Maxwell. *The Green Light Expedition*. 1975. Video available on YouTube: https://www.youtube.com/watch?v=pW4qAmfpjG8

The Báb. *Selections from the Writings of the Báb*. Haifa, Bahá'í World Centre, 1976.

Bahá'í World Centre. *The Bahá'í World: A Biennal International Record, 1930-1932, Volume IV*. Wilmette, Bahá'í Publishing Trust, 1933.

Bahá'í World Centre. *Century of Light*. Haifa, 2001.

Bahá'í World Centre. *The Bahá'í World: 1954-1963, Volume XIII*. Haifa, Israel, *Bahá'í* World Centre, 1970.

Bahá'í World Centre. *Messages from the Universal House of Justice 1963–1986*. Compiled by Geoffrey W. Marks. Wilmette. Illinois, Bahá'í Publishing Trust, 1996,

Bahá'í World Centre. *The Ministry of the Custodians: 1957-1963*. Haifa, Bahá'í World Centre, 1997.

Bahá'u'lláh. *Kitáb-i-Aqdas*. Bahá'í World Centre, 1992 edition.

Bahá'u'lláh. *The Summons of the Lord of Hosts*. Bahá'í World Centre, 2002 edition.

Bahá'u'lláh. *Tablets of Bahá'u'lláh Revealed After the Kitáb-i-Aqdas*. Illinois, US Bahá'í Publishing Trust, 1988.

Bahá'u'lláh. *Gleanings from the Writings of Bahá'u'lláh*. Wilmette, US Bahá'í Publishing Trust, 1990.

Bahá'u'lláh. *The Hidden Words of Bahá'u'lláh*. Wilmette, US Bahá'í Publishing Trust, 1985.

Bahá'u'lláh. *The Tablet of Unity (Lawḥ-i-Ittiḥád)* - translated by Moojan Momen. In Lights of 'Irfán, Book II. Evanston: 'Irfán Colloquia, 2001.

Bahá'u'lláh. *The Summons of the Lord of Hosts*. Wilmette, Bahá'í Publishing, 2002.

Bahá'u'lláh. *Tablets of the Hair.* Bahá'í News, 121, 1938. Available online at; https://bahai-library.com/bahaullah_alwah_shaarat

Balyuzi, Hasan. *'Abdu'l-Bahá*. Oxford, George Ronald, 1972.

Faizi-Moore, May. *Faizi*. George Ronald Oxford, 2013.

Fatheazam, Shahbaz. (2015). *The Last Refuge: Fifty Years of the Universal House of Justice*. Evanston, IL, Irfan Publication Occasional Papers.

Foucault, M. The Subject and Power. *Critical inquiry*, 8(4), p. 77-795, 1982.

Furútan, Írán. *Dr. Muhájir: Hand of the Cause of God, Knight of Bahá'u lláh*. London, Bahá'í Publishing Trust, 1992.

Furútan, Írán. *Hand of the Cause of God Furútan*. Wilmette, US Baha'i Publishing Trust, 2018.

Gail, Marzieh. *Summon up Remembrance.* George Ronald Oxford, 1987.

Handal, Boris. *In Memorian Mas'ud Khamsi (1922-2013).* Unpublished.

Handal, Boris. *El Concurso en Lo Alto.* Lima, PROPACEB, 1985.

Handal, Boris. *Eve Nicklin, She of the Brave Heart.* SC, CreateSpace, 2011.

Hornby, Helen Bassett. *Lights of Guidance: A Bahá'í Reference File.* New Delhi, Bahá'í Publishing Trust, 1983.

Interview with Mas'ud Khamsi. Tape provided by Masud Samandari.

Käfer, *Alex. Die Geschichte der Österreichischen Bahá'í Gemeinde.* Horizonte Verlag: 2005.

Khadem, Javidukht. *Zikrullah Khadem: The Itinerant Hand of the Cause of God.* Wilmette, Ill.: Bahá'í Publishing Trust, 1990.

Khamsi, Mas'ud. *Pioneering Services of Mas'ud Khamsi*, unpublished manuscript.

Mazandarini, Fazel. *Zuhúru'l-Haqq (The Manifestation of Truth).* Tehran, Vol 7, 1944.

Mihrabkhání, Rúhu'lláh. *Khándán-i Sádát-i-Khams.* Darmstadt, Mu'assassih-'i `Asr-i Jadid, 1994.

Mírzá Yahyá 'Amídu'l-Atibbá Hamadání. *Memoirs of a Bahá'í in Rasht: 1889-1903* (Translated by Ahang Rabbani). Vol. 9, Explorations in Bahá'í History, 2007.

Momen, Moojan. *The Bábi and Bahá'í Religions - 1844-1944.* George Ronald Oxford, 1981.

Momen, Moojan. *The Bahá'í Community of Iran.* Oxford, George Ronald, 2015.

Rivadeneyra, Adolfo. *Viaje al interior de Persia.* Madrid, 1880.

Root, Martha. Pilgrimage through Persia. Part 3: Qazvin and Tihran. *Star of the West*, 21, 6 (September 1930).

Sabet, Habib. *Memoirs,* 1989. Available online from: https://archive.org/stream/HabibSabetMem/HabibSabetMem_djvu.txt

Shahvar, Soli. *Forgotten Schools: The Bahá'ís and Modern Education in Iran, 1899-1934.* I.B.Tauris, 2009.

Shoghi Effendi. *Citadel of Faith: Messages to America 1947-1957.* Wilmette, US Baha'i Publishing Trust, 1953.

Shoghi Effendi. *God Passes by.* Wilmette, US Bahá'í Publishing Trust, 1979.

Shoghi Effendi. *Messages to the Bahá'í World: 1950–1957.* Wilmette, US Bahá'í Publishing Trust, 1971.

Shoghi Effendi. *The Promised Day Is Come.* Wilmette, US Bahá'í Publishing Trust, 1980.

Shoghi Effendi. *Directives from the Guardian.* India/Hawaii, 1973.

Siegel, Jennifer. *Endgame: Britain, Russia and the Final Struggle for Central Asia.* IB Tauris, 2002.

Taherzadeh, Adib. *The Revelation of Bahá'u'lláh*, vol. IV. George Ronald Oxford, 1987.

The Compilation of Compilations: Prepared by The Universal House of Justice (vol. 2). Maryborough, Victoria, Bahá'í Publications Australia, 1991.

The Compilation of Compilations: Prepared by The Universal House of Justice (vol. 3). Maryborough, Victoria, Bahá'í Publications Australia, 2000.

The Universal House of Justice. *Century of Light.* Wilmette, Bahá'í Publishing Trust, 2001.

The Universal House of Justice. The importance of Obligatory Prayer and Fasting. *The American Baha'i*, 31:7, pages 3-6, 2009.

The Universal House of Justice. Messages from the Universal House of Justice 1963–1986. Compiled by Geoffrey W. Marks. Wilmette, US Bahá'í Publishing Trust, 1996.

The Universal House of Justice. *Wellspring of Guidance: Messages of the Universal House of Justice 1963-68*. Wilmette, US Baha'i Publishing Trust, 1969.

The Universal House of Justice. *Wellspring of Guidance: Messages 1968-1973*. Wilmette, US Bahá'í Publishing Trust, 1976.

US Bahá'í Publishing Trust. *Bahá'í Prayers: A Selection of Prayers Revealed by Bahá'u'lláh, the Báb, and 'Abdu'l-Bahá*. Wilmette, US Bahá'í Publishing Trust, 1991.

Zinky, Kay. *Martha Root, Herald of the Kingdom*. NewDelhi, India: Bahá'í Publishing Trust, 1983.

www.ingramcontent.com/pod-product-compliance
Lightning Source LLC
Chambersburg PA
CBHW020316010526
44107CB00054B/1866